LISA MILLAR is the co-host of ABC TV's *News Breakfast*. Millar returned to the ABC in Australia after finishing a decade-long posting as bureau chief in both Washington, DC and London covering some of the world's biggest stories. She began her career at *The Gympie Times* in 1988 and has worked in print, TV and radio. She won a Walkley Award in 2005 for investigative reporting.

# LISA MILLAR

## Daring to Fly

The TV star on facing fear
and finding joy on a deadline

## hachette
### AUSTRALIA

Published in Australia and New Zealand in 2021
by Hachette Australia
(an imprint of Hachette Australia Pty Limited)
Level 17, 207 Kent Street, Sydney NSW 2000
www.hachette.com.au

10 9 8 7 6 5 4 3 2 1

A catalogue record for this
book is available from the
National Library of Australia

ISBN: 978 0 7336 4718 5

Cover design by Christabella Designs
Front cover images courtesy Millar family collection; Shutterstock
Back cover image by Will Belcher, Sheer Will Photography
Internal images courtesy Millar family collection; John Bean, Dan Sweetapple, Kim Landers, Max Futcher, Cameron Bauer and Emily Smith; and Prince Harry image © WP#JRAK.
Typeset in Adobe Garamond Pro by Kirby Jones
Printed and bound in Australia by McPherson's Printing Group

*In memory of Clarrie and Dorothy Millar,*
*the best support crew a daughter could have*

# CONTENTS

Prologue                          1

1 Finding a Course                5
2 Lift-off                       14
3 India Echo Charlie             24
4 Instruction Manual             37
5 Our Magnetic Compass           49
6 Pitch                          60
7 Crosscheck                     70
8 Taking Off                     82
9 Engine Failure                 94
10 Buckle Up                    112
11 On Approach                  135
12 Return Ticket                149
13 Winging It                   158
14 Catastrophic Loss            168
15 Full Throttle                185
16 Emergency                    208
17 Controlled Airspace          216
18 Rapid Descent                235
19 Crosswinds                   258
20 Inflate Lifejackets          281
21 Final Approach               294
22 Juliet Oscar Yankee          299

Acknowledgements                307

# PROLOGUE

WE SPOKE TWO languages in our family – English and aviation. Spot tests on the pilot's phonetic alphabet could come at any time.

'W?' Dad would ask.

'Whiskey!' We'd call out in response.

'D?'

'Delta!'

We had our own small plane for nine years and it never crossed my mind that flying was anything but the most natural way to get from one place to another.

Then, in 1993 while I was the ABC's North Queensland reporter, a six-seater plane we had chartered for work was caught in a heavy storm. While rain was lashing my window, there was a sudden loss of power and the motor on the left spluttered and died. The drop in altitude hit my gut so fast my brain couldn't understand what was happening. The engine on the right revved like mad trying to keep us airborne.

We made it safely to the ground but I was shaken by the experience.

After that, fear began stalking me. It was in the shadows initially, but it slowly became a constant, aggressive presence. It culminated when I was covering the Queensland election campaign in 1998 as the state political reporter. We were due to fly on a charter flight with the premier at the time, Rob Borbidge. I had been feeling sick about it all day. I drove towards the airport and the skin on my palms grew prickly.

Coffee and plain Arnott's biscuits were on offer when we arrived at the charter company's small office. There was always a wait as camera crews from different networks turned up and heavy camera gear was packed onboard.

I was starting to sweat and people's voices became indistinct, a hushed blur of noise. I went to the bathroom and wondered if vomiting would help spew out the torment I was feeling.

Finally the call came to load and leave. I put one foot in front of the other – there were only a few dozen steps from the small shed where we'd been waiting to the bottom of the plane steps.

'Come on, you can do it,' a colleague said.

Up the stairs, through the cabin door and just two more steps to my seat.

But I was physically incapacitated. I couldn't fold my legs or bend my knees to sit on the seat. I was locked with fear – every muscle in my body was spasming. I walked past my seat and lay on the floor at the rear of the twenty-seater plane.

Rob Borbidge bounded up the stairs and gave us a cheery 'G'day'. The pilot turned around to greet the premier and instead saw me, spread out on the floor. Borbidge knew I was a fearful flyer but the extent of it, on show for all to see, was news to him.

I wasn't humiliated. I didn't care. I was beyond caring about anything other than the fear.

# CHAPTER 1

# Finding a Course

THERE NEVER SEEMED to be a time when my family didn't talk about flying.

Dad had wanted to be an aviator in World War II but it wasn't until he was in his forties that he got his pilot's licence. My eldest brother, Robert, learned to fly small planes the year after I was born. My other brother, David, always the contrary one, preferred to jump out of them. My big sister, Wendy, gazed longingly from her bed at boarding school at the planes flying overhead and dreamed of being an international flight attendant.

They were almost grown-ups by the time my little sister, Trudi, and I were born. She was the happiest of passengers. And me? From the first take-off as a child, I simply loved being airborne.

Whether it was the soothing sound of propellers on a small plane as they found their rhythm and synced their spinning blades, or the high-pitched whine of a Rolls-Royce engine on a jumbo jet before it surged into life and lifted its load higher and higher, flying was a joy.

I was always torn between the anticipation of an exotic destination and the desire to stay aloft forever. But it was Dad who really started the flying dream – it made him happy and no one would have begrudged Dad that happiness. His childhood had been anything but.

\* \* \*

Dad was born in 1925, in Adelaide in an era of great confidence. The city was vibrant and trams vied for space on the boulevards with bicycles and a growing number of cars being churned out at the Holden factory.

Dad was named Percival Clarence, after his father, but he was always known as Clarrie. He adored his father who was a conductor and then driver on the trams. Dad and his siblings, older sister, Joan, and younger brother, John, would try to outrun each other to deliver their father's lunch at the tram terminus. If they were lucky and he was in good spirits, which he often was, he'd let them pull the cord and ring the bell.

They lived in a small brick home north of the city centre, a contented family with both sets of grandparents nearby. It was a happy childhood, but that didn't last long.

Deep in the back pages of the *Adelaide Advertiser* on 31 July 1935 was Percy's death notice. The 'dearly loved husband of Elsie Turbill and loving father of Joan, Clarence and John' had died at their Augusta Street home. There was a set rate for death notices if they were kept to a maximum of five lines but the family spent an extra sixpence to add the final detail – he was just thirty-four.

Anyone reading the paper that day wouldn't have had a clue about the heartache that had enveloped that Augusta Street home. Percival had suffered from tuberculosis, his lungs filling with blood, his wet hacking cough keeping the family awake at night with worry.

It was a painful and drawn-out way to die and his final gasping breath was taken in the arms of his wife. His children, waiting outside, heard her wail, 'Oh Daddy, oh Daddy,' and they knew he was gone.

For the rest of his life my father would recount the pain he and his siblings felt as they hovered on the other side of the door listening to their mother's grief.

Elsie, young and widowed with three children under twelve, decided she needed to find another husband. Things might have been different for the young family if she hadn't settled on a bloke named WD Millar – a 'gadabout' whose peripatetic approach to life had an immediate and distressing impact on the children.

WD met and romanced Elsie and then they packed up for Melbourne, leaving the children behind. Joan was placed with her paternal grandmother, a widow herself who was still grieving the loss of her son, and the boys went to stay with Elsie's friends. The unexpected stay lasted long enough that the children were told they'd be sent to an orphanage if their mother didn't come and collect them.

When Elsie and WD did return, the newly formed family of five began a migratory existence of short stays in boarding houses and flats in country Victoria and Melbourne. One boarding house owner, doubting he'd ever be paid, took a box brownie camera from young Clarrie's hands and said, 'I'll hang onto that, sonny.' The camera had been a gift from Dad's grandparents, one of the only things he truly possessed and he was mortified.

The family all adopted WD's surname – Millar. But even that was surrounded with mystery and suspicion. WD and Elsie hadn't ever married – as far as anyone knew – and the spelling didn't make sense. He was a blood relation of Keith Miller, an Australian test cricketer who played with Sir Donald Bradman in the era of the Invincibles. But why did WD spell his surname with an 'a'? Dad thought he was probably adding another layer of subterfuge for the endless debtors trying to track him down.

The family was always on the move: in the space of three years the children had changed homes four times and schools three. By the time they reached the small town of Rosebery in north-west Tasmania, Clarrie was thirteen and picked out by the head teacher for a job lugging bags of ore to the ovens at the zinc and lead mine – the same place WD was working as a mechanic. They offered Clarrie ten shillings and sixpence a week – a fortune for a teenager. It was his birthday when he delivered the news to his mum that he was leaving school and offered to pay her five bob a week rent, half his salary. She burst into tears at her son's generosity.

It wasn't long before the family was on the move again, to Queenstown and then south to Hobart. Dad, who was now fourteen, and his twelve-year-old brother, John, were again separated from the family and put up at the Sailors' Rest at Salamanca down by the harbour for a while. As the name suggested, the four-storey narrow brick building, with a ship's anchor painted on the front, was a place for mariners to bunk down. Groups of men lounged on the wooden bench outside. It was not a place for children. Four years later it was closed down for good after being declared 'unfit for human habitation'.

In quick succession, courtesy of WD's inability to pay rent, the family moved from one home to another, ending up in a boarding house in South Hobart.

Clarrie began work at the Brownell Brothers department store on Liverpool Street. Despite his youth, he took the role seriously. He was a stickler for rules and not even his mum's familiar face changed his approach.

'Yes, Madam, how may I help you?' he greeted her one day.

His mother responded with a quizzical look.

An opportunity then came up for him to join the Postmaster-General's Department (now Australia Post) as a telegraph messenger. Two hundred sat the exam and thirteen were appointed. Clarrie was one of them. The job came with a sombre responsibility. The faraway battles of World War II were creeping closer and the messengers would pedal their bikes up and down the hilly streets of Hobart day and night, summer and winter, to deliver telegrams.

The soldiers couldn't reveal much about their movements and the messages to their families were short and to the point, with military-approved phrases that at least let their loved ones know they were alive. But as the enemy advanced on Allied troops, families began dreading the sight of the young uniformed cyclists coming down their street.

When Clarrie knocked on people's doors, the words contained in the telegram would go through his mind – he knew them by heart: 'The Minister for the Army regrets to advise you that your husband/son has been killed/wounded in action.' Sometimes wives would collapse in a torrent of grief before he'd even got back on his bike, their wails reminding him of his mother's pain when his father had died in her arms.

There was no counselling for the families or for the young messengers like Clarrie whose duties weighed them down. They were another part of the collateral damage of war.

Despite what he witnessed, Dad was desperate to go to war and was worried it would end before he was old enough to enlist. He wanted to fly with the RAAF but his mother begged him not to. Even though he was eighteen and didn't need her permission, he couldn't break her heart. She'd suffered so much already.

Instead he was promoted to the operating room where morse code was translated into English for the telegrams. He then trained to become a radio operator at Shepparton in Victoria where he was taught to salute, bayonet the enemy and reverse-butt them in the face with the rifle.

It was the end of 1943 and the Allies in the Pacific were beating back the Japanese. General Douglas MacArthur seconded Australia's best and brightest wireless operators to intercept the Japanese *katakana* messages and translate them into English. Dad was one of them and they were sworn to secrecy, operating out of the Northern Territory, north Queensland and Brisbane. MacArthur credited them with having shortened the course of the war by twelve months but the clandestine nature of their work meant they returned to civilian life with little celebration of what they had achieved.

It was only decades later when the then British prime minister, Gordon Brown, thanked the Australians for their work and bestowed on them war medals that those wireless operators felt they could speak publicly about their war efforts, despite Dad having shared some of his stories with us privately over the years.

Dad never let on if he was fearful at all during those war years. But his voice trembled when he talked about his mate Victor. Vic had initially trained with Dad at Shepparton and had gone on to do what Dad had desperately wanted to do – fly. The two of them were based in Darwin, Dad at the Central Bureau's intercept unit and Vic flying Spitfires.

On 15 August 1945, the day the Japanese surrendered, Dad rushed to relay the message to Vic but was told by the commanding officer that he was on a mission. Vic never came home. His plane was shot down just as the war was ending.

'Poor, bloody, Vic,' Dad would say, the pauses accentuating the emotion that slipped out of each word.

After the war, Dad returned to Sydney, where his mother and WD had taken over a small shop in the northern suburb of Wahroonga near the train line. His brother, John, was now working in a shoe shop and Dad began working in the telegraph branch of the GPO in Sydney. Before he returned to civilian life, Dad had tried to push for a promotion, sending letters asking for specific training opportunities. But he was knocked back. While his bosses described the 21-year-old as 'keen, conscientious and reliable' they noted he hadn't served overseas during the war and would have to wait his turn behind other veterans who had. Little did they know the extent of his wartime service.

At night Dad started trying to catch up on the schooling he'd left behind when he was thirteen, completing his high school certificate and concentrating on economics.

After the excitement of his role during the war, Dad's daily duties must have felt mundane. Each day he'd walk through the operations room, not realising there were a few female eyes following his path.

'Hey, that little blonde over there fancies you because she thinks you look like James Mason,' one of the women finally told Dad, pointing at my mum, Dorothy.

The English actor James Mason was one of the UK's biggest box office drawcards after the war.

Mum wasn't lacking in movie star qualities herself. Her skin was tanned from long hours spent at the beach, her figure trim and her hair neatly coiffed.

Dad took her to the pictures for their first date, although it wasn't a James Mason film. Maybe Dad didn't want to take the chance he wouldn't shape up in comparison. They saw *The Jolson Story* instead, a biographical film about the American singer and comedian Al Jolson who starred in Hollywood's first talking picture, *The Jazz Singer*, two decades earlier.

It wasn't long before they were married, and a year and a half later had their first child, my eldest brother, Robert.

Mum and Dad were living with Mum's mother – Ida Cooper – in the leafy Sydney suburb of Pymble when they decided to head north to Queensland for a holiday. Dad's mother and WD had ended up in the centre of the state, a few kilometres out of Biloela, the largest town in the Banana Shire. They were living on a piece of land that Dad's brother, John, had started working.

If Mum and Dad thought they'd be driving through banana plantations on their way north they soon learned otherwise. The shire was named Banana after an old yellow-coloured bullock who'd been a favourite of local stockmen in the 1860s and became part of the area's folklore.

Mum and Dad ended up spending a few years in Biloela, building a basic home with John, a dairy shed and telegraph lines to get a phone installed for the half-dozen other properties along Valentine Plains Road.

Dad had been dragged from one place to another as a child but, even as an adult, when he was the decision-maker, permanence didn't come easily. Within five years Mum and Dad were on the move again, to Brisbane, where Dad worked in real estate.

But he hankered for the land and made a decision that would eventually lead to the realisation of his flying dream.

# CHAPTER 2

# Lift-off

MY PARENTS, CLARRIE and Dorothy Millar, were still only quite young when they arrived in the small town of Kilkivan, three hours north of Brisbane and a couple of hours inland from Noosa. Back then the rich beachside resort town of Noosa consisted of a caravan park and a milk bar. And there wasn't much more to Kilkivan.

If you stumbled on Kilkivan at just the right time of year, when there was a combination of sun and warmth and rain, the green pastures would be filled with crops and fat cows, and the main street would be full with farmers doing business, making money. But Kilkivan could also be cold with early winter fogs sitting low in its gullies long after a weak sun had lifted itself wearily into the sky. The hard-set soil gave life to weeds and grasses with names that rang out like warnings – native panic, barbed wire, giant rat's tail. And in that grass lay two-metre-long venomous brown snakes ready to strike if disturbed.

This was all still to be discovered when Clarrie and Dorothy set up home in a two-bedroom cottage off Running Creek Road with three children under six. My eldest brother, Robert, had been joined by another boy, David, and then my sister Wendy. The two boys were given the second room and Wendy slept on a divan in the corner of the living room.

It was 1955 and Mum and Dad didn't have a lot of money, but they made up for it with an ambition to be successful dairy farmers.

Kilkivan was named after a Scottish farm that belonged to the father of one of the first settlers there. Its great claim to fame was being the first place where gold was discovered in Queensland in the 1860s – a question that turned up on more than one primary school exam.

There was only one dirt road into town and it became the main street before turning into the escape out of there, to towns further west like Goomeri and Kingaroy, their names inspired by the original inhabitants.

Like every mining town of that era, some of the busiest places in Kilkivan were the courthouse, the police quarters and the lockup. There were two pubs in town, although one later burned down in circumstances that were described in hushed tones as 'suspicious'.

By the time the young Millar family arrived, most of the businesses lining the main street focused on supporting the farms around the town. There was the local grocery store, owned by the

Wex family, who had the first television in town and displayed it in their front window.

My older brothers would hang around outside the shop on their way home from school to catch a glimpse of this new technology. If they were lucky, Mum and Dad would pile them into the car and they'd drive to a friend's house to watch episodes of *The Flintstones*. Eventually, they got their own television and stared at it even after the programs ended at 8.30 pm and all they could see was the test pattern into the wee hours.

Each morning, long before dawn, Mum and Dad would head to the milking shed, calling out to the cows, attaching machinery and avoiding the splat of manure hitting the concrete floor. It was often dark and the frost would crackle underneath as Mum walked up the hill. When Wendy was young, Mum would have to find a dry, high spot to put her. In winter it seemed to take forever for the sun to show itself. And even then it barely changed the temperature in the shed. It was rough but it was still a step up from Biloela in central Queensland – the cow shed there didn't even have a roof.

My brothers would get a lift home from school and head straight to the dairy, where they'd be on shovel duty to catch the poo before it hit Mum, who was busy drawing every last drop of valuable milk from the cows' teats. Wendy was too young to have chores in those early years but old enough to cuddle up to the cows for warmth. There was never any discussion with the children about money and it was only later that Wendy learned the pancakes drizzled with sugar and lemon that she thought were a treat were mealtime staples because they were so cheap.

One constant through it all was the presence of Mum's mother. Even when she wasn't within arms' reach, her moral and sometimes financial support gave them strength.

* * *

Mum's mother, Ida Emma Cooper, was a great traveller. She and her family arrived in Australia on a ship from England when she was just fifteen. It was 1911 and their first decade away from England was tumultuous.

Grandma worked as a stenographer for a tobacco company in Sydney and, while she was smart, there were no expectations she'd continue her education and work after marriage. Grandma was in no rush to marry, though. She enjoyed earning money and she liked her comfortable life in Sydney. But a young man returning from World War I soon changed that.

Alfred Cooper had grown up in Western Australia and his journey home from the war led him to Rabaul in New Britain. The island, now part of Papua New Guinea, was administered by Australia at the time and Alfred joined a new generation of Australians making their home there.

Alfred was fifteen years older than Ida when he met her on a trip to Sydney. It took him a few years to convince her but eventually Grandma married him and went north to New Britain with him, where Alfred had taken up a 99-year lease on a coconut plantation called Asalingi.

In 1927 the couple sailed into Rabaul. On land, the volcanic soil gave way to lush green grass and tropical flowering plants tended by local staff, who waited at the plantation house for the manager to return with his new wife. Palm trees rustled in welcome for the newest arrival.

The plantation was one of the larger ones in Rabaul and life was pleasant for the prosperous white farmers and their families. Dressed in starched white cotton suits and calf-length frocks, they sat on balconies in the cool breeze, enjoying high tea with liberal splashes of gin and tonic. The tables were laden with cakes and sandwiches.

The local tribes worked hard keeping the plantations profitable while their children played on the grass with the offspring of the newer inhabitants.

Grandma was soon pregnant with her first child and was reassured by the presence of Doctor Phyllis Cilento and her husband – medicos from Queensland who were living in Rabaul. But when Grandma went into labour Doctor Cilento was back in Brisbane, called away at short notice, and a local intern took charge. It was a long and traumatic labour and the birth became not so much a delivery of a baby but a violent extraction. The instruments used meant the baby, Thomas, suffered serious head injuries. He survived but was permanently brain damaged.

A couple of years later, Ida was pregnant for a second time and decided that she'd travel back to Sydney to give birth rather than risk another difficult delivery in Rabaul. Her daughter Dorothy arrived in perfect health in 1930 and the family were soon back on the plantation.

The effects of the Great Depression were arriving on the New Guinea shores as the price of copra, the flesh extracted from the coconuts, started falling. The plantations were vital to the local economy and Australia was being called upon to provide financial assistance. The tropical lifestyle became more frugal but was still idyllic and they imagined it stretching on for years. Except Alfred was now well into his fifties, and he was becoming frail and showing signs of a serious illness.

Ida and Alfred took their two children to Sydney for his treatment, hoping it was just another temporary diversion from their life in the north, but he died from cancer in 1939. Grandma was left a widow at forty-two, with two young children and part ownership of a plantation as the world faced another decade of turmoil.

A manager had been put in place to look after the plantation while Grandma and the children stayed in Sydney. But by the end of 1941 the Japanese were threatening New Britain and surrounding areas and the Australian government ordered civilians to evacuate by ship. Women and children left, but hundreds of men – plantation owners and government employees – stayed behind and attempted to fend off the Japanese invasion in January 1942.

Asalingi's plantation manager, Hugh Scott, did not survive. He hid there but was taken as a prisoner of war and was onboard the *Montevideo Maru* – a Japanese ship transporting POWs from Rabaul – when it was torpedoed by a US submarine. The Allies had no idea that a thousand Europeans and Australians were onboard.

Of the others who stayed around Rabaul, hundreds died from starvation and illness, including malaria, and hundreds of others were executed. The war left its brutal mark, both on the physical terrain and the population. Homes and roads were bombed and the plantations themselves were in terrible shape. Years later bullet holes could still be seen in the palm trees that had welcomed my grandmother at Asalingi.

Perhaps out of sentimentality for her past life and lost husband, and the fact that no one was wanting to buy into New Britain so soon after the war, Grandma hung on to her part ownership of the plantation.

By the 1950s my mother, Dorothy, had moved to Queensland with my father and my uncle Thomas was in institutionalised care. Ida, now in her early fifties, loaded her caravan in Sydney and hit the road, driving 1100 kilometres to Mum and Dad's farm at Kilkivan. It was a solo expedition that would have given pause to even the most adventurous man back then but Grandma had already proven little could faze her.

She decided to move permanently to Queensland, to Hervey Bay north of Brisbane – close enough for regular visits to her grandchildren. But she'd barely settled in when she was off again, setting sail across the world by herself, joining long cruises and indulging in her love of flying.

Postcards would arrive from Switzerland, Mykonos, Jerusalem, Nairobi and Durban. 'Dear David,' she'd write to my brother on a postcard featuring a photo of a 28-seater Sikorsky helicopter in the United Kingdom. 'How would you like a flight in this helicopter?

It takes twenty minutes from Penzance to the (Scilly) Isles. Quite an experience to be airborne without having to make a run along the ground.'

On occasion she'd travel on cargo ships with just ten or fifteen passengers. She was a woman with an appetite to do things a little bit differently, to gain another perspective. She'd try anything from riding camels in Baghdad to climbing high up rocky outlooks.

Another postcard read: 'Am writing this on the boat steaming up to Cologne. Have never seen so many old castles, a photographer's paradise.'

Grandma never went anywhere without her camera, whether she was on a global adventure or spending days on the farm. She sent us boxes of slides of her photographic efforts, dates and locations added in her cursive handwriting. Her true skill came in capturing people's faces, especially a passing moment of emotion, a wistfulness or flash of joy.

She would address her cards from abroad to the family, simply 'Kilkivan, Queensland, Australia'. Nothing more was required. The cards would arrive at the post office and Mrs Farrow would hand them over to the grandchildren, promising their reply letters would be swiftly dispatched.

At the farm, it was hard work and the return letters to stops along Grandma's route were filled with news of the daily grind. By this time, Dad and Mum had sold all but half-a-dozen cows and moved away from full-time dairy farming because, after years of milking cows, Dad had developed a skin condition. So they'd moved into crops – growing grain and lucerne and baling hay to bring in money.

Despite her seemingly constant international travels and trips around Australia, Grandma was still a regular visitor to the farm at Kilkivan. In the early days, she'd bring her caravan, towing it over the dirt road from her Hervey Bay home. She had to sleep somewhere after all and the family was already squeezed into the house with not enough beds to go around.

Mum was barely thirty at the time and longed for those visits from her mother probably even more than her children did. Warm and magnanimous, Grandma never left after one of her visits without depositing coins under the pillow of each grandchild. Robert always remembered the time when he was eight and Grandma asked him what he'd like as a gift.

'I'd like an aeroplane please,' he told her.

'Well, one day if you learn to fly we can look at that,' she said. If delivered by anyone else, it might have been mistaken as a patronising tone, but Grandma's words only stoked Robert's ambitions.

He and David would build billy carts to sit in, creating wings out of wood and material, hoping the small incline near the house would be enough to pick up speed and carry them away. 'It had a canvas cover and proper flaps as well as the wings and I'd tell David to pull like hell so I could fly,' Robert recalls.

They'd make complicated models of paper aeroplanes in the hallway until Mum insisted it was time for bed.

In 1967 Grandma was off again, this time to West Africa. But the plantation in New Guinea was on her mind and at the end of that year she suggested to my brothers that they travel to New Guinea with her. 'Nothing like the imprint of an owner's foot,' she told them.

They flew into Port Moresby from Brisbane and then on to Rabaul. The motel at Rabaul was surrounded by a sea of colour as butterflies landed lazily on bushy hibiscus plants and a cool breeze offered relief from the summer heat.

The boys sipped beer under Grandma's supervision. They stayed with friends at a nearby plantation, New Massawa, and swam in a freshwater creek, diving under the water to pick up remnants of anti-aircraft shells. It wasn't the only reminder of the horrors the island had witnessed during the war. They also found overgrown graves behind the house.

It was their only visit to the old plantation and a handful of years later Grandma finally parted with it, selling it to a Chinese Papuan before independence in 1975.

Grandma never discussed money with us so we never knew how much that plantation might have helped Dad realise the dream he'd been harbouring, that one day, he'd learn to fly.

# CHAPTER 3

# India Echo Charlie

IT WASN'T UNUSUAL in rural Australia to see light planes buzzing across the sky in those years. Once you moved an hour in from the coast there weren't a lot of roads that boasted bitumen and flying would save hundreds of hours in valuable farming time. Big-time graziers and smaller-time farmers would often have someone in their circle with a licence, and they'd rather fly than drive to cattle sales to buy new stock or down to the big smoke to talk to the banks.

One day, when the family was working on the farm and Mum had come down with sausages and spuds to cook on the hot coals, Dad sat back and declared, 'I think we should build an airstrip.'

The nearest airstrip was in Gympie, an hour away on dirt roads. Dad was convinced that an airstrip would prove popular to pilots zipping around Queensland. They'd need a place to touch down for a break or for fuel. There were still plenty of dirt roads on the trip to Brisbane in the mid-1960s and there were enough people in Kilkivan who felt they needed their own airstrip.

And he'd already found the perfect spot on the 260-hectare farm. It was flat and away from the deviation banks he'd built to channel water into the dam to prevent soil erosion. Those banks had been carefully calculated, something that had impressed other farmers. Dad's land management and attempts to reduce erosion and preserve water had also attracted the attention of the CSIRO.

At that stage, Dad had no plane – he didn't even have a pilot's licence. But he was a believer. And he'd loved the idea of flying from so early in his life that it had become a part of him.

He got council approval for the airstrip and suggested to them that the job would be done even quicker if they sent a few graders out for a day here and there. That's how things got done in the country.

The council were happy to help. They'd been trying to convince Dad to stand for council and perhaps hoped this might get him across the line, but he told them, 'I'm too flat out trying to make a quid on the farm to go into politics.'

Dad studied the aeronautical details of the venture, checking hill heights and prevailing winds. My two brothers helped slash the grass and Wendy, who was close to finishing primary school, was enlisted to remove large rocks.

Slowly one runway – from east to west – took shape, stretching for a kilometre. It was perfect but still not enough for Dad.

'Bugger it,' he said to Robert, 'let's build a cross strip.'

Dad knew any decent pilot would need to cater for all wind and weather conditions. A cross runway was created. At nine hundred metres, it was only slightly shorter than the original.

For days the family would walk in step up and down the two airstrips, removing any rocks or stones that could flick up into a propeller and cause catastrophic damage. The airstrip had to be smooth, completely smooth.

They didn't have a plane but that didn't stop them dreaming. Robert would sit in the front of the farm Land Rover as Dad gunned the engine, slowly releasing the handbrake as the vehicle bumped along the grass, thundering down the runway until they imagined themselves lifting off into the sky, only screeching to a stop when they got to the fence line.

When the hangar was built and the airstrip was finally operational, the family sat back and waited for the planes. Well, in fairness, there was never any waiting on the property. No one was allowed to stand still – except when they'd hear the sounds of a faraway engine. Then they'd stampede to the best lookout, bristling with excitement, to see if someone was going to land.

There was only one set of family binoculars and it was passed around with the greatest of care. 'Put the strap over your head,' Dad would command. Wendy, who was then still the youngest, would end up being the last to clutch onto them and by the time she fiddled with the focus the plane was well out of sight.

Once or twice a plane landed carrying the Queensland premier at the time, Joh Bjelke-Petersen, with his long-time chief pilot,

Beryl Young, at the controls. They would touch down for a school function or official event in the region and Dad or the local police officer would pick them up and deliver them the few kilometres into town.

You never knew who might turn up. Enthusiasts with the Royal Queensland Aero Club flew in one day and headed to our creek for a picnic.

Dad had friends who shared his fascination with flight. Peter Sparkes was the first to land on the strip. He lived on a property fifty kilometres away at Manumbar and owned not one but two planes – a Tiger Moth and a Victa Airtourer, a light plane manufactured by an Australian company that was better known for its lawnmowers. Peter had already been taking Dad on long-distance air races in the late 1960s in the Victa. The hairiest part of the race was touching back down on Peter's property where he'd made a makeshift runway that was a little on the short side and somewhat rough. The Millars' smooth grass runways were a step up from that.

Dad had eventually started taking flying lessons while the airstrip took shape. It involved an entire day away from the property, driving two hours to the nearest flight school at Maroochydore where the instructor would cram several lessons into one long day of study and practical experience. Dad's dreams were starting to come true but first he had a new arrival to celebrate.

\* \* \*

Joy had to end up in my name somewhere.

It had taken fourteen years after Wendy was born for my parents to have another child so it wouldn't have mattered if I'd turned out to be anything but joyful, the simple fact of my birth gave them reason to celebrate.

While my parents were happy, and Wendy was excited to have a baby sister, my older brothers were best described as nonchalant about the family addition. By the time the last of our tribe of five, my little sister, Trudi, was born two and a half years after me, Dad sent a telegram to the pub at Toogoolawah west of Brisbane where he knew our brother David would get the message. It read 'little sister born, all well'. Telegrams were pricey and every letter counted. There was no need for too much information anyway because David was not one to worry about the details. We'd never been a family to make much of a fuss.

Not long after my birth in 1969, Grandma made our family an offer. 'Why don't I buy a plane,' she suggested, 'and leave it parked in Kilkivan.' She was living in Brisbane by then and perhaps she thought this would make it easier to visit the farm to see her daughter and grandchildren.

Grandma had always been a generous woman, due in part to her own careful financial management of the plantation and a portfolio of shares that had grown rapidly over the years, but this was a new level of generosity, and it fulfilled her words to Robert all those years before.

Back then, buying a plane was less complicated than choosing a car but it still required kicking some tyres. There were two main plane brands in Australia – Cessna and Piper – and each worked hard to woo new customers. The sales representative would fly a demo model in, landing on Dad's airstrip at Kilkivan, to give him a chance to see the plane up close and take it for a fly.

The Cessna rep was confident he'd clinched the sale. But then the Piper salesman flew in, swooping down and neatly pulling up outside our hangar like he'd parked a Ferrari. It looked like a proper plane, Dad thought, with its under-carriage wings and sleek exterior. The deal was done and a little while later a brand-new four-seater, single-engine blue and gold Piper Cherokee, worth around twenty thousand dollars at the time, joined the family.

The plane arrived before Dad had finished his flight training but, because of the distance between the farm and the airport where he took his lessons, he was given an exemption to fly the route solo until he passed the navigation tests.

The evening before he and Grandma were due to take delivery of their prized possession, Dad was helping friends whose daughter had been admitted to hospital. As they waited for the doctor Dad whipped out his flying manual and began intently reading. He'd promised them one of the first joy flights and this last-minute study was making them anxious. 'Just brushing up on a few things, don't worry,' he told them with a smile.

In December 1970, the Piper Cherokee was registered as IEC – Ida Emma Cooper – in honour of the woman who'd made it happen. But we all knew the addition to our family as India Echo Charlie.

\* \* \*

India Echo Charlie was more than a plane to the Millars. We thought she was beautiful, with her sleek gold nose and the strips of gold and blue paint along her body. I was barely two years old but with India Echo Charlie's arrival my love of flying was born. Another Millar had been caught up in Dad's passion for flight.

And the connection between our IEC and Ida Emma Cooper, the only grandparent I ever knew, made it even more special. Money was still tight and, without Grandma, we knew we would never have had IEC in our lives.

We'd zip down to Brisbane in under an hour to pick up Grandma. If only those families squeezed into hot cars on a packed road below could see how happy and carefree we were.

Not that there was a lot of room inside IEC. She was, after all, only a four-seater. Dad would carefully pack the bags underneath the cabin and then reinforce his instructions for us to avoid the 'No Step' sign on the wing. I'd be strapped in on someone's lap and we would sit there on the grassy airstrip on our deserted farm waiting for Dad to do his final check.

Despite there being no other human life within cooee, Dad would open his window and loudly call out, 'Clear prop!'

The Kilkivan folk were both impressed and bemused by Dad's flying. When he stepped onto the pitch at a charity cricket match they called him 'Clear Prop Clarrie'.

Even though we flew regularly, we were never away for long. There were too many things to do back in Kilkivan. IEC would go back into the big steel hangar that was her home and I'd always wonder if she was a little lonely there when the sun dropped away and the chill of the evening set in. The sliding doors into that hangar were huge and heavy, and the next time we opened it, when the keys went into the lock and the latch flipped open, I'd take a step back and hope that snakes hadn't made their way in.

The fuel drums were the size of wine barrels but were filled with Avgas, a smell that would trigger my memories for decades to come. If I was lucky I'd get to open the valves and start pumping the red orange liquid that fed IEC.

Dad loved sharing her with others and would take friends on flights. One time he took graziers Pauline and Ian Fitzgerald to Brisbane for business and on the trip home the clear skies disappeared and they were surrounded by dense clouds. They couldn't see a thing and the conversation inside the plane's cabin dried up.

Dad wasn't endorsed for instrument flying which meant he was only licensed to fly if he could see where he was going. But he always did his homework and leaned over to Ian and said, 'We should shortly be over the summit of Sinai Mountain.'

A small gap in the clouds confirmed the mountain was directly under them. They made it home but good weather was never taken for granted.

Around this time, Robert, my eldest brother, was finishing a stint as a bank teller at the Commonwealth Bank in Mount Isa. There were a couple of options for kids growing up back then – stay on the farm or see how you went with the high school bank exam. Robert had done the exam and then worked in a bank in Gympie before moving to Mount Isa. At night he'd pull beers at the Barkly

Hotel so he could afford a flying lesson each week. He'd spend his spare time hanging out in the control tower at the small airport.

That's what Millars did.

There was only one flight a week from Brisbane to Mount Isa but light aircraft would fly in and out every day. Dad and Grandma decided to go and pick Robert up in IEC. It was a long trip from Kilkivan and Dad and Grandma touched down in Longreach to refuel before tracking north to Mount Isa.

Robert was watching the radar and could see a massive storm was moving in. He knew Dad wouldn't take risks, but he started getting worried.

And he was right to worry.

Inside the tiny cabin of IEC Dad and Grandma were feeling the turbulence. Sweat beads spread across Dad's forehead but Grandma sat there peeling an apple. It was her way of letting him know she had absolute confidence in his piloting skills.

When they touched down in Mount Isa, they taxied past the wreckage of several small aircraft that had been flipped over. The storm had been so wild the aircraft control operators were amazed they'd made it through. It was so remarkable a camera was immediately summonsed, and photos were taken of India Echo Charlie and its occupants parked among the debris.

'If you worry you do not trust; if you trust, you do not worry. Why pray if you worry? Why worry if you pray?' was the saying Grandma would often repeat. She was a woman of great faith in the power of positivity. And she had the ability to make you feel she had great faith in you.

While India Echo Charlie brought us all great joy, it was also a working member of the family and it had to earn its keep. Dad was now flying graziers to cattle sales as he looked for opportunities to make the most of IEC and the airstrip he'd created. When he returned, he'd fly over Kilkivan and waggle the wings – a universal sign for 'hello'.

Word about the farmer who'd built an airstrip was starting to spread. In December 1974 a skydiving team had just taken out the Australian Championships and was looking for somewhere to train ahead of the world competition in what was then West Germany.

Annie, the girlfriend of the team's captain, asked around at Archerfield, Brisbane's secondary and smaller airport, and was told there was a farm a few hours north that might suit them. The Kilkivan Council readily gave permission and the skydivers moved in to the showgrounds just down the road from the airstrip and our home. There were seventeen of them in total – including ten in the skydiving team, the pilot, two girlfriends and the captain's mum who was 'chief cook and bottle washer'. For six weeks they lived at the showgrounds where they had basic facilities, tents and swags and an entire town of several hundred people cheering them on. The Kilkivan pub even held a fundraiser for this bunch of strangers who'd lobbed into town.

Skydiving had started becoming more popular in the 1970s because of the development of quick release mechanisms on parachutes. The team was highly skilled but the manoeuvres were also high risk. They'd jump from their Twin Beech aircraft with the aim of accelerating to earth as quickly as possible, while also forming a circle before deploying their chutes. The stopwatch would start the minute the first team member left the plane and it stopped when the last one joined the circle.

In Kilkivan they could practise without any prying eyes, and also not have to worry about clearances or the Civil Aviation Authority. Not that they were planning anything that wasn't completely legal but bureaucracy and extreme sport weren't a comfortable match.

I was only five and my little sister, Trudi, was just three, but the skydiving team always welcomed the young daughters of the airstrip owner. And they were more than happy to see our older sister, Wendy. She was nineteen and a nurse in Brisbane by then but would make regular trips back to Kilkivan, partly due to homesickness and also the appeal of playing with her young sisters.

We were deposited on a rug on the grass near the hangar while Wendy was given personal tuition on best practices for rolling up parachutes. The skydivers' jumps and the speed with which they'd form their circles would happen too high for our eyes but their colourful parachutes would soon come into sight, floating delicately back down before landing with a thump on the hard ground in front of us.

The team celebrated the end of their time in town with a farewell party at Goomeri, thirty minutes up the road. And they went on to take a silver medal at the world championships, thanking us for the small part we'd played in their success with a signed and framed colour photo of them forming their mid-air circle.

While they insisted they were indebted to us, we felt like a little bit of magic had been sprinkled on our airstrip in Kilkivan.

\* \* \*

With India Echo Charlie ready for departure at a moment's notice, we saw a little more of its namesake, Ida Emma Cooper. She wasn't the kind of grandmother to spend time in the kitchen on those visits and disappear behind the steam as she extracted a tray of cupcakes from the oven. What she gave us was attention. And lots of it.

There was no book she didn't want to hear us stumble through a thousand times, no early singing attempts she wouldn't listen to, no ballet steps she didn't marvel at, no billy cart she wouldn't climb into. She was a large-boned woman but would get into whatever contraption had been built and would urge her grandchildren to push hard and send her flying down the hill, even if just to prove our impeccable workmanship.

Whatever the adventure, Grandma would always be part of it.

Grandma was never lean but I used to think her knuckles and joints were like the rings of a tree revealing the years of life that had challenged her. I inherited Grandma's sturdiness and the way our thighs morphed into knee joints and then into calves. Neither of us would have made catwalk models. But if inheriting Grandma's physical features was the trade-off for absorbing just a fraction of everything else about her, then it was worth it.

But things were changing for the Millars. India Echo Charlie was left at the strip without her propellers turning for months on end as Dad's career began going in another direction, a political one that would begin to take him far from home.

Planes were meant to fly and it felt cruel to keep IEC locked away in the hangar. After nine years she was sold to a rural Christian organisation that visited remote properties offering pastoral care. It felt right.

# CHAPTER 4

# Instruction Manual

THERE WAS NO daycare or kindergarten in Kilkivan and my first day in grade one, a month before I turned five, was horrifying. The school seemed so huge even though there were only around 150 kids, and that included the high school. I saw a familiar face or two but most of us were strangers to each other. It would be years before parents discovered the concept of playdates.

My first classroom was on the ground level of a two-storey weatherboard building. This room became the gardening shed once we'd finished grade one, but while we were there our teacher taught us to make bright crepe-paper flowers and ignore its sterility. It worked well until the home economics students upstairs defrosted their fridges and the water streamed down our walls and wilted our flowers.

We had slates and chalk in an antiquated set-up that I only discovered much later was not routine for other first-year students in Queensland in the mid-1970s.

If you wanted to study past grade ten you caught the bus for an hour to another town further west or you went to boarding school, as many country kids did.

\* \* \*

By the time I started school there was only the one pub in town, not that we spent much time there, and when we did it was only for a raspberry lemonade in the ladies' lounge out the back. The barmaids would come and serve you and it felt downright posh sitting there in a grown-up's chair with my legs dangling towards the floor.

The ladies' lounges were a fixture in Queensland pubs because, until 1970, women weren't allowed in public bars. Even the sign pointing you to Kilkivan's ladies' lounge was on the side street to avoid any accidental passageway through the public bar. The absurdity of it was reinforced when I returned in my forties and had a drink at the front bar for the first time.

Mum was working every day, hauling hay and milking cows alongside Dad, but if they went to the pub she would have been separated out the back with the 'ladies'.

The post office was run by the Farrows and my schoolmate Desley's mum also operated the telephone switchboard from there. We had a heavy black phone at home with a clear plastic circular disc with holes for you to stick your finger in to turn and dial the number. Most phone numbers in the area were a maximum of four digits so they weren't hard to remember.

It sounds basic now but it was a step up from the party line country towns used to have. That was a telephone circuit loop shared by multiple locals which ran the risk of offering zero privacy. Anyone who shared your party line could pick up and join in, or inadvertently catch the conversation, including the switchboard operator, who'd be in the process of connecting you with plugs and leads.

The public hall was the biggest building in the main street but any aspirations of grandeur were dampened by the fact that it couldn't be called a 'town' hall because Kilkivan was too small. It was important enough though that the education minister came to open it in the 1960s and it became the centre of the town's social life.

It was a simple pale-brick building with polished wooden floors and a stage at one end with thick red velvet curtains that dropped from the high ceiling and provided the backdrop for the ballet teachers and debutante ball instructors who'd gaze down on us.

When I was around ten we had a junior debutante ball there. Our teachers and parents must have been looking for an excuse to hold a dance because we were all too young to be 'coming out into society', which debutantes did in their late teens.

My parents were protective and not keen on me going, thinking it was peculiar that children were being encouraged to pretend they were debutantes entering adulthood. They relented slightly and agreed to me being an escort for the girls, walking them along the red carpet to their waiting partners. My friend Robynne's mother had the same dim view about the age-inappropriate deb ball so she ended up with the same job as me. We were happy to at least be involved. Another bonus was that we didn't have to wear the pastel-coloured dresses that made the other girls so unhappy. Instead, our mums stitched some material to the bottom of two white flower girls' frocks and we were ready for rehearsals.

Robynne was the kindest girl in the school and she had two great skills none of us could match: she always won the prize for best cursive handwriting at the Kilkivan Show and, better still, she had blonde hair so long she could sit on it in class.

But scandal almost derailed the junior deb ball. One of our classmates had discovered a magazine under her parents' bed and brought it to school for the kind of closer examination only ten-year-olds can give. We huddled in, thoroughly engrossed in the nude pictures, when Robynne's cries of 'I can't see, I can't see' attracted a teacher's attention.

Thoroughly chastised, we were told to confess to our parents or the teachers would talk to them instead and the junior deb ball would be cancelled.

There was no choice but to fess up – parental conversations we were still too pained to talk about decades later.

Outside the public hall, there was a garden that seemed dark and mysterious, full of vines and trees that provided hiding places for children playing tag and teenagers taking drags on their first cigarettes.

But the real treasure was inside the public hall: the shire library, a cavern of books, cushions, chairs and calmness. Every Friday after school we were permitted to borrow two books. The librarian, Elizabeth Leyer, was a kindly older woman who loved her young readers and the joy we showed when she pressed her heavy stamp on the slip inside the book cover.

Reading was never a chore because the library visit itself was such a treat. I thought I was roaming free in that place, making independent decisions, choosing books at will. But years later Mrs Leyer confessed to me that our mother had had a heavy hand in our reading choices. 'She made sure you could never find *Where the Wild Things Are* because she thought you'd be afraid,' she told me.

Afterwards, we'd make a stop at the Wex's store for twenty cents worth of mixed lollies, which always included a confectionery called 'Fags', white musk-flavoured lollies that looked like cigarettes and even came in a little packet like cigarettes. No one at the time seemed to think it was odd to be offering these to children.

Then we'd throw our school bags into the Datsun 120Y and tumble in after them, smelly and hot, our scuffed leather shoes leaving a trail of dust while we desperately tried not to start reading the books or consuming the lollies before reaching our dirt driveway.

The drive to our house on Mudlo Road seemed to stretch forever but it was not much more than a kilometre out of town. If you continued down the road you'd reach the creek and the Kilkivan Showgrounds, the scene of one of the great Millar family triumphs.

My older sister, Wendy, had been something of a tomboy, taking her horse Angus and disappearing for hours as she roamed across the countryside. When she was thirteen she'd decided to enter the horse-riding competition at the annual show. She'd borrowed another horse, worried that Angus wasn't up to the task of winning a ribbon and when the judges called her out from the circle of prancing riders no one was surprised.

Except when they declared her with great flourish 'the best boy rider'.

She stuck out what chest she had and informed them she was not in fact a boy. That was news to the judges who sent her back into the ring only to announce her moments later as 'best girl rider' and present her with a blue velvet ribbon and a dollar note that she promptly delivered to the man whose horse she'd borrowed.

Dad would later proudly declare it only went to show she was the very best rider on the day but that didn't stop us all teasing her long after she was a grown woman.

Trudi and I were a bit of a novelty to most people in Kilkivan, given Mum's age and the fourteen-year age gap to our next closest sibling. By the time we were at school, Robert, David and Wendy had long left home. We shared the same parents but at times it felt like we were two separate families.

David would return home occasionally and plonk me between the handlebars of his motorbike, deliberately roaring past Mum's tennis ladies, revving the engine just enough to drown out the tsk tsking.

Every family has a joker and David was ours. He was the brother who'd dress as Santa Claus but add his own slapstick antics that would have us weeping with laughter. He had the added benefit of being not only funny as a teenager but good looking. That had pluses and minuses for his education. To break the boredom of life in a boys-only boarding school he developed friendships with a different girl in each of the other schools. He was popular at dances as long as none of the girls crossed paths. The time he spent crafting love letters improved his English results, but keeping a check on the number of girls he'd befriended failed to help his maths, which he failed.

Maybe it was the farm upbringing, but David always seemed destined to work outdoors. Not long after he'd finished school he was laying sewerage pipes in Kilkivan. The company he worked for got a new contract a few hours south and he raced up the dirt road on his motorbike to tell the family he was heading off.

It was his eighteenth birthday and Mum had baked a cake. But he didn't have time for that and was gone. That was David.

I was only seven when I became an aunt for the first time when Robert and his wife Dot's first daughter was born. And Wendy, who studied nursing, was getting married as well and Trudi and I proudly walked down the aisle with her as flower girls. We were showered with love by our siblings and their spouses although it sometimes felt like we had too many sets of parents laying down the law.

\* \* \*

Among my family's closest friends in Kilkivan was Mary Green and her husband, Brian. When my parents met her, Mary already had her private pilot's licence, which was just one of several attributes that made her seem like an exotic creature in our midst. She also had a soft Massachusetts accent and could play the most complex piano pieces without so much as a pause. I only learned later she spoke impeccable French as well, as not a syllable was proffered, or needed, in Kilkivan.

Mary had been plucked from Texas where Brian, who had a much stronger American accent but was in fact a Kiwi, had been studying. Mary was working full-time and putting her husband through agriculture college. When he suggested she and their young son Philip move across the world to a place she could barely find on the map, she agreed. She was, after all, in love.

Mary, who was a decade younger than Mum, brought the smell of America with her. I didn't realise this connection until I lived in the United States twenty-five years later and felt a sudden homesickness for Kilkivan at a traditional Thanksgiving lunch as the large platters with the familiar American spices were placed on the table.

As children we would watch Mary set to work in her kitchen, wearing a knee-length apron, with her thick hair swept up into a loose bun. The aroma of cinnamon, vanilla beans, rosemary and sage would waft from her kitchen as she pulled muffins and pecan pies from her oven. Trudi and I were bug-eyed with astonishment. At home, Mum would occasionally put salt and pepper on the table but it wasn't encouraged and our idea of adding flavour was to splash our plates with tomato sauce.

The Greens had two sons and a daughter, all younger than me. Philip, the eldest in their family, was in Trudi's grade. They were further out of town than us and would normally catch rides to school with other farming families, except for Philip, who, even at a young age, was teased about being chubby, so started riding his bike the roughly eight kilometres into town. We thought he was so grown up.

The family built a home – a double-storey house made out of the palest of bricks with large white columns on the tiled front terrace. It was the first house I'd seen that wasn't a wooden Queenslander set above the ground on stumps that let the cold winter winds in through the floorboards.

The Greens' house had touches of Cape Cod architecture and a nod to their harsh new environment with the addition of a corrugated iron roof to catch the rain. They went through three builders in their attempts to get their home finished, the stress of that eased partly by the fact that each of the builders was called Dennis.

Trudi and I thought the house was a mansion. Mary, on the other hand, treasured the house we lived in, believing our low-set wooden house at the end of a long driveway was the nicest house in Kilkivan. It sat at the top of a small hill and the long dirt driveway circled around to the back of the house to deposit you near a beautiful old Chinese elm. The front of the house featured a pretty balcony and a view back down to the road and to the elevated paddocks in the distance.

Trudi and I would use the wide open runway between each doorway as our sprint track, running through the lounge room and then out the back and circling the house again and again until we were exhausted. There was risk involved if Mum had stretched out the hose between our circuits, or, as occurred on one occasion to me, if we misjudged our departure through the open sliding glass doors onto the veranda. My elevation was off by just a millimetre and I knew as I dragged my toes across the bottom metal track I was in strife. The blood seeped through the tea towel Mum wrapped tightly around my foot and, as she folded back a corner of the material and took a peep, she quietly announced there was a 'bit missing'.

Both David and Wendy were home that weekend and the search party was rallied. They didn't have to look far and the piece of flesh was put back on top of my toe and kept in place with surgical tape. Any medical issues in Kilkivan had to reach Millar family–certified emergency level to warrant the hour-long drive to Gympie and this was considered one of them.

Wendy, who'd been nursing for a few years, came for the ride and was delighted when the doctor asked if she would like to carry out the procedure on her kid sister. I thought he was joking but she scrubbed up and went to work on several very neat stitches, the scar still there forty years later.

\* \* \*

Mum had become obsessed with creating a lawn for our house on the hill. Perhaps she was inspired by the luscious green tropics of the plantation at Rabaul or the leafy Sydney suburbs where her family had returned before the war. But Kilkivan had none of the attributes of either of those landscapes.

Nevertheless, she got her lawn. It went around the house and extended to the first wire fence and unpainted wooden posts. It was hard grass that never softened under your feet no matter how liberal we were with the tank water. But it was the best the soil could muster.

Beyond the fence line was a paddock filled high with dry stringy grasses that looked more like weeds. The slightest wind would dislodge their gritty seeds and send them sailing towards the house.

Years earlier, in a fit of activity that would become a trademark, a teenage David decided to mow the paddock and get rid of the tall grass. It took him a day to push the mower up and down the hill, stopping just a metre from Mudlo Road. Everyone admired the end result but David then left for boarding school and it became Wendy's job to maintain the new lawn's appearance. She begged Dad for a ride-on mower, but he told her the chore kept her out of mischief so every few weeks she would begin what had become a two-day job: mowing the house yard, the roadside driveway and the front paddock.

Finally, when there were no more teenagers at home (and Trudi and I were too young), Mum took the job over and seemed to relish the harshness of the physical labour. She'd return to the house with the sun having burned its way into her shoulders, her legs pockmarked and bloody where the blades of the mower had spat out stone chips as if in protest at the savageness of the chore.

By the time Trudi and I were strong enough to push the mower my parents decided that it was too dangerous and that we were likely to lose a toe. We felt robbed but, in hindsight, the decision should have sparked celebration.

We eventually sold up in Kilkivan when I was about eleven and moved to Gympie which was more central for Dad. The prospective buyers, from 'elsewhere', wandered through to the kitchen in Kilkivan and asked Mum how she could possibly cope without flyscreens on her windows.

'Well, they fly in and then they fly out,' she told them brusquely, as if her standard of what was considered civilised life had been called into question.

There were plenty of flies in Kilkivan, I'll give them that. But they were sluggish enough on those long sweltering summer days to hit with the long-handled swatter. Those were the hot days when even the snakes couldn't be bothered moving when the thump of footsteps approached. I'd loved Kilkivan and didn't realise how special that country childhood had been. But it was also isolating and I never felt entirely comfortable with the darkness that stretched for miles around us as the lights were switched off each night. Gympie was a city. And I was about to become a city kid.

## CHAPTER 5

# Our Magnetic Compass

MY MOTHER HAD been outgoing as a child, growing up on the plantation in New Britain, skittering from here to there with the local children, diving into the deep blue waters of Lassul Bay, and playing hide and seek behind the huge trunks of the palm trees.

As a teenager she'd been cheeky, after discovering a pretty face and sparkling eyes looking back at her from the mirror. She'd had the confidence of a beautiful seventeen-year-old to let her workmates know that she was keen on the handsome young public servant she'd spotted walking through the post office each day.

As an adult though, she retreated. She saw the hard life her mother was living, a widow with a disabled son. She recognised the judgement of others, the sniggers of strangers at the gangly teenage boy so traumatised by his own birth. She became familiar with guilt, replaying in her head the selfish responses she'd given as a teenager to her mother's calm but repeated requests for help.

By the time she married Dad, she already carried great sadness with the early death of her own father and a brother who needed so much care. But that too was something she'd dismiss. 'Not like Grandma had to deal with,' she'd say if we ever wanted to talk about what she'd gone through as a child.

Mum always guarded her privacy, not in a dramatic manner but with quiet, tight lips that opened just enough for a small uncomfortable expulsion of air. Gossip irritated her, and she found it hard to contain her contempt for those who dallied with it to simply pass the time. 'Hmph,' she'd say.

My mother was a private person. So private that even writing these words makes me feel like I'm intruding.

Early in my career the Queensland newspaper *The Courier-Mail* decided to do a feature on me as the new host of *Stateline*, a weekly half-hour current affairs program. The photographer came round to my house and the journalist, Wayne Smith, chatted about my hopes and ambitions. I was twenty-nine and it was the first time I was on the other end of the questions.

Wayne asked me about plans for children and I fobbed off the question with a throwaway remark that Mum had given birth to me just after her thirty-ninth birthday and then gone on to have another child so I felt like I had time on my side.

The paper came out and I was featured on the magazine cover. I regretted some of the naivety of my answers but I was generally happy. Mum, however, was not.

She stopped talking to me. We'd been at loggerheads before but our relationship was good. I loved her dearly. I had no idea why she was so upset until Dad explained it was because I'd inadvertently revealed her age. I was twenty-nine and had proudly spoken of her being thirty-nine when she had me. It didn't take a maths genius to work it out.

Mum wasn't vain. She was simply private. And now the world knew more than she wanted it to know.

It was the only time we ever fell out and it only ended several weeks later after I'd sent her a heartfelt card pleading with her to forgive me. She didn't like to talk about things so nothing more was said.

For a short period when Trudi and I were not yet teenagers, we lived in a caravan on Mary and Brian Green's property in Kilkivan. It was the start of a short but turbulent disruption in our lives. The caravan was old and I remember the musty smell when we returned from school and opened the thin metal door. Mum never told Mary why we needed to stay there and Mary never asked.

Mary suspected Mum was not well. Mary's friendship with Mum was strong but Mum's desire for privacy was resolute. We eventually returned to our own bedrooms in Kilkivan and nothing more was said. Mum didn't want to talk about it then and she wouldn't if she was with us now.

There were moments when Mum would catch everyone off guard with a flash of independence. Once, she went to the small building society in the main street of Gympie. In a hesitant voice, she queried if a maturing $100,000 term deposit, an inheritance from Grandma, could perhaps be earning higher interest. She was led to the manager's corner office where, with a superior tone, he suggested she call her husband for guidance. One thing led to another and Mum withdrew the lot there and then. She never entered that bank again.

She never dwelled on these moments of decisiveness or explored what had been her tipping point. The only reason we knew she'd swept out of there having closed her account and with a bank cheque in her purse was because the manager had rung Dad before Mum got home to see if he could talk her round.

'I'm afraid that would return a negative result, my learned friend,' Dad would have told him.

Mum would get a bee in her bonnet that quickly became an entire hive buzzing with her fury. It also revealed itself when any of her 'babies' were under threat.

When we made the move from Kilkivan to Gympie, I was eleven and Trudi was nine. We were introduced to a school that felt ten times the size of the one at Kilkivan. The buildings were larger and there were more of them. There seemed to be so many students, we wondered if they'd combined two schools into one. And our new school had a pool, which was quite an accomplishment for a state school in a regional town in the late 1970s.

The pool would have delighted us if all we had to do was jump into the shallow end and, like monkeys, cling to the edge and make our way round the perimeter, patting ourselves on the back for our bravery when we reached the ladder to climb out. Unfortunately for the two of us, the school had a formal swimming program that everyone else had been compliantly following since grade one.

When we'd lived in Kilkivan the closest pool to us had been at Goomeri, thirty minutes' drive away, and while Mum had invested time in piano lessons, swimming classes hadn't been a priority. We'd splashed around in creeks, swinging out on ropes and dropping into the water, but we'd rarely swum in deeper water, like dams, for fear of getting dragged under by some mysterious farm-like version of the Loch Ness monster. And we didn't like having to tiptoe through moist cow patties of manure to get to the dam.

For country kids, learning to navigate the water was often more about what was necessary than a formal swimming program. Dad's friend Ian Fitzgerald had taught his kids how to wade across a flooded bridge with their books on their heads and their shoes in their bags. Ian would make the crossing first to check the current and then send the kids on their way to the bus. They practised, under their parents' gaze, falling into the river in their school clothes, learning how to dodge logs and float with the pull of the water until they got out. Their mum, Pauline, was so keen on a proper education that the water was rarely considered too high to warrant a missed day of school.

Our home in Kilkivan had been near Running Creek Road but the name became a misnomer as the seasons became drier and the water barely reached our knees. The only danger we faced was cutting our feet on the sharp edges of protruding rocks and the search for swimming holes got harder.

There was nothing fun about the pool at One Mile State School in Gympie.

For us two little non-swimmers it seemed to stretch forever with a bottom so deep I could only carefully shuffle myself to the edge to see if it actually had one.

All classes had an assigned hour in the pool each week and the kids would scurry down there so not a minute was wasted. The boys would excitedly punch and kick each other on the way, faking howls of pain, before dumping their gear inside the change room and bounding into the pool with as much velocity as possible, in a bid to spray the teachers standing guard.

The girls would approach the session a little more timidly, not because of any reluctance to get in the water but due to the pressure that came with undressing in front of others. And then there was the moment when we pretended to avert our eyes as at least one girl would hand over a note excusing them from the class because they were 'unwell'.

The swimming teacher, a woman in her thirties, was tall and muscly with a long thick blonde braid of hair that was secured at the base of her neck and then allowed to swing free. Her immaculate grooming reminded me of a show horse and her obvious attachment to her hair only confirmed my initial assessment.

No doubt she had the best of intentions when she decided the way to handle the two timid swimmers from Kilkivan was to plunge our heads under the water, holding us down until we spluttered to the surface. It had the effect you'd imagine. Not only were we now terrified of the expanse of water but we were scared of her as well.

It was only a matter of weeks before Trudi began begging off school with a 'sore tummy' whenever her class was scheduled to swim. And it didn't take long for Mum to put two and two together. She stormed up to the principal's office to lodge a complaint.

If only the principal, Mr Carter, had received forewarning from the bank manager who'd had a taste of Mum in full flight but, alas, he was oblivious and attempted to soothe her with reassurances that the swimming teacher was the expert and it needed to be left in her qualified hands.

Trudi was withdrawn from swimming lessons and miraculously recovered from her regular sicknesses while I persevered, knowing that I only had a few short months left at primary school before leaving for high school so there was at least an end in sight.

Forty years later, I returned to One Mile for its 150th anniversary. Trudi took her young family, and some old school friends joined me for the drive from Brisbane. They were eager to revisit classrooms and the concrete parade ground where we'd gather each morning to sing 'God Save the Queen'. A couple of hours later we'd have 'little lunch' and skip with pieces of elastic stretched between our knobbly young knees.

Trudi and I headed straight to the pool, our nemesis. We walked along the familiar concrete path, turned the corner and looked at each other in shock. The gigantic mass of water that had struck us down with terror had been replaced with a smaller pool. Or so we thought. Had we really been so frightened of that twenty-five metres of water, the lane markings set by ropes of colourful balls floating there so harmlessly?

The swimming teacher was also there that day, smiling and chatting to other former students who'd prospered under her coaching. But I couldn't bring myself to say hello. The years had not diminished my feeling of fear, or the loss of control I felt during those lessons.

The move to Gympie had been hard for all of us. Mum was often a solo parent as Dad spent time in his electorate and Canberra. Trudi and I didn't make it easier. We were the best of friends who could turn on each other in a flash, wrestling one day with such ferocity we left a crack in the plaster wall. I probably covered it with a Boy George poster. Each of us had dreams about the world that waited for us. We'd seen a glimpse of it through our travels with Dad to Canberra and we knew there was a bigger life to be had.

\* \* \*

Our grandmother Ida Cooper had been in her early seventies when I was born but she wore her age well.

She'd moved from Hervey Bay to Brisbane to get more help for her son, Thomas, as he grew increasingly unwell and his fits of aggression became more regular. He was in care again, this time at an institution in Wolston Park, and Grandma moved into the fourteenth floor of an apartment building on Moray Street, New Farm. It was in a leafy pocket of Brisbane sitting along the winding brown river just a couple of kilometres from the city centre.

The streets were dotted with beautiful old Moreton Bay fig trees whose roots would create miniature craters in the footpaths. She had a beautiful view of the river and the city.

Being on the fourteenth floor meant two things – Trudi and I would always fight over who'd get to push the buttons in the lift and who'd get to drop the rubbish down the chute and hear it bang from side to side as it fell into the bin in the basement.

Grandma's flat had a single bedroom that was separated from the lounge area with a heavy concertina blind that took all our strength to open. The combined bathroom and laundry, tucked away with no natural light, scared us both. But it was the magical world inside Grandma's glass cabinet that filled our hearts.

It was full of tiny delicate souvenirs, pieces of china, dancing ballerinas and enchanting music boxes from her travels.

Robert, David and Wendy had only been allowed to sit and gaze in wonder at the cabinet, letting their minds imagine the places where these marvellous objects had come from. By the time Trudi and I came along, years later, the rules had been relaxed and we could unlock the glass doors and carefully hold and admire the objects up close, no doubt as Grandma held her breath.

I imagined the countries they'd come from and wondered how long it would be before I could be a traveller in those foreign lands. The dream of great adventures was growing.

On one side of her building was the city of Brisbane, with the lights of the old Port Office and Customs House twinkling at night. The other side of the building led down to Moray Street and just a few blocks from there were the seedy laneways of Fortitude

Valley, where police corruption and illegal prostitution would be revealed years later.

Grandma's unit had been a refuge for my older siblings who escaped the confines of their Brisbane boarding schools on weekends for day excursions. Grandma gave them driving lessons as they crossed the city to pick up Uncle Tommy from the Wolston Park psychiatric hospital he was living in and then return him at the end of the day.

Years later, Trudi and I only occasionally saw Uncle Tommy when we visited Grandma's. He was in his fifties by then and his joy came from old records, movie posters and cigarettes.

The government had shut down Wolston Park where he'd been living and moved people with mental impairments into boarding houses in the city. It caused enormous stress for Grandma, who always worried what would happen to him.

Dad had been called in to help on more than one occasion when Uncle Tommy's episodes took hold. We'd learn he'd been kicked out of a boarding house, or caught running naked through the streets of New Farm. In the end, Uncle Tommy died before Grandma, of thyroid cancer, and while the family grieved, it also meant his mother's dilemma, of who would care for him when she died, disappeared.

A while after we'd moved to Gympie, Grandma came to live with us. She was well into her eighties and needed more care. Mum was adamant she would be the one to give it.

I was in high school and felt slightly resentful that Mum's priority was no longer us. Trudi and I suddenly discovered we had more freedom without Mum's watchful eye but we didn't know what to do with it. My closest friend, Sharon Steele, lived next door to a small grocery store with her widowed mum and we'd spend hours at her place or mine trawling over the details of our secret crushes on boys who didn't know we existed, writing love letters that were never posted. I studied diligently, loved English but hated maths, and ended up in an all-girl class at my mixed public high school which added to my shyness around boys for the rest of my school years. And that suited Mum and Dad just fine.

Grandma's strong limbs were failing her and Mum would take her for long drives that would sometimes last for hours, the car pulling into the driveway as the sun was setting.

A commode was moved into Grandma's room when she could no longer walk to the toilet and Mum gradually accepted that her mother's physical and mental health was in decline.

There was not a huge choice of aged care facilities in Gympie but the decision was still difficult to make.

I was fifteen and poured out my heart in a poem I then sent on a whim to *Dolly* magazine – a teenage girl's constant companion in the 1980s. The editor, a young Lisa Wilkinson who would go on to become one of Australia's most popular personalities, decided it was worth publishing and I received a typed letter confirming it would appear in the next month's magazine. I think I got twenty dollars for it but the money didn't matter. I'd been published and it was exciting despite the subject matter.

Watching such a vital woman age so quickly was hard, and writing about it had eased some of my teenage anxiety. Even in her decline, Grandma was still helping her family climb.

## CHAPTER 6

# Pitch

DAD CERTAINLY HAD a way with words.

'The sun is beating down with vexatious tenacity,' he'd remark to one of the farmers.

'Yeah, Clarrie, it's bloody hot,' the voice from under the hat would respond.

It wasn't that Dad tried to bamboozle people with how he used the words that had been swimming in his head since he was an avid reader as a child – he just didn't know any other way to communicate. We would sigh with frustration that he couldn't simply say it was 'bloody hot'.

Even when he exploded with anger, he'd do it with linguistic flair. 'Jesus Christ!' he'd say when dishes were banged loudly in the kitchen. 'We can only be thankful you're currently not employed in an ammunitions factory,' he'd declare in a somewhat Churchillian tone to whomever had made the noise.

Dad's involvement in local farm groups – and possibly his oratory skills – attracted the attention of senior Country Party officials. Everyone was impressed by what he said and how he said it, even if they didn't always know what some of the words actually meant.

It wasn't long before he was encouraged to put his hand up for preselection and was chosen to run for the party in the federal seat of Wide Bay. It was 1974 and Gough Whitlam had called a double dissolution after the Coalition leader Billy Snedden threatened to block supply. Whitlam had been prime minister for just eighteen months and, although he was in the middle of a recession and had faced an oil crisis the previous year, he wasn't expected to lose.

Wide Bay had become a safe Labor seat, held for thirteen years by Brendan Hansen who was considered a sure thing in the approaching election.

Dad was such an outside bet that the *Maryborough Chronicle* splashed its front page with the headline 'Clarrie Who?'.

The campaign team had a big job ahead convincing voters Clarrie Who was someone they knew. They didn't resile from the challenge and instead adopted 'Clarrie Who' as the theme.

The campaign involved Dad standing on the back of a flatbed truck, a microphone in his hand as the heavy-duty speaker crackled out his voice to unsuspecting shoppers in main streets across the electorate. Trudi and I posed for family photos with Dad in his safari suit, while Mum smiled in silent acquiescence.

Gough Whitlam won the election but Labor lost Wide Bay with a swing of almost seven per cent to a little-known farmer from Kilkivan, the new Country Party member.

Dad threw himself into his new career and we'd sometimes traipse along although the functions could drag on and prove boring. I was five when Dad was elected and for years Trudi and I would fall asleep in the car parked outside country halls, waking as the engine started late in the night for the long journey home.

I was fascinated though by the reporters I'd see turn up with their spiral notepads in one hand, a pen and a cigarette in the other. They were mostly men. And they brought photographers as well. Some had tape recorders and I watched as they challenged Dad over various issues related to the region: high unemployment, sand mining on Fraser Island, the quality of the federally funded highway.

The newspapers were big and filled with ads and thirsty for plenty of content from the new conservative MP. His staff kept all the clippings, folders filled with his views on all matter of things. He weighed in to whether the ABC Board should 'grant spouse entitlements to homosexual partners of ABC staff'. Dad was firmly opposed and the newspaper reported his belief that the Labor Government's 'layback [sic] attitude on such matters simply encourages the swingers to run wild'.

Swingers running wild! The very thought.

I loved this new thing called 'the media' and would try to replicate it at home. I'd hold a small tape recorder, one that Dad used for dictation, near five-year-old Trudi, waiting patiently for her attention. I would start by humming the ABC news theme, the well-known 'Majestic Fanfare', and then leap into my questions, mispronouncing Gough Whitlam's name as 'Whipham', and then butting in with another question the minute Trudi tried to answer in a low gravelly voice. It was a man's world. We didn't think either a journalist or the interviewee could be speaking in a female voice.

The family seemed to barely recover from one election campaign when the next would arrive. The historic 1975 double dissolution, which saw Gough Whitlam controversially dismissed and Malcolm Fraser go on to win government, came just eighteen months after Dad had entered parliament.

The farmer from Kilkivan was now in government and he was able to advocate for his electorate in a way he hadn't been able to before. When sand mining on Fraser Island was banned, he argued for a huge compensation package for the workers who'd lost jobs.

But Dad loved the parliamentary procedures of Canberra more than the politics. He corrected people who called him a politician. He considered himself a parliamentarian.

And the words he had discovered deep in those books he'd devoured when he was younger now found a home in the pages of Hansard. Tintinnabulations. Propinquity. Germane. Concomitant.

His speeches weren't scripted and he mostly spoke without notes. The stenographers must have sighed a little on the inside when Clarrie took the floor. 'Legerdemain' made its way into Hansard, courtesy of Dad, for only the second time in Australian history. The word means deception or trickery. The other time it was spoken inside the chamber was in 1905 by a former prime minister who was described as 'quirky'.

Particular quotes were considered worthy enough to be repeated to us back in Gympie. 'Parliamentarians fall short of that which we expect of them simply because they will insist on behaving just like people,' he'd say to loud groans from Trudi and me.

'We know, Dad, we know.' But on he'd go.

'They warp logic and reason for their own desire and have a preoccupation with the next election whilst the next generation goes down the drain.'

Later, when we were teenagers, he'd use parenting analogies in parliamentary speeches as his concerns over the financial direction of the country grew. 'I am convinced that there is only one point of difference between governing a country in a democracy and bringing up a family where the youngsters know in an instant what they want.

'The parents, hopefully having acquired a modicum of wisdom through experience, have to make a judgement essentially on two points: firstly whether it is good for them, and secondly, whether they can afford it. If the answer is "no" on either point, the youngsters instantly hate their parents' guts but they cannot vote them out at the next election. That is the only point of difference.'

He was praised in parliament but his audience at home was less than enthusiastic on his return. We'd grown used to not having him there. He'd come home and drop his brown briefcase with a gold embossed H of R on the floor and, on occasions, we'd barely glance up from whatever we were doing.

We started spending school holidays in Canberra. Sometimes our visits would include Mum, sometimes not. It was not a world she was interested in, or had coveted, and she felt she had little in common with the other wives of politicians. How she longed to be back on the farm at Kilkivan, her body strained from the manual labour but her mind free of the stress she now endured in this new role.

Initially the thrill of Canberra revolved around rides on the carousel in the city centre but, as I grew older, I became fascinated by the press gallery. It was the clearest example of what being a journalist was about, asking questions, forcing answers. I'd always been curious about the world and here in front of me was the career that was going to let me explore it. I was just a young, naive teenager from Gympie but I longed for a larger life.

Dad wasn't an enthusiastic backer of my journalistic ambitions initially but he soon saw how enthralled I was. I'd sit there during question time watching the faces of the journalists as they jostled for seats in the gallery upstairs. The politicians, my dad's colleagues and friends, were of less interest.

Space was tight in the old parliament house and it was often standing room only as the journalists rushed in as the last bells sounded. There was Laurie Oakes, Peter Harvey, Paul Kelly in his dark high-neck skivvies, and Michelle Grattan. I knew their faces from the newspapers and TV. But my eyes would dart along the row looking for one of my favourites, Richard Carleton.

I was seventeen by then and had been watching him on the ABC's nightly current affairs program he hosted with Max Walsh called the *Carleton–Walsh Report*, or as it was nicknamed, 'Carwash'.

Tall, dark-haired and totally intimidating, Carleton was most famous for a question he'd asked of Labor leader Bob Hawke in 1983. The former leader Bill Hayden had resigned earlier that day and Carleton asked Hawke how he felt about having blood on his hands. Hawke blew up at what he called Carleton's 'damned impertinence'.

Dad knew I was a fan and one day asked Richard if he might have time to speak to his teenage daughter who was interested in journalism when she was next down in Canberra. It was 1986 and Queensland politics was about to upend the federal arena.

The premier, Joh Bjelke-Petersen, had wielded his power on the conservatives for almost two decades. His reign would end ignominiously, and he would go down in history as one of the most controversial figures in Australian politics. But before the stench of corruption brought him down, he was plotting to enter federal parliament and become prime minister.

Behind the scenes, the 'Joh for pm' campaign was taking shape and Dad's seat was a crucial element.

The federal seat of Wide Bay took in Joh's hometown of Kingaroy so backers of the 'Joh for pm' campaign, which included wealthy Gold Coast businessmen who were nicknamed the 'White Shoe Brigade' because of the way they dressed, schemed to remove Dad.

The role of Queensland Agent-General in London was floated as an enticement for Dad to step aside. It was a government job that involved promoting Queensland's interests overseas and would have been highly sought after. But he wasn't interested in having anything to do with getting Joh to Canberra.

'Joh is Not My Leader', the front-page headline in *The Courier-Mail* read, quoting Dad, as the pressure ratcheted up on him to quit his seat. Dad believed the voters had put him there and only they could decide to remove him.

In the end Dad stood firm, the Joh campaign collapsed months later and Bob Hawke was re-elected in May 1987, thanks in part to the disunity within the ranks of the Coalition.

That bizarre episode in Australian politics, and Dad's involvement in it, was still to come when he stopped Carleton in the corridor.

Richard Carleton was enthusiastic. 'Give me a shout when she's down,' he said, no doubt thinking it was useful to keep a Queensland conservative MP on side for down the track. He kept his word and the encounter had an impact that lasted long beyond the few hours I spent with him.

I arrived at the ABC's Northbourne studios in Canberra where the *Carleton–Walsh Report* was broadcast and asked for Mr Carleton. He suggested I make an instant coffee for him, which was probably an accurate assessment of the extent of my abilities at that point. But mostly I just sat and listened and watched.

As the show went to air live that evening I sat with mouth open and mind in overdrive. Everything about the studio, with its lights and camera operators and floor managers, was thrilling. And as Carleton farewelled the audience and the program credits rolled over a wide shot of the desk, he indicated to me to sit on the other stool and just nod and talk.

It was just a matter of seconds but I'd made my first appearance on the ABC and I was hooked.

Carleton drove me back to the motel where I was staying with Dad, and offered a final bit of advice. 'If you're going to be a journalist, aim for the top. If you're just going to be a mediocre journalist, forget it. There are thousands of them out there. Aim for the top, as far as you can go, and you'll make it.'

We called Mum with instructions to record the show on her chunky VHS tape, which she wouldn't see for another hour because of the daylight saving time difference between Queensland and the ACT.

*Don't be mediocre.*

Richard Carleton quit the ABC the next year and joined *60 Minutes* where his style of reporting attracted plenty of critics but I remembered the time he'd given me and the genuineness of his advice.

When I was in the US on my first overseas posting for the ABC I vowed to send him a note and let him know his words still sat with me.

I never did. And in 2006 Richard Carleton collapsed and died of a massive heart attack during a press conference at the scene of the Beaconsfield gold mine disaster in Tasmania.

I regretted I'd never told him his advice had driven me through the first decade and a half of my career.

Peter Harvey, his colleague at Channel 9, said, 'Whatever Richard was, he was not a shade of grey, he was a primary colour.'

Just a couple of years after I'd met Richard Carleton Dad began suffering worrying medical incidents. His brain started playing tricks on him. He'd be mid-sentence dictating notes to his secretary and he'd have mini blackouts that were almost imperceptible.

One of those blackouts, lasting longer than the others, happened in front of the television cameras at an event in his electorate. For someone who'd prided himself on his ability to comprehend and communicate it was devastating.

Mum, Dad and I were in Canberra in early 1990 for a parliamentary sitting week when Bob Hawke called an election for March. It would be Dad's seventh if he stood again. But instead, at sixty-four, he decided to call an end to his parliamentary career. It was the day before my twenty-first birthday and we celebrated and commiserated at the Tang Dynasty, a Chinese restaurant in the suburb of Kingston.

Dad had often despaired at some of the behaviour of the parliament, but he loved the institution and believed in its traditions and its central role in creating the future of the nation. It was going to be a very difficult goodbye.

Even more devastating for him, he decided to hand in his pilot's licence, no longer able to trust his brain to keep him and others safe. There were no tears from this man though.

It would be another two decades before I ever saw him cry. He was hovering near the stereo as he pressed the play button for *Evita*'s 'Don't Cry for Me Argentina'. He'd turned the volume up to a level just high enough for the neighbours to hear but not too loud to cause a complaint and, as the tears welled in his eyes, he turned to me and said, 'That's just beautiful, isn't it, lassie?'

I'd wondered if there was something else hidden in the music that had moved him so much but he didn't reveal anything more and we let the music fade to its natural ending.

# CHAPTER 7

# Crosscheck

LEAVING GYMPIE IN my teens for university was not the smoothest of departures. I was thrilled to be finally putting dreams into action and had succeeded in getting a place to study but not a place to live.

The solution came in an advertisement buried in the classifieds at the back of *The Courier-Mail* that thumped onto the lawn in Gympie each morning shortly before six. The deliverer would slow his car just slightly, wind down his window and hurl the paper without a backward glance. If Dad was home he'd be first out the door. His insomnia meant he was always up before any of us, but he was also keen to check if the marksman had taken out another of Mum's roses with his dodgy aim.

'Private board for two quiet country girls,' the ad read.

The Christmas holidays had sped by and I'd been desperate to know if I'd been accepted into the journalism course at Queensland's Institute of Technology. The practical hands-on nature of the course meant it spat out a steady stream of students who were quickly snapped up by the commercial TV networks and big newspapers. But, due to its popularity, the entry score required was approaching the same level as a medicine degree and therefore completely out of my academic league.

I shouldn't have been surprised when the rejection letter slid into our small pale-brick letterbox, but it sparked a torrent of tears that only a hormonal sixteen-year-old could deliver. I was convinced my career had been ruined before it had even begun.

Mum raised an eyebrow and waited a few days for calm to be restored. I soon realised the alternative offer – a Bachelor of Arts from the University of Queensland – wasn't so bad. It did mean, though, that by the time I saw the ad for board in the paper, things were starting to get a little desperate.

The ad offered breakfast and dinner and a shared bathroom for a weekly rate of eighty dollars in a large sprawling wooden house in Brisbane's upmarket western suburbs. The house was home to two middle-aged soon-to-be empty nesters who had just one son still with them.

It was appealing on a few levels. I was still only sixteen and a little daunted at leaving home. I'd started grade one earlier than most kids due to a quirk of the Queensland school year and my February birthday. When I was four that had been a relief for Mum because the lack of preschool or daycare in our small country town meant she was struggling to keep me occupied. But it also meant I was always a year younger than my classmates.

It hadn't really mattered in Kilkivan where most of our classes were a mixed bag of ages and abilities.

But when we'd moved to Gympie, I was suddenly sitting next to thirteen-year-olds who could have written a manual on modern romance in the 1980s, they seemed so grown up. My afternoon homework involved ploughing through year-old copies of *Dolly* magazine that I'd bought from the second-hand bookshop in town so I wouldn't feel so naive among the other girls, let alone how I might have felt among any boys.

There'd been a murmur or two, within earshot but not involving me, as to whether holding me back a year might be wise. Thankfully they held off but it did mean I was heading to university in the city as a very young sixteen-year-old.

Part of my lack of life experience came from the fact I hadn't been allowed to have too many experiences. Mum and Dad's approach to strictness was pretty straightforward – you couldn't have too much of it.

While neither of my parents was as heavy with discipline with Trudi and me as they had been with my older siblings, they were still very protective. As well as being obsessed with flying, Dad was obsessed with safety, whether it was with flight or his family. 'You can't wrap us in cottonwool,' my sister and I would say when yet another outing or adventure or sleepover at a friend's place had been canned.

I'd once begged my parents to let me go to a party after the last performance of the school musical I'd been in. The arguments went on for weeks and not even my grade ten debating team skills could convince them they would ruin my life if I couldn't go. I was petulantly resigned to having lost the fight, but Dad was taking no chances and delivered the ultimate embarrassment by firmly taking my hand and walking me out of the school hall at the end of the performance.

There was no doubt they loved us but we were always their 'little girls'. Dad made this clear when he gave a speech to the school's thousand-strong assembly in his role as the local federal MP and told them his 'little chickens' were both students at the school, not that anyone could see me at that point since I'd slid down under the seat.

So the idea of sending me off to board with a family in Brisbane appealed to my parents due to the extra protection it might offer. The other reason my parents and I liked the ad in the Saturday paper was because we had exhausted all other options.

My meticulously crafted letters of inquiry to the residential colleges that lined the sweeping roads around the university were met with swift rejections telling me all rooms had been taken months earlier and if I intended to reapply for the following year I would do well to take a more expeditious approach.

What were we to know? I was the first in the family to go to university and we were all a bit clueless.

It was 1986 and my older siblings were all living and working in Brisbane by then with young families squeezing into small houses in faraway suburbs. Boarding with them wasn't an option.

In early February I packed my suitcases, tossing in a teddy bear my brother Robert had given me as a baby, along with my portable red cassette player with two tape decks and an FM radio that a few years later would be more excitingly referred to as a 'boombox'.

I looked so young that Carolyn, the other 'quiet country girl' who'd arrived to claim her room, took a look at Mum, Trudi and me and thought Trudi, who was two years younger than me but two centimetres taller, was going to be her new housemate.

Carolyn's parents had also thought boarding privately with a family would be the perfect transition for their daughter to life in the big smoke. She had long, thick red hair and was petite – a body shape neither of us could claim by the end of that first year of living away from home. She was already seventeen and lived in Bauple, a one-pub town further north up the Bruce Highway from Gympie. Her dad had been a long-haul truckie but had suffered from the hours on the road and had retired early. Her mum worked at the Department of Social Security in the nearest big town, Maryborough.

Carolyn was an only child, or so I thought, until she confided in me later her older sister had died of leukaemia and that she'd shared my name, something that had made her mum baulk on first meeting me.

Carolyn had also applied to the residential colleges and missed out, although she'd steered clear of the ones that encouraged some evidence of a religious education. I was so naive I didn't even know some of them were aligned to churches, which made me relieved I'd been too late with my applications.

Our family had always had a little bit of an ad hoc approach to religion. Mum firmly believed in God and spent her life scribbling out notes of particular verses that might give her strength depending on whatever challenge she was facing. But her belief in the bricks and mortar of churches was not so inviolable.

Mum and Dad had attended the Anglican Church in Kilkivan when they'd first arrived in the 1950s. It was a white wooden building sporting a couple of small crosses above its doors and lacking any of the stained-glass windows or embellishments you'd find in bigger towns.

Robert, David and Wendy all went to Sunday school and threw themselves into it with such relish that Robert and Wendy became junior instructors. But the church coffers weren't in great shape and the pastor suggested Dad might like to add a little more to the plate if he wanted to guarantee a proper burial under God's gaze when the time came. Dad, then only in his late thirties, wasn't planning on dying anytime soon, and he was also dead broke. So my parents packed up their bibles and moved down the road to the Union Church where their meagre but enthusiastic contributions to the weekly plate and the church community weren't questioned.

Later, Trudi and I were regular Sunday school attendees at the same church although by then it was called Junior Friends and had been moved to a Thursday afternoon, to make it more palatable to a new generation.

We would gather in a room that doubled as the venue for our weekly ballet lessons. These were taken by a rather stern woman who, despite being married with children, was referred to as Miss

Williams. She drove from Gympie once a week determined to encourage a bunch of tomboys into tutus.

I was not particularly successful at either of the ventures that took place in that room but while Mum recognised the futility of the ballet lessons her commitment to faith didn't falter.

When we moved to Gympie Mum did a bit of church window-shopping and landed on another denomination altogether – the Church of Christ on Horseshoe Bend, which apparently had the added appeal of a weekly gathering of pious young girls called Girls' Brigade.

I didn't mind the idea, although I was equally happy not to go because it was late on a weekday evening when I'd rather be home watching telly.

While Mum was keen for us to continue having some sort of Christian education, the experience ended when I dobbed on the girls who were regularly ducking out the back of the church to have a ciggie. It was a tough decision for Mum, who had to weigh up her concern for her young daughters' spiritual upbringing versus her scorn of smokers. The scorn won.

When I moved in with my fellow 'quiet country girl' Carolyn years later in Brisbane I confessed smoking had been considered such a life-threatening transgression that I'd been too scared to ever show a moment of teenage rebellion and try one.

Carolyn was way ahead of me. When she was fifteen a friend of her parents came to stay in Bauple and brought her daughter, who was a few years older than Carolyn. The two of them would sneak off into the bush behind the house and smoke cigarette after cigarette. The visit only lasted a few days but Carolyn was convinced she was addicted by the time they left. There wasn't much she could do about it though, given there was only one shop in Bauple and any cigarette purchase would be immediately reported back to her parents.

But in Brisbane we had a new freedom to play with.

The problem was we were completely lacking both sophistication and fake IDs. You couldn't buy cigarettes if you were under eighteen. Carolyn decided to write to her friend Bruce, who was studying at university in Rockhampton, to ask him to post us some cigarettes.

The back and forth communication via snail mail took several weeks. Bruce responded asking if we preferred a particular type of cigarette. Once that was sorted (we, of course, had no preference and no clue) Bruce took our request at its most literal and two cigarettes turned up in a regular white envelope in the letterbox.

We located some matches and sought the privacy of the oval at Indooroopilly State High School to inhale. I coughed my way through my first cigarette and decided it was probably a habit I was happy not to adopt.

True to our parents' hopeful expectations, our lives in Brisbane as first-year university students were sheltered. Inside the house at Indooroopilly our lives fell into a predictable rhythm.

The owners of the house, Arnold and Nancy, had given us the back end of their home – two bedrooms and a shared bathroom, as advertised. My room had a sliding door to the veranda and a window that looked out over a lush green backyard.

Nancy and Arnold seemed old to us at the time but they were probably only in their fifties. Their son who still lived at home, Andrew, was in his twenties and we'd occupy ourselves watching him potter in the garden and then run for cover when the automatic sprinklers came on.

They had three other adult children who would arrive for dinner on occasions. Their son David brought with him an exotic bohemian girlfriend with long dark hair who wore trendy flipflops and rings on her toes, a daring act of fashion that left us wide-eyed with awe.

Their children's arrival would warrant takeaway for dinner and we'd always be invited to join them. Our favourite was from a restaurant that combined the cuisines of Indonesia and India and whose dishes were a complex array of spices foreign to both of us. For 'two quiet country girls', our host family's seemingly blasé approach to ordering takeaway, let alone from countries we'd struggle to pinpoint on a world map, was yet another example of the different lives we'd been leading.

In the 1970s and 1980s, most country towns in Australia had one of three kinds of takeaway food options. Depending on the size of the town, you could end up with all three. There was fish and chips at a burger joint, a pizza place and, if you really wanted to splash out, Chinese. Gympie's Chinese restaurant was called Sun's and was in the main street a few doors down from the second-hand bookshop that had been my source of out-of-date teen-girl magazines. We went so rarely that when I was in Brisbane Chinese takeaway continued to be something I thought you only got on special occasions.

It wasn't that Nancy didn't cook. She often did; after all, they'd offered breakfast and dinner for their two boarders so there was probably some pressure to deliver that nightly meal. Not that she needed to stress on my account. I'd come from a home where any meal planning occurred in the minutes before the fridge was opened and generally only after we'd whined about being hungry. The content of Millar family meals was often an afterthought.

Mum hated being cooped up inside the house and would stay in the garden until long after the sun had disappeared. She could rattle off the botanical names of all her plants and was an attentive green thumb. But bad luck for any plant that failed to thrive because there was rarely a second chance. A look of disgust would pass Mum's face before the pitchfork went in and the plants were ripped up and tossed out.

There'd be some evenings where Trudi and I would tentatively walk in the dark out on the dewy grass and follow the sound of the hose to locate her in our backyard, which was threatening to become a forest.

'What's for dinner?' we'd ask, and she'd sigh. Scrambled eggs was a regular go-to. She'd often slice a tomato in half, add cheese on top and put it under the griller, remembering to turn it off before the food burned. But on more than a few occasions, we'd find the tomatoes days later, having been completely forgotten once the griller had gone off.

As well as cooking for us in Brisbane, Nancy was completing more study. To what end, we were never sure but university education was free and she wasn't the only empty nester we saw at lectures.

Arnold was always deep in literature, either reading it or writing it. On one occasion I arrived home to find the renowned Australian writer David Malouf sitting at the kitchen table, in quiet conversation with Arnold. I had only just been introduced to Malouf's novel *Johnno* and felt lost for words in the presence of a real-life poet and playwright.

Twenty years later our paths would cross again in a lecture hall on the other side of the world. Malouf had been invited by the Australian Embassy in Washington, DC, to address a crowd of around a hundred expats to mark Anzac Day. He gave an evocative speech and one line in particular leapt out at me, so much so I quietly fossicked around for a pen in the bag at my feet and wrote it down on a slip of paper.

'There's something disconcerting that history is made while we're asleep,' he said, explaining what it meant to be Australian – to live at the 'arse end of the world' as former prime minister Paul Keating was reported to have said – to turn on the morning radio news and discover countries were at war, bombs had been detonated, legends had died and critical global decisions had been made. All while we slept.

He wasn't to know but with a handful of words he'd offered me at once both comfort and clarity. It suddenly made sense why I'd always felt the inner gnawing to leave Australia's shores, why I'd longed for the life of a foreign correspondent – to not only live a bigger life but to be reporting on it, on a different world that was awake while Australia slept, a world where history was being made.

Malouf was whisked away and I never got the chance to tell him how his words had allowed me to comprehend what had driven me.

My desire to go overseas was already strong when I started university but there were a few challenges to confront before I was ready to take flight – like catching a bus to uni.

# CHAPTER 8

# Taking Off

CAROLYN'S FIRST LECTURES at university began an hour earlier than mine but for the first few weeks we travelled together because neither of us had taken public transport on our own before. Carolyn had spent her years getting the school bus to Maryborough but I hadn't done that in Kilkivan or Gympie, unless it was with a friend to one of their farms.

Gympie High was one of three high schools. There was a Catholic private school at the top of town where we were convinced all the good-looking boys went and James Nash High, which was named after the gold digger who'd discovered rich gold deposits in the 1860s and sparked one of the wildest rushes in Queensland history. James Nash had been built just a few years before I started high school but it was on the other side of town and, despite it being completely presentable, we gave it the nickname James Trash and began a fierce rivalry with it.

All three of the high schools in Gympie were massive compared to the tiny school I'd attended in Kilkivan. Every morning swarms of buses would pull up disgorging farm kids and beach kids and kids whose parents had simply dropped out of the rat race, from Wolvi to Widgee to Rainbow Beach. Gympie was surrounded by agriculture, and 'townies' like me were the minority at the high school.

We lived less than a kilometre from the school's back gate but Mum would drive us there and back each day, concerned about the heaviness of our backpacks and the steep hills between school and home.

No matter how organised we were there was always something that delayed us, whether it was forgotten lunches or searches for homework.

One morning Mum remembered she'd left the water running on a rose bush, whose thirst would have been well and truly quenched by the time she'd returned. 'Jump out of the car and turn off the hose,' she said to me, expecting me to jump back in at the end of the driveway.

Unfortunately that wasn't what I'd been expecting to do and, as she reversed out of the garage, her foot heavy on the accelerator, the car door I'd left open in my dash for the hose crashed into the side of the garage, the sound of crunching metal echoing down the street.

We didn't bother stopping to survey the damage but it was a silent trip to school. We knew it was bad.

It was the second time I'd been responsible for what we referred to as 'car incidents'. The first was in the days after Mum and Dad had taken delivery of a new car that had electric windows rather than manual handles – something quite foreign to us. We were on our way to an evening rehearsal for the upcoming eisteddfod at the Gympie Civic Centre when I wondered out loud, 'What would happen if you put all the windows down at once?'

Not one to wait for answers, I proceeded to hold all the buttons down and blew the fuse, leaving all the windows stuck open. It was the middle of winter and the days it took for that 'incident' to be rectified felt like months as we rugged up for even the shortest of journeys.

While my track record with cars didn't improve I had no history with public transport so those first few weeks with Carolyn, negotiating tickets and coins with the driver while impatient city workers tapped their feet behind us in the queue, was nerve-racking.

Carolyn and I stayed in almost every night that first year, either studying in our rooms or watching *Moonlighting* and *LA Law* on the TV in Andrew's downstairs retreat. Our meals were already paid for and our parents kept a tight rein on our finances which meant we were constantly short of money. We had no extra cash to go out.

Not that we wanted to. A young woman had been attacked nearby in the previous months and each day at university we'd watch protests organised by the student union demanding better security and policing in the suburb.

Occasionally we'd venture out to the corner store to get an ice-cream after dinner but the return trip involved a steep hill up Whitmore Street and we often debated whether it was worth the effort.

My years at university coincided with the last three years of free university education. At the time we had no idea how lucky we were. The Higher Education Contribution Scheme was introduced in 1989 and the cost of going to university has climbed ever since.

We didn't think about getting part-time jobs in that first year, partly because we were young and lacking confidence in a foreign environment and also because our parents expected us to return home to Gympie and Bauple during term breaks and for long weekends.

We'd sometimes take the bus into the city, although this was before Queen Street became a mall and a destination for bored teenagers. If we had the money or had found a discount coupon we'd go to the movies but mostly we'd just aimlessly wander around the shops, rarely buying anything. That's what Carolyn was doing when she was approached by a young woman who offered her a haircut at the famous Queensland chain of hairdressing salons owned by a colourful Lebanese businessman called Stefan. The woman said she could have it for free if she was happy for a trainee stylist to be in charge of the scissors.

Her long, thick and curly red hair must have posed quite a challenge to the apprentice because they took the path of least resistance and chopped most of it off.

It wasn't the result Carolyn was hoping for but at least it was free, I told her, after I discovered her hiding in the wardrobe reading a romance book back at the house. She recovered enough to go back a second time, although this time to a different trainee, after weighing up the cost–benefit of a free haircut.

Carolyn, who was also studying a Bachelor of Arts, and was hoping to become a teacher, stumbled on another money-earner when she learned you could sign up to take part in practical experiments undertaken by undergraduate psychology students.

You never knew what you might face as a guinea pig for fellow students.

One of the tests involved trying to answer simple maths questions orally while listening to weird noises being pumped through headphones. It was a lot harder than it sounded like it would be and, while she got twenty dollars for her time, she left the room feeling stupid and forever after struggled to count by threes.

We did better in our English and literature classes, even if we had to laboriously handwrite the assignments because we didn't have a typewriter. Thankfully Carolyn had made friends with another student whose mother ran a business called St Lucia Secretarial Studies, mainly catering to academics. Helga would patiently take our scribble, whip it up into a format suitable for our lecturers and hand it back stapled and bound in a plastic-covered folder. We got mate's rates, if we paid at all, but we'd try to coordinate our drop-offs and pick-ups of the material to avoid extra bus trips and fares.

Carolyn and I would spend our days poring over our study books or doodling on notepads on the third floor of the undergraduate library. I was always hoping the boy with brown curly hair would be there. He was cute and I was happy to let hours pass pretending to study and keeping an eye on who stopped by his cubicle to say hello. Hmm, girl with the Culture Club T-shirt has circled back twice; 'caught him laughing, could be girlfriend' I scribbled down so I could go over the details with Carolyn later that evening.

Clearly my gaze had burned a hole in the back of his head and one day he wandered over to my desk and suggested I meet him at the rec club later that afternoon. 'Sure,' I said, rapidly nodding. The rec club was the university bar and was generally always full by mid-afternoon as students sat in the sun and drank beers and copious amounts of Strongbow cider. Or that's what I'd heard because I hadn't actually been there. I was still underage but this boy was worth the risk of getting busted for not having ID. That afternoon I set off for the rec club, only to discover I wasn't entirely sure where it was. I gave up when I realised I'd be making such a late entrance that it would be simply adding to the embarrassment I already felt – that's if I was able to even get in.

My love life never took off in that first year, but things did start improving. We got our own typewriters, which halved the work time but also challenged our touch-typing abilities. Excessive use of liquid paper – the white correction liquid we used to brush over errors before retyping – was a punishable offence for some lecturers and you never wanted to take a risk on which authoritarian might be marking the assignment.

We met a fun crowd, most of them through a friend I'd made in my first economics lecture. That course, EC101, focused on microeconomics and was an introductory subject, or so the course profile declared, but within minutes of the class beginning I knew I'd be needing a pre-introduction to the introduction. Despite having done relatively well in high school economics, I was out of my depth.

I had also felt ridiculously out of place after realising that most of the others in the class were beautifully dressed while I was still wearing the animal-print shorts I'd started making at high school. The material had been cheap and colourful and mostly featured cartoonish figures and oversized giraffes. I'd completed a couple of years of home economics at high school which had given me enough confidence to take two pieces of material and stitch them together with elastic at the top.

Pockets and a zipper were not part of the quick and easy pattern I followed but I thought the shorts were more than adequate so I knocked off a few more pairs in preparation for my first months at university. I didn't count on sharing classes with private school girls who'd gracefully swan in, sliding into the narrow lecture seats, wearing beautiful tailored trousers and crisp, collared Country Road shirts.

I felt out of sync with those around me, like a country bumpkin who'd wandered into a black tie dinner wearing an Akubra. I wanted to wait until the others left the class before I got up and revealed what I was wearing.

The butterflies of inadequacy swirling in my stomach reminded me of a birthday party in Gympie I'd attended in the last year of primary school. Sharyn was a new friend, as they all were then because I was the new girl, and she was turning twelve. Mum drove me to the small wooden house on Rifle Range Road and I nervously walked in clutching my carefully chosen present. I knew immediately I'd made a mistake when I looked around and saw a gaggle of girls in dresses, the colours and frills making me dizzy with embarrassment as I tried to hide my legs poking out from a pair of child's shorts.

It wasn't just the shorts. Everything started to feel wrong. My freckles were too dark, my front tooth stuck out even more than I imagined, my hair was chopped short, adding to my sense of awkwardness. I was angry at Mum for not having foreseen the situation, of not checking with Sharyn's mother and for not realising this wasn't a playdate for kids but a young lady's birthday party.

But at university I had no one to blame but myself. I had packed the bright shorts away after the first few weeks and tried to fit into this new world, adopting the fashion of calf-length pants and big loose tops billowing out from wide belts slung low and angled over hips. It was all pastels and perms and I fell into line.

A tall, slim teenager took a seat near me in one of those early economics lectures, his long legs knocking into the woman in front as he dumped a messy pile of papers on the seat to his right. I thought he looked like Tom Cruise in *Top Gun*, although later, when we became friends, that idea seemed silly.

He had a wide smile and an infectious laugh and also looked as if he hadn't spent a lot of money on clothes so I instantly warmed to him. And his name made me realise I had little to worry about if homemade animal-print shorts were my burden to carry.

Cyril Jinks had not had an easy childhood thanks to the popularity of a game show called *Blankety Blanks* on Channel 10. During the show, entertainer Graham Kennedy would put a panel of celebrities through their paces, asking them to fill in the blanks to questions he'd pose. Most of them were double entendres. *Joan and Paul went to bed and Joan asked Paul to BLANK her.*

It was basically a platform for Kennedy's style of comedy which was heavily laden with sexual innuendo. He specialised in jokes like this: 'I walked into the bedroom last night. My wife ripped off all her clothes, threw herself on the bed and said, "Do what you want." I said, "Really, do anything?" "Yes," she said, "absolutely anything." So I put on my jacket and went to the pub.' Cue the canned laughter.

The show's currency for cheap laughs came from a catch phrase delivered in a super camp voice by Kennedy who'd say 'Cyril said ...' with a lisp on the 's' for added effect. It was a ratings bonanza, screening each night at 7 pm. And it made my friend Cyril's life hell.

He was constantly bullied walking home from school as his tormentors yelled in their sing-song voices, 'Here comes the poofter, Cyril's a poofter.'

He lived in Inala, which was then one of Brisbane's poorest suburbs and just as rough. School became a warzone for him.

His Irish mum, who was five foot four, solid and strong, couldn't bear it anymore and said she'd follow him home at a distance so the kids wouldn't see her. Like clockwork, the bullying began until Mrs Jinks walked up to one of the boys and slapped him hard across the face. 'You come near my son ever again and it'll be more than a slap you get,' she threatened.

Cyril's dad, on the other hand, felt contrite that they'd burdened him with the name and offered to help his son change it via deed poll. It was a pivotal moment for the thirteen-year-old, who, rather than leaping at the opportunity, was affronted by his dad's suggestion and thought, 'I've come this fucking far, dealt with this much shit, there's no way I'm changing it now.'

He outsmarted and outplayed the bullies through high school. He was cheesed off, though, when he won a phone-in competition on an FM radio station and they refused to hand over the prize – an album by the band The Police – because they didn't believe Cyril Jinks was his real name.

But by the time he walked into that university lecture he had cast off his past life and felt a freedom that was heightened by the fact he was the only student from Inala who'd been accepted there. Cyril's zest for each new day was infectious and Carolyn and I were soon part of his quickly growing group of friends.

By second year Cyril had moved into a house with friends after discovering that his ninety-minute bus, train then bus commute from Inala to university made him eligible for a weekly fifty-dollar payment, which he promptly used to leave home and spend on rent instead.

The group house he lived in was just down the road from where Carolyn and I were now sharing a flat. We had both turned eighteen and Mum and Dad were feeling comfortable about loosening the reins a little and allowed us to say farewell to the only Brisbane home we'd known. We may have started out as quiet country girls but we were ready to start making a bit of noise.

Both our sets of parents were still keeping a close eye on our bank accounts which meant we had to get creative with our adventures. A night of dancing at a club involved turning up hours before the DJ clocked on and the music got going simply so we could avoid the five-dollar cover charge.

As well as becoming the central focus of our group of friends, Cyril was also very good at economics and became my informal tutor, helping me pass subjects I'd been destined to fail. He charged others for his coaching services and took a part-time job at Myer as well. He and his commerce friends combined their saved money and started buying shares, which they sold at a profit. The boy from Inala was always hustling and years later became the richest person I knew.

There was little chance of that kind of financial gain with my career choice. Even back then a career in journalism was predicted to have a short shelf life and our first lecture started with a warning that there was a significantly high failure and dropout rate. 'Look to the left and right of you, in front and behind,' the lecturer said. 'Only one of you will be here by third year.'

There was no question in my mind it was going to be me. They didn't know I'd been putting family members on the spot with my tape recorded interviews since I was seven.

I was diligent with my study at university but I wasn't enthralled. I was desperate to be a working journalist and still felt out of place among the more urbane students who were busy setting up work experience opportunities at *The Courier-Mail* and the ABC. These students referred to the commercial stations and their newsrooms at the top of Mt Coot-tha as if it were a given that that's where they'd start their careers.

It's hard to overstate the feeling of being so out of place. The fit wasn't right. But it wasn't long before I found my tribe – and, oddly, it was back in Gympie – where I'd spent so many teenage years plotting my bigger life.

# CHAPTER 9

# Engine Failure

I ALMOST KILLED my mother once.

The enormity of what might have been sat with me for a long time, despite her protestations about there being no need for me to feel any guilt. 'It was an accident, it could have happened to any of us,' she would say whenever it was raised, which, to be honest, wasn't often, despite how significant a shadow it cast over Trudi and me at the time.

But I couldn't help noticing the grimace she'd make as she filled the kettle with water and strained to lift it from the sink up onto the bench, letting the weight of it drop into position with a plonk. She'd switch it on and then stand there, her hip resting against the white laminated kitchen bench, watching the steam rising, as if the simple act of making a cup of tea had sapped her energy. Or perhaps she was contemplating what plant was going to get her attention when she returned to the garden, picking up the trowel with her left hand to give the right a rest.

I doubt she would have been thinking about the accident. Mum didn't like to spend time reflecting on the past, not even happy occasions.

'Why do you want to do that?' she'd ask, when boisterous family barbecues would end with calls to pull out old photos so we could laugh at our adult brothers showing their baby bottoms, or Wendy on her horse proudly trotting around the farm.

Mum was not a small person, but she could make the space around her shrink if it enabled her to retreat.

When family conversations were peppered with 'Do you remember when?' she would slip silently away, her vacant chair on the back veranda quickly taken advantage of by a young grandchild whose searching fingers were spotted creeping towards the soft adult's cheese in the middle of the table that was strictly out of bounds.

And then someone would say 'Where's Mum?' and a search party would find her in the front yard of whichever sibling's home we were visiting, doting on a grandchild or watering a plant and pulling weeds with a concentration that made it appear to be the single most important duty she had that day.

'Come back to the group, Mum, it's no fun without you,' we'd urge. But she'd shake her head and we'd return to the crowded family table, our search and rescue mission only partly successful.

I never understood Mum's reluctance to talk about the past. Perhaps it was because the memories from her time on the properties in Biloela and then Kilkivan with her young family, before Trudi and I were born, were her happiest and she couldn't find a way to appreciate what had been without being left mournful for what was no longer.

Mum didn't want to talk about the past and she didn't want to talk about how she felt, despite our persistence. So I never knew if she thought about how close to death she came on an August day in 1989.

\* \* \*

Mum and Dad were still living in Gympie, Trudi was finishing grade twelve and I had just been promoted to a D grade reporter after serving a year on the Gympie paper.

In 1988 when I was halfway through my third year at uni, I switched to doing my course externally and part-time to take up a cadetship at *The Gympie Times*. I'd stumbled into the job after applying for work experience there during the mid-year holidays. My arrival coincided with a disagreement between the cadet, an Irishman, and a senior editor over the inability of the local coppers to understand his thick accent. The debate ended with the Irishman quitting in a huff and decamping to the pub across the road. The editor turned to me and inquired, 'Do you want a job?'

I couldn't say 'yes' fast enough. I was over the moon.

It was pretty much a given that you'd make the next step up at the paper, as long as you completed a test showing your T-Line shorthand speed was 120 words a minute and you were showing some aptitude for the career you'd chosen.

One of my first stories about an infestation of head lice at a primary school had been received well and I was asked to do daily vox pops or quick surveys of shoppers on particular subjects. For example, I had to ask people if they felt enough was being done to make the street accessible to wheelchair users. I approached six different people of different ages, asked the question and then got the staff photographer to take headshots of each of them, ensuring their names and ages were correctly recorded. Then I borrowed a wheelchair from the hospital and proceeded to try to 'shop' in the main street, discovering of course that it was damn near impossible since ramps and consideration for the immobile hadn't been high on anyone's agenda.

The photos of my efforts were ridiculous and the way in which we approached it, as something of a laugh as I tried to spin the wheelchair in a 180-degree turn on the footpath, would have no doubt upset those who actually faced that challenge every day. But I was rewarded with my own regular column with a black-and-white photo at the top and the original title of 'What's On With Lisa Millar'.

It was meant to be a must-read calendar note for locals but it was often a wildly diverse affair with events that ranged from volunteer callouts for Meals on Wheels to details of a 1970s dress-up night at the roller-skating rink, which attracted mostly teenagers who wouldn't have even remembered what the 1970s looked like. The roller-skating rink soon closed down and was turned into a clothing factory where they made KingGee workwear so that was one less thing on my 'What's On' list.

There wasn't a lot happening in Gympie, especially during the week, so I would often add a few flourishes to the submitted handwritten copy from readers to bulk up the word count and fill the acres of empty white space on the page. 'Ever wondered why so many people are flocking to lawn bowls? Want to finally learn about bias on the green? Edna at the Albert Bowls Club in River Road will show you what it's all about on the dwarf green at 10 am as excitement peaks ahead of this weekend's competitive RSL Open Pairs event. And don't worry about the soaring temperatures set to hit us this week, they have shade shelters and an open bar where the beer will be frothy and cold,' I would write.

My little column was unlikely to ever attract anyone new to lawn bowls in Gympie but Errol and Edna and Frank, or whoever's turn it was, would submit their neatly written note each week on blue lined paper, having probably mulled over the wording for some time beforehand. 'Albert Bowls Club. 10 am. Wednesday. All welcome.'

I wasn't the only one to 'embellish' our written copy. My friends Dean and Nathan were always keeping us entertained in the newsroom with their wicked sense of humour.

One of our daily tasks was to create a little column called 'Today in History' using the AAP wire copy that would churn from the dot matrix printer in a long cascade of paper throughout the day. It didn't take much brain power and Dean started adding in his own fictional moments in history. He ended up with a following of cricket mates who'd look for clues of his mischievousness with entries like '1859 – First McDonald's opens in Moscow' or 'Pope John Paul's son leaves home on an adventure'.

It was all going splendidly until the editor walked in one day and called the newsroom to attention. 'OK', he said with his sternest voice, 'who wrote that on this day Wordsworth and Coleridge attended a cricket match?'

The game was up but Dean earned our admiration.

To give you an idea of how 'local' the paper was, when Pizza Hut opened its first restaurant in Gympie (albeit on the Bruce Highway on the southern outskirts of town, therefore attempting to appeal to travellers rather than establishing itself as a hangout for locals), it made the front page of the paper. No longer were 'all you could eat salad buffets' and West Coast Coolers, the sweet alcoholic sparkling drink that appealed to a generation of teenagers, the preserve of city folk. Gympie had made it.

The arrival of the first (and only) Pizza Hut franchise was considered such a significant news event that it also featured twenty-five years later when the paper published an article looking back at historical events worth revisiting.

The reporter at the time detailed the fact that Peter Southern, a Bundaberg resident, was going to manage the new restaurant making him, at twenty-one, one of the youngest Pizza Hut managers in Australia.

It was also noted that they were planning a bake-off among the newly employed casual staff for the invited guests, of which the editor was one. Pizza Hut no doubt had spent a small fortune on advertising which may or may not have influenced the newsworthiness of that front-page decision.

I'd left the paper before the Pizza Hut front page, but we'd never have thought about questioning the editor's judgement. I also didn't question the sexism or racism that existed at the time.

I remember the day I saw a body for the first time. It was a woman who appeared to be on her side with her knees slightly bent. The police had placed a tarp over her, little snatches of brown hair escaping from the top.

She was on a grassy slope just off Nash Street in Gympie, a couple of blocks from the paper's office.

I'm not sure how we heard about her, perhaps a phone call from police. Bigger newspapers had police scanners but we knew all the cops well enough to rely on a call. I even dated one policeman for a few months until his country posting ended and he headed back to the city and his old girlfriend.

Not many people died in Gympie, at least not in ways that made them newsworthy. Highway car accidents or farm drownings were guaranteed to make the front page.

But the death of an Aboriginal woman, with immediate assumptions it was probably domestic violence, didn't warrant the attention of one of the more senior reporters.

'Send the cadet,' they would have said.

I was nineteen and didn't want to confess to my work colleagues that I'd never seen a dead person.

I don't remember even getting her name or asking many questions of the police. The story didn't make the front page although there would have been a few paragraphs somewhere in the paper.

We rarely wrote about domestic violence unless it ended in death and the victim and perpetrator were white, or it ended in the magistrate's court with a charge of assault – and only then if it was a well-known businessman or local identity.

It was the kind of paper where the editor brought back page-three girls in the late 1980s – photos of semi-naked young women that were the fodder of tabloid newspapers. A freelance photographer called Bernie would take the photos. 'Bernie's Birds' they called it.

I should have considered myself lucky. A previous editor had sent a cadet out to file a story on the drought and told her to wear a bikini and stand on the river bank to give readers a proper perspective of how low the levels were. She obeyed but was thankful for whatever reason the photo didn't run.

That was the era.

One of the older employees at the paper told a younger reporter who'd remarked on Whitney Houston's beauty that he supposed she was okay 'if you like your meat barbecued'. There was no admonishment or tsking. It would have provoked a few laughs in that knockabout aren't-we-all-good-blokes kind of way.

There was no hesitation when a local personality, in front of a group of people, looked at an Indigenous man and said, 'He's a funny little coon.' It's shocking to even write those words now, so out of place and jarring today. And I sought advice from three friends to ask if even repeating the words here would cause offence in their communities. They encouraged me to tell these stories to remind people of the kind of casual racism that not so long ago was part of everyday conversations.

\* \* \*

I was mostly occupied with trying to complete my Bachelor of Arts degree at Queensland University. This was the pre-email, pre-internet days when large brown envelopes were mailed back and forth between students and lecturers so I spent late evenings typing up assignments about global economic reform and world politics at the little desk next to my single bed, which was still in my original childhood bedroom.

I wasn't earning enough to live away from home although I was sorely tempted. I was discovering a new group of friends through *The Gympie Times* – young reporters who were driven about their careers – and our conversations were filled with talk of how quickly we could get to a bigger regional newspaper.

We'd occasionally eat out at a Mexican restaurant on the Bruce Highway near Gympie's tourist drawcard – the gold museum and duck ponds. The restaurant was called Burritos and the food had all the authenticity of a Mexican restaurant run by white Australians. But the owners were entertaining hosts and the salt-rimmed margaritas were generous both in size and the ratio of alcohol to mixer.

None of us ever had enough money to cover cabs, dinner and then a nightclub. That would blow a cadet's wages in one night. So we tended to only do one or the other.

Klyx was the town's first nightclub and, just like the arrival of Pizza Hut, its 1988 opening was greeted with appropriate fanfare. It later went through a series of name changes – Phantoms, The Shaft, Tremors – but the small-town nightclub vibe remained the same. It was a place for hook-ups and cheap liquor. And dancing.

And that's what was calling me.

I don't recall there being a cover charge at Klyx but there must have been one. Unless they made enough from the drinks, which in that era all seemed to have been tinged with a red mixer. Or you could buy beer on tap. Although even the beer would sometimes get the raspberry treatment if they thought the intended drinker was a woman.

The dance floor was at the back, furthest away from the entry and past bar stools and hip-high tables. There were no low lounge chairs or comfortable places to sprawl out and talk. It didn't matter because we'd spend hours swirling ourselves into a sweat in the crush of people. We'd pause and glance at each other as each new song began, waiting for the first few beats to decide if we'd stay and dance or inch to the edge of the laminated dance floor and maybe to the bar for drinks of water.

There were two songs on high rotation during that period and I can remember the chorus to each of them. Neither were terribly complicated.

'Boom Boom (Let's Go Back to My Room)' seemed to fit the theme of a Friday night out for a lot of the locals. It was a hit that sent the drunks into a trance-like callout and the more sober dancers running for cover. The other song, 'Ride on Time', released by Italian house trio Black Box, had lyrics that were just as basic but stayed with me through the decades. DJs knew it was guaranteed to have people slamming down drinks on the table and rushing back to the dance floor.

There was no musical intro but a woman's low voice chanting about getting up half-a-dozen times. She pulled you along, teasing you with the slow build-up to the screaming crescendo you knew was coming. It arrived with a bellow and a throbbing beat that seemed to pass right through you. The bass and piano raced each other to the powerful high as the voice belted out the words from the song's title, 'Ride on Time'.

It became a hit single around the world but I had no idea what it meant. And neither did the Italians who produced it. They later said they'd misheard the original lyrics by an American artist who was actually singing 'cause you're right on time'. And it turned out they hadn't got permission to sample her voice and so the whole song was mired in controversy and lawsuits.

Not that I cared.

For the next thirty years it would be my anthem, the one song guaranteed to lift me, almost hypnotically, from my seat and pull me onto a dance floor, no matter what country I was in or who was with me.

Years later it was also on high rotation on Coles supermarkets' in-house radio playlist. I could be completely absorbed comparing the sodium content in yoghurt pots but when I heard those first few words I'd grip my shopping trolley and grin at the overwhelming urge to break into a euphoric dance in aisle nine.

But back then, as a nineteen-year-old back living at home, I couldn't make Dad understand how we could all occupy ourselves at Klyx until well after midnight. When he was home and not travelling for work he would wait up for me, sipping a whiskey and completing a crossword in the paper. When satisfied I was home in one piece, he'd switch off the lights and retire. I wanted to be treated as a grown-up but Dad remained vigilant in his role as protector.

My petulant threats to move out never went much further than just that, and Dad's absences in Canberra meant we had time to moderate our demeanours in between encounters.

My university studies finally came to an end and I was given a graduation date – 18 August 1989. Mum drove Trudi and me down to Brisbane, where we were going to meet Dad, who was flying in from Canberra, and my sister Wendy, who was living in the city with her husband and two young children.

I'd hired a black gown with the gold trim that designated I'd be collecting a Bachelor of Arts degree. I placed the hard board cap that came with it carefully on the back seat. It was exciting.

The weather in August was predictably cold with the Ekka winds blowing off the river. The Brisbane Exhibition – the annual two-week agricultural show where city folk were promised a taste of the country – also heralded a winter weather pattern referred to as 'the Ekka westerlies'. The photos from my graduation ceremony showed my newly painted nails gripping my cap so it wouldn't blow away.

My results were never more than a bit better than average but I'd worked hard to complete majors in both journalism and economics remotely while starting my first full-time job and I felt proud. Dad wore a suit and Mum's shoulder pads seemed to stand to attention as they linked their arms through mine with smiles that revealed they were proud too.

While Mum and Dad might have originally held reservations about the necessity of a university degree, they couldn't have been more supportive in the end. We celebrated that night, happy to be together for dinner at what we all considered a 'posh' restaurant.

The next morning we woke early to go our separate ways. Mum, Trudi and I would return to Gympie. And Dad would catch a flight to Canberra for another week of parliament.

It was meant to be a quick trip home, heading north up the Bruce Highway past Burpengary and through Nambour, past the Big Pineapple and the Yandina ginger factory, where we used to take visitors and I would consume so many dried sugared ginger cubes that I didn't touch them again until I was in my thirties.

We'd driven this road hundreds of times. The Bruce Highway was a money pit for Queensland's Main Roads Department. They kept completing small projects, realigning the road, removing single diversions and straightening the highway to avoid small country towns. The service stations where we used to stop for a sausage roll and a can of Coke on special occasions on our trips up and back from Kilkivan had long been bypassed and slick new highway rest stops had replaced them.

But the work barely kept up with the steady increase in traffic as the population in south-east Queensland boomed. As a child I'd done the trip so many times before dawn when Mum sought the company of her grown-up children on weekends to escape the isolation of the property. And I'd been completing the trek by myself more recently to attend a handful of compulsory lectures.

I was nineteen and a half and had been driving long enough that Mum didn't think twice about handing me the keys on that morning after graduation. She sat beside me in the passenger seat and Trudi behind her in the back as we debated whether we played Mum's cassettes or listened to the radio.

It was raining heavily but I don't recall feeling any anxiety. Mum's Mazda wasn't new but it was well serviced and felt solid. The traffic on the southern side of Nambour started to slow but this was a new section of road with two lanes on either side and a concrete barrier in between. The steep incline meant the heavily loaded semi-trailers ahead of us were grinding their way to the top and spraying us with dirty water from the road.

I tapped the indicator and accelerated to overtake one of the semis. I don't know what happened next, whether we made it past that truck or whether our car left the road before I'd reached it.

We hurtled through the air, the sedan spinning down into a gully, hitting something on the left-hand side before slamming backwards into a tree, stripping its bark as the car's boot took the impact and was crushed open, sending our suitcases flying.

Mum's right hand shot up to protect her face but it found the broken glass of the passenger window instead.

The engine was smoking and I recalled ridiculous Hollywood movies where cars exploded and victims survived an initial accident only to be burned alive. Neither Mum nor Trudi could open their crumpled doors so they clambered over the seats. We'd dropped twenty metres down from the edge of the road. The grass was slippery but we grabbed hold of long reeds and tried to heave ourselves up. Mum could use just one hand as the other was bleeding badly.

I made it to the top of the bank and realised no one had stopped. Had no one seen us go over? I stood there in my blood-stained yellow woollen jumper, which I'd pulled on over my pyjamas just two hours earlier, and waved frantically at cars racing by on the slick road, flicking up sprays of water as they passed.

It would only have been a matter of seconds before a car pulled over in the rain, a young mother behind the wheel, with two children in the back seat. I pleaded with her to take Mum to Nambour General Hospital – about five kilometres away – and to tell them to send an ambulance. Trudi seemed okay but the car was a write-off and I wasn't sure of anything at that moment. Mum was groggy but conscious enough to be dismayed she was getting blood on the woman's car. The rain was still pelting down on this sorry group of women.

I said, 'I love you, Mum,' and shut the door. For a split second I let myself wonder if I would ever see her again. I had no idea how badly injured she was.

An ambulance arrived within minutes. Someone had seen our car careen off the road and had sped off to get help. When Trudi and I arrived at the hospital they wouldn't let us see Mum or tell us what was happening, other than that she was on the operating table. There were no other details.

The hospital rang Dad's office in Maryborough and got through to his secretary, Mary-Anne, who'd known us since we were toddlers. There were no mobile phones back then and my bag with my address book of phone numbers was back at the crash site.

At Brisbane airport, Dad had settled into his seat on the Boeing 737 bound for Canberra and the door had been closed ready for the plane to taxi out for departure. Mary-Anne called Qantas and asked them to get a message to the plane. Her timing was perfect, although the way the message was delivered couldn't have been more dramatic. The cabin door opened and a staff member hustled over to Dad. 'Mr Millar, I'm afraid your family has been in a car accident. You must come with me,' they said.

Dad rented a car and sped up the same highway, knowing that he was risking his own safety but driven by a desperate urge to get to us. 'I went like a bat out of hell,' he would tell us later.

When he walked in the door at Nambour Hospital Trudi and I fell into his arms.

Mum was released from hospital five days later. She had concussion and needed stitches in her face. The nerves in her right hand had been severed and it would continue to ache and cause her difficulty for the rest of her life, not that she ever dwelled on it. I felt terrible that I'd been responsible for the accident but knew how lucky we were it hadn't been worse.

My older brothers surmised that the car had aquaplaned in the rain and I hadn't been experienced enough to know how to handle it. It was enough to put me off driving in the rain for at least a year.

Mum's car was replaced but I went back to driving my small Mitsubishi Galant which was now close to fifteen years old. It was brown with a steering wheel that was so narrow in width it sometimes felt like you were holding onto a piece of plastic not much more secure than the handles of a skipping rope. The car had belonged to Grandma in the 1970s, but had been sold to a family friend who then sold it to me for $2100. I'd borrowed the money from Dad and was paying it back bit by bit, with interest. It was my first car and I named it 'Alf' after the popular American TV series.

But I wondered, if we could be at risk in the rain in a solid sedan like Mum's, then what hope would I have in my car, with its thin metal doors, manual wind-down windows and the type of windscreen that would shatter into small thick pieces of pale green glass?

Alf would take me to *The Gympie Times* and back but it started spending most of its time parked outside Mum and Dad's house.

Around this time, my university friend Cyril turned twenty-one and wanted me to come to his party in Brisbane. The theme was *The Rocky Horror Picture Show* but I'd never actually seen the movie. When it had first been released in 1975 my mother thought it was scandalous.

We only had reception for two TV channels in Kilkivan, the ABC and the local regional commercial station, SEQ, that broadcast from Maryborough.

SEQ was going to show the movie and every time an ad came on featuring the mad scientist Dr Frank-N-Furter in his jocks and garters and fishnet stockings Mum would leap in front of the television, spreadeagled, to try to block as much of the screen as possible, convinced our young minds would be tainted with even the smallest glimpse of a protruding groin.

By the time I was old enough to make my own decision about seeing it I couldn't be bothered. Although I had expended plenty of energy dancing to 'Sweet Transvestite' over the years.

But Cyril's birthday came and went and I begged off. I just wasn't confident enough to get behind the wheel again. I kept thinking how happy we'd all been the night of my graduation and how, twelve hours later, we could have been dead.

If I'd tapped the accelerator a moment later or sooner, we might have hit the tree. Then it wouldn't have been the boot copping the brunt of the force but the side of the car with Mum and Trudi. There might have been seconds between life and death. I couldn't shake that feeling.

# CHAPTER 10

# Buckle Up

IT WAS AFTER landing a dream job for a young journalist – as the ABC's North Queensland reporter based in Townsville – that my sense of safety was even more deeply challenged. The reporting patch stretched from the Whitsundays to the Torres Strait and out to Mount Isa. I worked with a camera operator called Pav, a Melbourne import who loved the lifestyle North Queensland offered his family.

The distance to the bosses in Brisbane was 1300 kilometres and we could go days without speaking to them as we roamed across the vast north of the state. Occasionally the chief of staff, Albert Asbury, would catch me on the phone and ask, 'What's cooking, blossom?' but mostly he let us follow our noses, filming stories on wild pig hunting or mating butterflies or mango farmers looking for wives.

Sometimes we'd get the call to do a 'pick-up' which involved filming an interview or pictures for someone else's story around the network. A senior reporter for the then state-based *7.30 Report* in Brisbane was chasing a story about miners being drug-tested and had been given the nod to get a camera crew to the Peak Downs Mine in central Queensland. Who knew that phone call to us in the Townsville bureau would set off a chain of events that would have a decades'-long impact on my life and rattle my faith in flight.

Pav and I clocked up thousands of kilometres every year on the road, knocking over the ten-hour drive to Mount Isa often enough that we knew the best roadhouses for an unbeatable sausage roll. But if the network needed stories quickly we chartered planes. On this day, the twin-engine Beechcraft Baron sat near the hangar with its doors open in a fruitless attempt to catch a wisp of breeze in the cabin.

We loaded the camera, tripod, extra tapes and batteries and a playback machine to watch the footage on the flight back and timecode clips to feed to Brisbane via satellite that afternoon.

It was a clear day and as we took off I leaned into the window and felt the comforting vibration of the propellers shift into an easy hum. We had a couple of hours on the ground, filming the massive trucks lumbering up to the top of the mine face and interviewing the mine manager.

We were packed up and ready to leave when we were told, for safety reasons, to delay our take-off until after planned detonations at the mine. Our pilot was watching a line of afternoon storms moving across our flight path but I wasn't worried.

Bad weather wasn't necessarily fun but I'd flown enough with Dad to feel at ease being tossed around a little. When it was time to go, I sat in the back of the six-seater and strapped in. Pav pulled on the passenger's aviation headset in the front next to the pilot. Large cushioned headphones covered my ears as well but they were connected to the portable playback machine we'd brought and I started checking the footage.

I could hear the engines straining and the wings dipped one way and then the other as the pilot plotted a path through the storm cells. We were using a lot of fuel and the pilot switched to the reserve tank. But an airlock starved the left-side engine and it stalled, while on the right, its mate strained to keep us airborne.

My head snapped up and Pav spun around.

How long did we sit in that suspended moment?

It could have been five minutes but it wouldn't have been. It could have been a second or two. And it probably was.

The pilot was silent until we landed. 'Sorry about that up there,' he said as he walked away, job done.

'That was bloody scary up there,' I murmured as we walked to the cars.

'Yep, it was,' Pav replied.

We packed the gear into the ABC's four-wheel drive and started up the engine, forgetting we'd been listening to loud music when we'd last left it in the car park earlier that morning. 'Bloody hell,' we yelped as a screeching guitar filled the car.

The next day, we were back on another charter plane, this time to Thursday Island, no more than a thirty-minute flight from Townsville.

It was a larger plane and there was a pool of reporters and camera operators onboard. I sat at the back and felt something new – a gnawing sensation of uneasiness.

On charter flights after that, my fear began slipping out occasionally when a storm was forecast, or a pilot seemed too inexperienced, or a plane too old. I'd feel the release of a hundred butterflies in my stomach as a cabin door opened, and I'd catch the whiff of the stuffy air of a plane that had sat for hours on the hot tarmac. And my mind would race – what would happen if we hit a bird on take-off in this single-engine plane? How was the pilot going to find this airstrip in Roma once the sun had set? What if someone had sabotaged this engine while it had been sitting unattended on a remote airstrip?

The scenarios I was running through my mind became more and more extreme. I'd replay that flight from the mine in central Queensland and repeat the story to people, convinced that no one else could have experienced something so terrifying. But every time I told the story the fear became less of a stalker and more of a constant presence.

I began actively trying to talk the ABC chief of staff out of hiring charters and had a list of reasons why a seven-hour drive was more sensible than a forty-minute flight to get to a story.

Each flight taking off from Townsville involved a different plane model, forcing me to do more preparatory research to ensure that if another 'incident' happened I'd be ready.

Ready for what, I didn't know. Did I think I was going to be able to take the controls if the pilot had a heart attack, or that sitting on the left or right in the back would increase my chances of survival if we crashed?

I would pepper pilots with questions, often finding the answers completely unsatisfactory. The fear became aggressive in its possessiveness, not content anymore to stay in the shadows. It was no longer just small planes that caused anxiety but commercial airlines as well. It would start taunting me not just for hours but for days before a scheduled departure. The butterflies disappeared and were replaced by muscle spasms that sparked diarrhoea and gastro.

I always got on the plane, mostly because they were work jobs and I didn't want to let people down. But my God, sometimes it was the most unbearably difficult act to simply walk up the steps into what I now saw as a death trap. My legs would shake and I could barely find the strength to grip the stair rail.

The fear had been born in a matter of minutes high above central Queensland but it was maturing into an all-consuming takeover. Every flight was destined to be my last. I didn't think I was going to die. I knew I was going to die.

Despite this I was still on cloud nine as a young reporter. My stories were filled with beautiful pictures of the reef and rainforests, of waterfalls and wallabies. I was loving it all. What I didn't know was that these stories were going national and I'd come to the attention of the network editor in Sydney.

\* \* \*

In 1994 I was offered a job covering federal politics for the ABC. I'd only been in Townsville for nine months, and I was happy. I certainly hadn't been looking for another job. I'd never been to the ABC's Sydney headquarters and was clueless about the hierarchy. In fact, I was so naive that the first time the network editor approached me I just forgot about it. I didn't even know who this guy was until Pav the camera operator rolled his eyes and explained that if the big kahuna was asking to see a job application, you didn't say no.

Saying goodbye to my life in Townsville was tough, but Canberra was now my focus. I'd taken a room in a share house in Kingston opposite a cricket field. It was a beautiful spot and within walking distance of Parliament House. Not that anyone walked back then. And while the house was quaint, only the lounge room was heated.

I'd left Townsville on a sunny day with the temperature nudging 26 degrees but it was already single digits in Canberra when I arrived and the trees were blanketed in red and orange autumn leaves.

The house might have been cold but the two camera operators who'd offered me their spare room were utterly delightful. John Bean also worked for the ABC in the press gallery so, depending on our shifts, we saw each other most days in the office. Ben Curry worked for Channel 7, just across the corridor.

Their friends were keen to adopt me as well although one of them, Stephanie Kennedy, gave me an early lesson in dressing for the new climate. She'd decided to take me out for brunch soon after I'd arrived. I opened the door to her gasp of 'You can't go out like that' as she looked down at my feet. I was wearing sandals and she insisted I at least add socks. So off we went, my new friend and I, with me wearing socks and sandals because I'd arrived from Townsville with no enclosed shoes. All I could think was it was lucky the animal-print shorts were long gone.

John and Ben organised a dinner out the following Friday and I offered to drive. I'd sold Alf by then and was driving a second-hand Holden Nova which had the added bonuses of a stereo system and air-conditioning. I was still getting the hang of the vast network of roads that crisscrossed through endless roundabouts in the nation's capital. Ben sat in the back while John gave directions and ran me through the personality traits and romantic liaisons of each of their friends I was going to meet that night.

We were travelling around eighty kilometres per hour down a perfect stretch of road, past native bushland into the suburb of Woden, when suddenly there was a huge bang.

Had we hit something on the road? Had we blown a tyre?

Ben was in the back firmly calling out, 'Don't hit the brakes, don't hit the brakes,' and I tapped them gently until we slid to a stop, the loose gravel crunching under the car's wheels as I edged it over to the side of the road.

Ben couldn't open the back door and we realised that whatever had hit us had concertinaed the car like a soft drink can that had been squashed and tossed from a car window.

We saw flashing lights back towards the top of the hill we'd just come down and an ambulance arrived to take us to hospital. We'd been hit by a speeding drink driver with no headlights. He'd come out of nowhere but the ambulance officers had seen him roar through an intersection further back and began following him while calling for police back-up.

We stayed at the hospital till the early hours. The medicos were confident we were suffering nothing more serious than shock and mild concussion.

The answering machine at our house flashed thirteen missed calls. The early messages were full of laughter and ribbing about keeping our dinner companions waiting. The final messages, tinged with panic, told us they were trying to call hospitals and were fearing the worst.

John, Ben and I spent the next day hunkered down on the couches in the one warm room in the house eating Chinese takeaway and drinking vodka and tonics, and reliving that split second where we went from happily sharing gossip about friends to being in the back of an ambulance.

A split second.

I felt like I'd dodged another moment of life and death and, once again, I was behind the wheel of a car that was written off. What if I'd survived and Ben or John had been killed? Just like Mum, they insisted I should feel no guilt. It wasn't my fault. But did the fact that, on each occasion, I was supposed to have control but didn't, make it worse? Maybe I could have reacted differently in that first accident, not overtaken, reduced my speed. But in the second accident there was nothing I could have done differently other than not be on the road at that precise moment. Our lives had been in the hands of someone else who was making bad and reckless decisions.

Was it starting to gnaw at my sense of security? If I couldn't drive ten kilometres to dinner through suburban Canberra without ending up in a car wreck where could I be safe?

The night of that accident in Canberra was my third life-threatening experience in the space of five years. The accident with Mum and Trudi. The plane with the stalled engine. And now this.

The accident with Mum and Trudi had an even greater impact because it came hours after one of the happiest moments in my life at that point and I saw how quickly joy could be stolen from you.

The mid-air scare in North Queensland had happened eight months before my car was written off in Canberra. In 1994 I hadn't developed the full-blown psychological paranoia about flying although I was certainly feeling uneasy.

But did the accident that night with John and Ben trigger a subconscious reckoning about danger?

I wasn't the pilot on that flight in North Queensland when the engine stalled in a thunderstorm and we lost altitude. I didn't know how to fly a plane. I had given my safety over to someone else, hoping they would do the right thing. But even when I was driving a car and I did have control, I couldn't prevent something terrible happening.

* * *

Thankfully most of my work in Canberra was ground-based. The official title of my new role was 'junior reporter' but we were more commonly known around the gallery as 'door-stop dollies'.

We pounced on politicians as they arrived each morning and peppered them with questions on the news of the day. We'd arrive at 7.30 am and stay for an hour or so waiting for the official government cars to pull up. I'd quickly flick through a small book of headshots of the MPs to work out who was who but often the camera crews, who'd spent years on the job, would identify them first and leap into action. Some of the pollies would try to rush past while others, with an eye on climbing the party ladder, would stop and regale us with their views on numerous subjects. The TV networks would divvy up who would go where and we'd pool our material.

The commercial TV reporters always arrived looking beautifully groomed and I only learned later it was because they had their hair blow-dried professionally each morning on instruction from their bosses, a luxury not even contemplated at the ABC.

Friendships were solidified outside the doors. So were competitive frictions as we jostled for position to get the best eyeline of an arriving politician.

I'd dread being assigned to the Senate doors in winter when I could see the snow on the mountains and the chill would seep through the soles of my shoes. The House of Representatives side of the House caught the morning sun and had the added benefit of being the spot where you were more likely to create news. Leadership rumblings were born at the doorstops outside the House of Reps and disgruntled backbenchers would vent for the cameras. Not that there was any rush to put this to air.

There was no 24-hour news channel or social media or live blogs on internet sites. The radio reporters might file a story or two but they'd return to the office to do that. Mobile phones were still to come. We had pagers instead that would beep with a message from the chief of staff to pack up and head upstairs where we'd thaw out while the editors began the laborious process of swapping material between the networks, dubbing the tapes in real time.

Only then would I sit down to write a news story for *World at Noon*, spooling through the interviews to select the best quote or 'grab' as we called them.

I'd arrived just a few days before the Federal Budget and thankfully wasn't expected to join the ABC troops in the traditional lockup. I could barely find my way around the building let alone the Budget papers. Most of Dad's time in politics had been in Old Parliament House down the hill and I wasn't as familiar with the new building and its interconnecting passages.

Paul Keating was prime minister, having stamped his hold on the job at the 1993 election, while John Hewson, the vanquished Liberal leader, had chosen to stay on at the helm in opposition. His party eventually decided that wasn't the path to any future victory and just two weeks after I arrived in Canberra a leadership spill was called and Alexander Downer emerged as the victor.

It was a less than successful period for the man who'd later become foreign minister and after a series of missteps he was booted from the job after eight months and replaced by John Howard who led the Liberals back to power in March 1996.

I was in Canberra for less than two years but witnessed three leadership battles and a change of government. It was a steep learning curve and my boss, bureau chief Russell Barton, and the political editor Jim Middleton were terrific mentors. The top TV jobs in the gallery were dominated by men – Paul Bongiorno, Laurie Oakes, Peter Harvey, Glenn Milne and Alan Sunderland.

The door-stop dollies rarely got a starring role. The Sunday shift was my chance to shine and was one of the few times I'd get a story on the 7 pm news. It was a vastly different job from what the younger reporters face today. Now they're starting by 5 am, filing for ABC *News Breakfast* and radio news, tweeting and writing for online, publishing news as it happens.

It could be a brutal environment back then. I remember being horrified when my friend Helen McCabe at Channel 7 was summarily dismissed via fax when the new CEO decided on some old-style bloodletting that was fairly common in commercial TV. Helen wasn't the only casualty but news of the brutal manner of her sacking travelled quickly through the gallery.

A lot has been written about sexism at Parliament House and my time there was certainly a period of gender imbalance. There weren't a lot of women who worked in television and we were all in junior roles. The camera crews were mostly men as well and some of them would enjoy pulling rank on us, merely by the fact they were male. But the blokeyness of the place wasn't something we ever discussed. And while I recall a few leering politicians and odd characters who'd pop up as lobbyists I was still pretty naive and probably missed even the most overt signs of sexism. I was also distracted with a new relationship.

I'd met a newspaper reporter, Sid Maher, at a cheap and noisy restaurant in Canberra with a bunch of other friends from the press gallery a few months after I arrived. We were seated next to each other which allowed me to catch his witty *sotto voce* appraisals of the conversations bouncing back and forth across the table. He played guitar, which was great, and golf, which was less impressive. But he certainly knew how to make me laugh. And he was also another country kid, having grown up in Stanthorpe, in southern Queensland.

\* \* \*

Most journalists in Canberra lived for leadership challenges and elections. My last assignment in the job was the 1996 election campaign between John Howard and Paul Keating. The senior journalists stayed in Canberra while the junior reporters raced around Australia filing material each day. I desperately wanted to be part of it but a deep dread was building.

It was an historic campaign but I remembered little of that. Instead I recall the gripping panic of a daily flight with dozens of press gallery colleagues and of not being game to take a sedative that might help because I knew that on arrival I would have to begin doing my job.

If it was a night-time flight to relocate us for a morning campaign event I would have the luxury of being able to drink. Back then the air force staff on the government's Boeing 727 still served wine and small bottles of vodka that could help numb me. Few people knew what I was facing each day as I forced myself to join in the friendly joking in hotel lobbies with the travelling media pack before climbing on the bus for the airport.

A journalist from Channel 9 in Sydney, Fleur Bitcon, had been assigned to cover the campaign. She wasn't a press gallery regular and I didn't know her well but, even at twenty-six, her formidable reputation made her intimidating. She surprised me on one of those flights by plonking down in the seat next to me before leaning over to quietly ask, 'Does it help if I talk to you while we take off?'

It was all I could do to give her a small nod of relief.

My father, who'd instilled in us our love of flight, was mystified by my fear and tried his best to encourage thoughts of safe take-offs. 'Lassie,' he'd say, a term of endearment he used for all his daughters, 'flying is safer than driving. We can't have you torn up like this.'

I moved back to Brisbane with Sid after the campaign to become the ABC's state political reporter and there was no escaping the regular flights required around country Queensland. Some I handled. Others, like the moment on the flight with Premier Rob Borbidge when I couldn't physically fold my body into the seat, were devastating.

Sid and I had been together for a couple of years by then, so he knew how scared I'd get as a day of departure approached. He'd try to comfort me but that would just make me more irritable.

And when you're facing extreme fear, there's no room for other emotions.

When I was on a plane, I couldn't read to distract myself. My eyes wouldn't focus. I couldn't listen to music because it stopped me hearing the sounds of the engines. A fearful flyer always listens for changes to the rhythm of a plane because a fearful flyer needs to know how close they are to death.

Something had to give.

The trigger was an event that should have been filled with happiness. My former Canberra housemate John was marrying ABC reporter Pip Courtney. They'd asked me to give a reading at their garden ceremony near Launceston where Pip had grown up.

I didn't know it then but I was reaching what would be the peak of my fear.

In the days before Sid and I left Brisbane for the wedding I snapped at small things and then the diarrhoea and fear-induced vomiting began. We'd planned a driving holiday around Tasmania before the wedding but once there all I could think about was the agony of the flight home.

I checked if it was possible to take the *Spirit of Tasmania* ferry to Victoria and rent a car and drive eighteen hours up the inland highway to Brisbane and make it back in time for work.

I sat on the edge of the bed and asked Sid to wait another ten minutes while I checked weather forecasts, again, for the flight, which was still days away. I was angry and tired. And so was Sid. He'd been dealing with my fear for five years.

One morning in a small hotel near Cradle Mountain, he turned and looked at me and shook his head.

'This. Cannot. Go. On.'

\* \* \*

Bizarrely, it had never crossed my mind to attempt to eradicate my fear rather than just suffer through it, not until that defining moment.

When I had to fly, I preferred Boeing over Airbus and distrusted the Australian airline Ansett because it had such a complex mix of planes in its fleet that I feared their maintenance teams would miss a crucial part of their checks. The fear wasn't logical.

Ironically, despite my hesitation about Ansett, they were the airline that offered the most convenient course to overcome my fear of flying. When the airline first put the call out for fearful flyers it was with a small classified in *The West Australian* in the 1980s that simply asked, 'Want to fly but afraid to do so?' It had an office number with no corporate branding. It was so discreet and ambiguous in its language it could have been mistaken for an adults-only activity. A few course participants even thought they'd signed up to study *Fear of Flying* – Erica Jong's hugely popular novel about female sexuality.

But there was a reason Ansett wanted to fly below the radar with their course. The airline, which operated in Australia for sixty-five years before it was grounded by bankruptcy in 2001, was concerned about having its image closely aligned to a course about fear.

The original classified ad might have been small but the response was not. The course expanded to other states and was still hugely popular when the airline folded.

An estimated quarter of the population is nervous about flying and many of those have a genuine fear. I was one of them when I signed up in 1999 to the Ansett course created by clinical psychologist Neil McLean.

The meeting room at Brisbane airport was plain with white walls and no windows. It could have been anywhere but, little did we know, we were already starting the course, simply by being exposed to the environment that caused us so much stress.

There were half-a-dozen people in the room when I walked in and dropped my bag next to a chair towards the back. Completing the course with others was a tactic as well. Ansett wanted you to realise you weren't alone in dealing with this fear, that you weren't 'silly'.

Like an Alcoholics Anonymous session, we circled the room detailing the origins of our fear and why we'd reached the point of taking action.

The courses were run over five weeks, one night a week. Or, for the impatient fearful flyers, like me, it was an intensive three-day weekend, ending with a graduation flight to Sydney on the Sunday.

Pilots and engineers and flight attendants were brought in to answer all our questions. Can a plane glide if the engines stall? Can a plane take off on one engine? Can planes be hit by lightning? How is fuel load calculated? What happens if the fuel gauge flashes 'empty'?

They were passionate about the job. Like dog owners who want everyone to love their dog, these aviation employees wanted us all to love their planes.

There were two Ts at the heart of most people's fears: take-off and turbulence. Fearful flyers would see lightning and think, 'God, we're flying through a thunderstorm.' But the pilots would patiently explain it was in the distance, that they weren't avoiding it because it was dangerous but because they wanted to make the flight as comfortable as possible.

Planes love turbulence, they told us, painting a picture of a large jet swooping and dropping on air currents like a seagull over water. But passengers hated it, and they were the ones paying for the ride.

The instructors explained how much information they gathered from radars and how many hours before a flight they studied the meteorological charts.

While flying was becoming safer, Neil McLean believed the number of Hollywood disaster movies being made wasn't helping fearful flyers. 'If people are constantly exposed to films where wings fall off in turbulence, then that's what they'll start believing will happen,' he said.

One thing the course instructors never took for granted was the courage and trust it took for people in the grip of an anxiety to even show up. And that was at the heart of a fear of flying – anxiety. So they approached the course with a theoretical framework around cognitive behaviour therapy.

'Your anxiety is totally understandable given your understanding or misunderstanding of the flight,' they told us. They assured us that if they were getting on a flight with the same genuine belief we all held (that they'd die), then they'd be scared as well.

The problem was that the premise of our fear was wrong. Our body would switch on an anxiety response if it received a message from our brain that there was a threat. But what if your brain was raising false alarms based on your lack of knowledge about flying?

The first task for instructors was to correct all our misinformation and then help us learn to process that while we were flying. If your brain started telling you there was something to fear, you could run through the palm cards they suggested you carry onboard and repeat the facts as a way of reassuring yourself.

On the day of the graduation flight usually around seventy-five per cent of course attendees turned up. A couple might not because they had other flights booked. Occasionally someone would start having second thoughts but Neil would find a way to get them onboard.

It was a regular commercial flight and the flight attendants knew who the fearful flyers were but not the other passengers. That resulted in a memorable moment for Neil McLean once when one of his fearful flyers sitting behind him stood up before the plane started taxiing. He stepped out into the aisle to check if she was okay but she stopped him in his tracks, in full view of the rest of the plane.

'Get out of my way, I want to get off. If you don't get out of my way, I'm going to hit you,' she seethed at him as the other passengers held their breath wondering what had sparked this outburst of plane rage.

Thankfully for Neil McLean that was a one-off.

When he told me the story, my sympathy was with the woman. I had been that person once, raging internally at being forced to board a plane and face a clear and present danger that would inevitably end in my death as we plunged from the sky.

Aviation had become a victim of its own safety. When rare accidents did happen, they were big news, even if the number of victims was much lower than the annual road toll in Australia.

Flying continued to become safer in the decades after the demise of Ansett but fear of flying experts around the world noticed an odd correlation between safety and the demand for courses.

Psychologist Les Posen, who spent six years conducting the Ansett program, was part of a conversation at the World Conference on Fear of Flying in Montreal in 2007. They'd assumed after the September 11 terrorist attacks in 2001 that 'business would go gangbusters'. But instead there was a significant drop in the number of people signing up for courses.

'The reason was that you were perfectly justified in being afraid of flying after September 11, so it felt normal and not something you needed to fix,' Les said. 'They weren't thinking, "What's going wrong with me," and so you discover that business actually goes up when flying becomes safer and there are fewer accidents or incidents.'

That was when people would say to themselves, 'I know flying is safer, so why am I so fearful to fly, I don't get it.'

One of the benefits of the Ansett course was that my boarding passes carried a stamp indicating I was a fearful flyer, giving the flight attendants a heads-up. In the years before September 11 it meant instead of turning right to economy on a domestic flight you were asked if you wanted to sit in the cockpit.

I always said yes.

I was still far from fully cured and wanted to ask pilots for details on their flying hours, rest times and when the jet had last been in maintenance.

'When was the most dangerous time during a flight?' (TWA 800 in 1998 exploded twelve minutes after take-off from New

York killing all 230 onboard. It confounded investigators who finally agreed that fumes in the near-empty centre wing tank had ignited.)

'How quickly would you know if there was a fire in the wiring?' (In 1998, 229 people died in Swissair 111 when faulty wiring ignited insulation above the cockpit and the fire slowly burned out of sight until the pilot's controls were crippled.)

'Why are there crashes on runways with the technology that you have?' (US Air 1493 in 1991 hit another plane waiting for take-off at LA, killing thirty-five people.)

I was the Rain Man of plane crashes, able to rattle off the details of most major incidents, how many had died and how survivors had made it out. I would follow investigations through to their conclusions often years after the event. The vast bulk were caused by human error and I didn't trust humans.

Most of the Ansett staff were helpful although one pilot hadn't got the corporate message. He was French and a product of a national airline strike in the 1980s which saw foreign crew and the military brought in to fly Australian planes.

'Is it true that a jet can still take off even if it loses power in one engine?' I asked (already knowing it was true but needing constant reassurance).

He chortled and in a thick accent replied, '*Oui*, it is possible, but it would not be pretty.'

It was the only time I sought the refuge of my economy class seat, worried that any more time in the cockpit on that flight might set me back.

One of Les Posen's first jobs was helping passengers who'd been onboard United Airlines Flight 811 on its regular flight from LA to Sydney in 1989. The cargo door on the Boeing 747 malfunctioned causing an explosive decompression that blew a hole in the body of the plane, taking out seats in business class and killing nine people.

Les went on to treat everyone from pilots who'd misjudged landings or felt the mounting pressure of being responsible for hundreds of passengers to a seventy-year-old who had never managed to get on a plane.

I used my homemade palm cards for years after the course. 'The pilots have maps of where all airstrips are, no matter how small, so they can land in an emergency,' I'd written on the pieces of cardboard I was gripping in my sweaty palms.

I'd keep reminding myself of the key message they'd given us all – that we'd been cultivating and nurturing fear for years. Getting rid of it would take work.

Fear of flying courses continued to adapt as travel became safer but demand from flyers remained. When I finally tracked down Neil McLean, twenty years after I graduated from the fear of flying course he'd created, I felt overcome with emotion. On our video call, I blurted out, 'You changed my life.'

And he had. The course was the springboard to the big life I'd aspired to. Without him I wouldn't have been able to follow my dream of being a foreign correspondent. It was a dream that I only dared to imagine as a girl in country Queensland. I never lost sight of it but the fear had made it feel out of reach. Neil McLean's work enabled me to take on three different postings with the ABC and travel to dozens of countries covering some of the most important stories of our time.

He smiled and said he'd had more feedback from happy customers from that course than at any other time in his career.

There were so many people who felt just like me. One of those he remembered fondly was a primary school principal, a Francophile who'd never left Australia because she was too afraid to fly.

After the course she sent him an Eiffel Tower keyring from a trip to Paris.

I knew how she must have felt.

Recovering from a fear of flying was the most empowering thing that had ever happened to me and it led me down a completely unexpected path a few years later in Washington, DC.

CHAPTER 11

# On Approach

EACH OF MY jobs – in Gympie, Brisbane, Townsville and Canberra – had offered their own challenges but mostly they'd been enormous fun. And they'd proven to be great building blocks towards that dream of reporting overseas.

In mid-2001 I felt ready to start the process even if I knew the competition would be tough. I'd had my eye on a position in the US bureau so I threw myself into preparing the application.

It had already been a big news year in the US. Americans had been working themselves into a frenzy during what was dubbed the Summer of the Shark. A child had been bitten by a bull shark in knee-deep water in Mississippi and *Time* magazine had a menacing shark on its cover ensuring Americans approached their beach holidays with trepidation.

American Timothy McVeigh had been executed for carrying out the deadly Oklahoma City bombing six years earlier. In DC, a young intern, Chandra Levy, who'd been working on Capitol Hill had gone missing. Rumours were rife after it was revealed she'd been having an affair with her boss, a Californian congressman. He was cleared of any involvement but it would be a year before her body was found. And columnists were still debating whether the scandal involving Monica Lewinsky and Bill Clinton had damaged Al Gore's chances in the 2000 election.

Back in Brisbane I was reading up, taking notes and trying to anticipate the questions that might come from the interview panel. That was the peculiar thing about overseas postings. All of the emotional energy that went into applying for the job and gaining a deeper understanding of the country you were hoping to report on could sometimes be immaterial by the time you touched down as a newly minted foreign correspondent.

It could be months between those nerve-racking moments in front of the selection panel, getting the job and then your eventual departure.

There was the emotional tug of renting your home, selling your car, pulling kids out of school and farewelling family.

And then there was the check list for the ABC. Visa applications and hostile environment training, laptop upgrades, dental checks and medical appointments that involved needle jabs for an array of possibly threatening viruses. It was only once you'd ticked all the boxes that you were considered ready to launch.

By the time you boarded the flight you were often torn between relief that you'd managed to navigate it all and mounting apprehension about what lay ahead.

When I applied for my first posting in 2001 I was partly driven by a need to prove that I was successfully, albeit slowly, overcoming my fear of flying. The instructors who took the course had warned me that it would take a while to feel comfortable again in the air given the level my fear had reached.

My bosses at the ABC had approached me a few months earlier about applying for a job in Moscow but I'd declined. They never knew it was because I'd committed every Aeroflot crash to memory, and I felt ashamed by the possible lost career opportunity. While I tried to remind myself of all I'd been taught in the fear of flying course, Russian air travel was a flight too far.

I knew I needed to apply for the job in the Washington bureau when it came up even if it was to simply prove I was a serious contender. So when the phone call came telling me I'd actually got the job, I babbled a few words of thanks and hung up. All the details and plans and starting-date negotiations would come later.

I was sitting in the windowless office of the *7.30 Report* in Brisbane where I'd been working for the past year. I picked up the desk phone and punched in Sid's number.

After being together for five years, Sid and I had married in a garden ceremony at a hotel near the Botanic Gardens in Brisbane. His dad had died when he was a teenager and his mother made up for it by doubling her level of care and protectiveness of him. She was hoping for grandchildren. Instead, her only child would move across the globe, not for his own career but his wife's.

At that point we'd been married for two and a half years and we'd talked about this possibility but now, as I almost whispered the words into the phone, I wondered what he'd think.

'I got it,' I said.

The Washington bureau was considered one of the most sought-after postings. It was unusual for any overseas posting, let alone the Washington one, to go to someone from the BAPH states – what people called the ABC's smaller capital city offices, an amalgam of their first letters: Brisbane, Adelaide, Perth and Hobart. It was a nickname that came loaded with negative connotation. We felt we were regarded less highly than the mighty triangle of power formed by Sydney, Canberra and Melbourne.

Sid was the chief of staff on Queensland's only daily newspaper, *The Courier-Mail*. We didn't talk for long and, while he'd supported me applying for the job, he hadn't really contemplated what would happen if I actually got it.

A couple of ABC reporters whipped across the road to the Regatta Hotel in Toowong to buy bottles of sparkling wine and we splashed it into plastic cups and celebrated a success for the Brisbane newsroom.

It was 7 September 2001.

Four days later, I watched the September 11 terrorist attacks on television, like everyone else. And I knew that my posting had fundamentally changed before it had even begun.

It was late at night in Brisbane and Sandra Sully was fronting Channel 10's national evening news as the first reports started coming in. She was our conduit in Australia to an event that would have devastating ramifications for decades to come.

Sid had raced back into work to help rewrite the front page when we thought a small plane had crashed into the first tower and it was still simply a terrible accident. As another plane hit the second tower I sat on our lumpy blue striped couch by myself and pulled a blanket up to my chin. It wasn't cold but I was shaking. I called my parents and woke them. Turn on the TV, I said.

The next day I rang the international editor Bronwen Kiely pleading with her to get me there, to let me start my job, desperate that the story would be over by the time I arrived. That was the last thing she and her team had on their minds as they coordinated coverage of the biggest story in the world.

As my planned December departure date approached I was comforted to know I wouldn't be the only new correspondent. My friend Leigh Sales had also scored a posting in the DC bureau and we were booked on the same flight.

The northern winter had well and truly set in when she and I touched down at Dulles International Airport, on the western outskirts of Washington. We'd packed what we needed in our suitcases until the rest of our belongings, and our husbands, arrived a few weeks later.

The ABC's office manager, an American who was renowned for his fastidiousness, told us to look for a driver holding a sign with just one of our names on it. His attention to detail had involved him emailing us before we left Australia to ask which of our names should be on the hand-held sign since both wouldn't fit. We'd laughed about it at the time but later discovered his thoroughness, which on one occasion involved asking me to repay by cheque a three-dollar debt to the ABC for stamps I'd taken, would be a constant test of patience.

It was twelve weeks after the September 11 attacks and the heavy military presence at the airport gave a glimpse of what was ahead. Fighter jets flew constant loops over Washington, DC. They hadn't been scrambled in time to prevent the attacks so for months a roster of crew kept patrol.

Conversations with new acquaintances would soon slip into discussions about memories of where they'd been that day and escape routes out of DC if terrorists struck again.

It was only a few weeks after we'd arrived that Leigh and I went to the movies on a Saturday afternoon. Leigh was on call for emergencies so when her Blackberry started vibrating she crept out. The international desk in Sydney said there'd been another suspected terrorist attempt on a passenger plane. When we learned the full details it was horrifying to know what might have been. A man later known as 'the shoe bomber' had tried to detonate explosives he'd packed into his shoes on a Miami-bound jet with nearly two hundred people onboard. He only failed because passengers restrained him when he struggled to light the fuse.

The fires at Ground Zero smouldered for months after the World Trade Center was obliterated and Americans could do little but think and talk about the impact on their country. They followed the colour-coded alert system as closely as the weather reports. It swung between orange (high risk of attack) and yellow (elevated) for the entirety of my posting.

Our ABC office on the corner of F and 14th streets was just a couple of blocks from the White House, putting us at the heart of an area considered high risk.

Another accused terrorist was arrested in 2002 over plans to build a dirty bomb. The fear of a radioactive explosion in downtown DC saw a run on duct tape and plastic at hardware stores after the government warned people to shield their windows. We doubted the efficacy of that given our proximity to the White House and while our office manager wanted to ensure our safety he was also concerned the price for plastic may have skyrocketed because of demand and he'd wait until there was more in stock.

The initial scare had lessened by the time that happened and we never bothered with it.

Sid and I discussed what we'd do if there was another attack and phone networks went down. He was trying to fill his days, entertaining visitors, playing guitar in a band, as well as some casual work at the World Bank. But visa restrictions meant he was limited in what he could do as my spouse in the US and while I enjoyed having a stocked fridge and dry-cleaning picked up, I knew he wasn't entirely happy.

The terror alerts also threatened to derail my steady recovery from the fear of flying. It had been a year since I'd done the course and I was working hard to change the way I felt about air travel. But it was hard to deliver my internal mantras with confidence.

Thankfully I had an ally in Janet Silver, the ABC's producer in Washington. She was a Canadian who, with her husband, had been working and living in America for a decade. She had two young children and a sympathetic nature that extended to her reporters.

Janet was chief wrangler of interview guests, story producer and logistics queen. She was a pro at nabbing cheap flights for our work trips, sometimes saving hundreds of US dollars on one assignment.

The trouble was I was more worried about safety.

A flight on AirTran to Miami seemed harmless enough but I was able to remind her AirTran was simply a rebadged ValuJet that had sent Flight 592 into the Florida Everglades killing 110 people five years previously.

Initially she'd pause and wonder just how difficult it was going to be to find a flight for this new correspondent. Eventually we found a compromise and a group of budget airlines that I was comfortable with was classified in her notes as SFL – Safe For Lisa. Little did the airlines know they'd move up and down my top ten based on their safety record and, sometimes, whether the paint on their aircraft was chipped or tired. 'If they can't keep the planes properly painted,' I thought, 'what else is lacking?'

Southwest Airlines won my approval by being the milk run of American skies, taking off and touching down more times than any other airline, therefore ending up with more experienced pilots. United Airlines got a tick for having a channel on their inflight audio that allowed you to listen to all communications between pilots. I found the calm voices about planned movements reassuring but it didn't stop me obsessively looking out the window to see if the approaching jet was lifting its altitude to 30,000 feet as it had been told.

Decades later when an aircraft model that I had been reluctant to fly – the McDonnell Douglas MD-80 series with its awkward-looking design and engines tacked on the tail – was finally retired from the Delta fleet, Janet and I shared an email remembering the efforts she went to in avoiding ever booking me on that plane despite its good safety record.

It was an expensive business having a team of ten in the Washington bureau, especially when the exchange rate for the Australian dollar was sitting around fifty cents.

Later that decade the ABC would reduce the number of staff in DC but at the time there were four reporters, two camera operators, an editor, two producers and the office manager.

Cost wasn't an issue for one of my first stories out of the bureau. It simply had to be done. It was January 2002 and an Australian, David Hicks, had been transferred to the US military base at Guantanamo Bay after being picked up in Afghanistan. He was accused of fighting with Al Qaeda. Getting to Gitmo, as it was known, would eventually become such a well-travelled route for lawyers, media and military that commercial flights, with government-approved manifests, would fly between Miami and the US base on the southern tip of Cuba.

But back then, Gitmo had only just been reactivated as a detention camp and we joined a dozen US media on a three-hour Hercules flight from a military airfield in Maryland.

We weren't the only arrivals into Gitmo. Alongside us the huge military transport planes were coming in from Kandahar in Afghanistan.

We were taken to the edge of the tarmac to watch as the prisoners, in their orange jumpsuits with their hands and feet shackled, were led off the plane to their cells. We weren't allowed to film but the US wanted to convince us they were treating the prisoners well. They led us through a makeshift tent hospital, past the beds of eight or nine Taliban prisoners, medical staff hovering over them.

Those who were well enough were taken to Camp X-ray, a collection of outdoor wire cages with concrete floors. It had been rushed into service and would soon be replaced by a purpose-built detention centre. But back then I could get close enough to see various prisoners pacing in their cells and speaking to marines who were standing under a tree out of the warm Cuban sun.

We were the only Australian media on the trip and information on David Hicks had so far been scarce. I had a satellite phone to file live radio reports and told presenter Eleanor Hall on *The World Today* that the marines had described him as 'a bit of a loudmouth' initially but he'd been sitting very quietly in the corner of his cage, praying five times a day and constantly reading the Koran. I also told the Australian audience he'd asked a few questions of the marines, including when he might be able to go home.

It was a rare snippet of information that was republished by other media in Australia.

Hicks would end up spending five years at Gitmo and even today, twenty years later and despite attempts to shut it, dozens of prisoners remain.

I was back on the island later that year but this time in 'real' Cuba and not the US military base. It was my first chance to film a documentary for *Foreign Correspondent* and producer Vivien Altman was flying in from Sydney to meet me, our American sound recordist and editor Woody Landay, and camera operator Dave Martin.

Dave had been with the ABC for decades and his passion for filming was matched only by his passion for skiing. He suffered a terrible memory, though, a condition attributed to a car accident when he was younger. He'd find a way to make us laugh about it but we all had stories of backtracking to pick up forgotten tripods or tapes left at train stations.

The schedule was thrown out on the first day of travel when we were forced to divert to Jamaica because of an approaching hurricane. Our equipment remained in customs at the airport but we were bussed to an all-inclusive resort near Montego Bay where we were presented with coloured wrist bands to indicate our stay would not only include all-you-could-eat but all-you-could-drink.

I'd just finished an exhausting few days reporting on the first anniversary of the September 11 attacks and I couldn't believe my luck at the enforced downtime.

But it meant that when we eventually got to Cuba time would be tight. It was exactly forty years since the Cuban missile crisis and this was an anniversary piece. Timing was everything.

We were desperate to snare an interview with then President Fidel Castro but our requests were knocked back.

We'd fill each day filming young hip hop musicians and democracy activists and Havana's streets with their old American cars held together with wire and hope.

Castro was seventy-six and a grandfatherly commander-in-chief who generated mixed emotions. As our trip neared its end, we headed to the first US–Cuba trade show in forty years – odd in itself that American and Cuban businesses were talking trade when relations between the two countries at a government level were still chilly.

The indoor convention centre was filled with hundreds of people.

Suddenly, President Castro arrived and we joined the mob of cameras around him.

There was no doubt he knew we were the Australian TV crew who had been trying to talk to him all week. After he'd finished patting some cows and the heads of children – I called out with my best fake Spanish accent, 'El *comandante* – Australian TV', and he stopped and looked at me.

And truthfully, that is where my contribution ended.

Vivien, our pocket-sized producer who was fluent in Spanish took over, struggling to keep her head above the rough and tumble of the crowd around her. She fired off half-a-dozen questions and he answered each, offering observations for an Australian-only audience and remarking more than once on his admiration for swimmer Susie Maroney who had become the first person to swim the 180 kilometres of water from Cuba to the US five years previously.

Finally, he was done with indulging us and was gone. Vivien, Dave, Woody and I all looked at each other as if seeking confirmation – did that just happen? Did we just interview Fidel Castro?

Another hurricane delayed our departure from Cuba but our story went to air a week or so later. We all moved on to the next assignments but never forgot that encounter with Castro.

It was the fallout from the September 11 attacks that dominated my first years in the US. I spent months at the United Nations in New York following the debate over America's claims of weapons of mass destruction in Iraq and the huge protests that followed.

My high school friend Sharon was planning a wedding and asked if I could make it back to Sydney to be her maid of honour. But even the quickest of trips was ruled out by the Sydney bosses because of the impending invasion of Iraq.

I interviewed soldiers going off to war and met the widows and widowers of those who never returned. The deployment farewells and epic homecoming ceremonies would each reduce me to tears.

And I'll never forget the high school near Fort Hood in Texas, America's biggest military base. Almost all of the students were army kids and as their parents deployed for Iraq and Afghanistan they would write their names on cardboard stars and hang them from the school's main corridor. Dave and I followed the school's principal under thousands of twinkling blue and silver stars spinning on string. They looked like Christmas decorations but signified such sadness. As we reached the end I looked up and asked the principal what the gold stars were for.

'Oh,' she said, 'they're for the ones whose parents have died. Would you like to interview them?'

Dave and I felt weighed down by the intense sorrow contained within those school walls.

Later that night at the hotel we debriefed on the futility of it all while we downed beers and watched a DJ set up a karaoke screen.

'Wanna sing, Dave?' I asked him, looking around at the smattering of business travellers loosening their ties.

We might have been out of tune, but we made up for it in volume as we belted out Men at Work's 'Down Under'. If the others in the bar had known we were in town to report on the growing toll of America's involvement in Iraq and Afghanistan they'd probably thought of us as insensitive.

But we needed to shed some of the grief we'd absorbed that day. It had been three years since I'd arrived in America. Sid left six months before my posting ended to take a job on a newspaper back in Brisbane. And after that day in Texas I was thinking it might be time for me to go too.

CHAPTER 12

# Return Ticket

FORMER CORRESPONDENTS OFTEN joke that returning from a posting is often harder than starting one. It can take a while to settle back into the groove and find a job as exciting as the one you left. And you quickly discover life in Australia has moved on without you.

When I returned to Australia in 2005 at the end of that first posting to the US my marriage was disintegrating, so I happily signed up to be a fly-in, fly-out reporter for breaking stories in the Asia–Pacific.

There were assignments to Bali in May of that year for the trial of drug trafficker Schapelle Corby and back again to the holiday island for another terrorist attack. Three suicide bombers attacked two sites, including a beach resort near the Four Seasons hotel, and killed twenty people. It wasn't as bad as the 2002 Kuta bombing that killed 202 people but it troubled security experts.

It was 2 October and the international editor called me in the early hours to see if I could get the first flight to Denpasar. I was home alone. Sid had left two weeks earlier after a final failed marriage counselling session that signalled the end of our eleven-year relationship, six of them as husband and wife.

Being alone was still so new to me that on the way to the airport at 5.30 am I rang Mum and Dad and asked them to cancel a bikini wax appointment I'd made at a beauty salon and to tell the Brisbane Writers Festival I wouldn't be on the panel they'd asked me to MC that day.

I travelled alone but there was a small team of colleagues waiting in Bali including our Indonesia correspondent, Tim Palmer. We worked through the night to file for the morning programs, walking brazenly into hospital wards, approaching family members of the injured and pushing them for interviews. It sounds heartless but there was so little time to think things through. We hadn't slept and the deadlines kept coming.

Police were still trying to identify the bombers and their networks so they gave us square coloured cards the size of a pack of playing cards with photos of the three suspected suicide bombers. The heads were all that were left of their bodies after the bombings and the photos were bizarre in their gruesomeness, with hollowed eyes, bloodied necks, no bodies.

I walked back into the hotel room one afternoon and realised I'd left the cards face up on the table where they would have been immediately seen by the unsuspecting Balinese housemaids. I hoped they hadn't been horrified by my insensitivity. The Balinese were devastated that trauma had been inflicted on so many innocent people again.

I was back in Brisbane within a week, arriving at the airport looking like a tourist returning from a few days at the beach – my legs and face brown from sun exposure, my bag heavy with dirty clothes.

I dropped the bag into the second bedroom, which had been emptied of any signs that another person had once shared the home. I'd been surrounded by people, under pressure, each day disappearing in a swirl of dust and noise, trying to remember complex names of terrorist cells and suspects for endless live crosses. I stood there in the lounge room of the apartment, the carpet soft under my feet, twisting the wedding ring still on my finger and was swamped by a sudden emptiness.

I kept turning up for work each day, but I felt like an empty shell. Within weeks I was saved again by another assignment – this time to Singapore.

Our Asia correspondent Peter Lloyd normally covered the patch but there'd been a sudden development on a story and he was back in Australia for the Walkley Awards.

Van Nguyen was a 25-year-old Vietnamese–Australian who'd arrived in Australia as a baby onboard a boat with his mother and twin brother – escaping their country in search of a better life. But both boys grew up facing troubles. Van had financial debts and his brother, Khoa, had been a heroin addict.

In December 2002 Van left Australia for the first time since he'd arrived as a tiny refugee. He was bound for Cambodia to pick up drugs with instructions to take them back to Melbourne via Singapore. If successful he'd been promised not only would his debts be paid but he'd clear his brother's as well.

On 12 December 2002 he left Phnom Penh to begin the journey home.

Singapore airport is a huge metropolis with upmarket shops and manmade rainforest escapes alongside the ubiquitous smoking rooms. Van had a four-hour stopover. When he passed through security to reboard his flight, the metal detector was triggered and the drugs were uncovered.

Of all the countries to have his poorly planned virgin drug-mule efforts unravel, Singapore was the worst. The death penalty was mandatory and his trial was swift, with the Singaporean High Court sentencing him on 20 March 2004.

Van Nguyen had been on death row for twenty months. But after appeals of clemency from Amnesty International, the Holy See and even the conservative Australian prime minister, suddenly his date of death had been set and his mother was on her way to Singapore. That was when the foreign desk called me to see if I could get there. It was 21 November and they'd booked me on an Emirates flight to Dubai that stopped in Singapore.

I threw jeans, jackets and skirts into a suitcase before shutting the door on the empty apartment again. My colleagues in the office were printing every word that had been written about Van Nguyen so I could brief myself on the plane. Not only had I never reported on the ground in Singapore, I was coming in completely cold on the details of the story. I told myself I'd have at least seven hours on the flight to get up to speed.

Camera operator Rob Hill was flown in from Darwin. He was a blond Welshman with a build so slight you wondered how he lifted the camera and held it steady on his shoulders. He was young and talented and in Australia because he'd fallen in love, and was keen to prove he had the skills to go further. By the time I arrived at the hotel he'd turned his room into a portable studio and was already transmitting footage back to Australia. He'd filmed Van Nguyen's mother, Kim, arriving into Singapore.

I introduced myself before dumping my laptop and notebooks on his bed.

The next day we ordered a cab to take us to Changi Prison, where we set up for what would end up being a two-week watch and wait. Sometimes we'd catch glimpses of Kim's daily visits to see her son. Other days it would be his lawyers from Australia. He had two female friends, Bronwen Lew and Kelly Ng, who'd flown in from Melbourne. They were among his loudest campaigners, trying to win support from Australia, delivering letters of hope and encouragement from strangers.

The then presenter of the ABC radio current affairs program *AM*, Tony Eastley, had rung to offer encouragement and support. He'd covered the hanging of Australians Kevin Barlow and Brian Chambers in Malaysia nearly two decades earlier and cautioned me about not underestimating the impact of covering someone's death, planned in such a barbaric way.

That kind of wise counsel has been invaluable throughout my career and part of the camaraderie and support that so many more experienced journalists offered me.

The media pack was growing outside the prison. The ABC had sent another reporter, Shane McLeod, to add to our coverage.

Knowing that her pleas to save her son were now hopeless, Kim Nguyen asked for one last favour – that she be able to hold him before he died. In an act I regarded as bastardry, the Singaporean government refused. In the final hours of Van Nguyen's life his mother was allowed to touch her son's face, reaching her hands through the bars of his prison cell.

Back in the hotel room, as we recorded the track for the TV story, my voice faltered each time I attempted to read the words on the page, explaining that last touch of a mother. I apologised to Rob, knowing he'd also struggled with our role over the past ten days.

Even now, writing these words, it is hard to think of Kim Nguyen's soft skin stretching between the metal to clasp her son's cheeks, letting her fingers fall away for what she'd know would be the final time.

We didn't sleep that night, heading back to the prison and then following leads that illicit candlelit protests were being held in nearby neighbourhoods, groups of supporters gathering, knowing that their own actions were risky and the Singaporean government would have no tolerance.

By 4 am we were back outside Changi as the car arrived carrying the newly appointed hangman – the previous one sacked after an unauthorised media interview.

Candles were lit along the fence and, as dawn broke over Singapore, Van Nguyen was hanged.

It was 6.07 am Singapore time and I was live on radio with Fran Kelly describing the scene around me. Back home at the church where his mother had prayed, twenty-five bells rang out for each year of his life. An hour later, an official notice confirmed the young Melbournite was dead.

Van's lawyer, Lex Lasry, emerged from the prison to give a short statement, his words almost lost as the media pack pushed and shoved. He said Van had accepted his death with grace and dignity, and was comforted by other inmates singing 'Ave Maria' as he walked towards his maker.

'Ave Maria' – a humble Catholic prayer set to the stunningly beautiful music of Schubert.

*Hail Mary, Mother of God,*
*Pray for us sinners,*
*Pray, pray for us;*
*Pray, pray for us sinners,*
*Now and at the hour of our death,*
*The hour of our death / The hour of our death,*
*The hour of our death / Hail Mary.*

The last words heard by a 25-year-old Vietnamese–Australian man whose life began with hardship and was ending at the hands of a hangman.

We filed our stories and that night Rob, Shane and I drank vodka martinis in the hotel bar, clinking our glasses, talking about Van Nguyen, trying to understand what we'd just witnessed.

I woke the next morning with a hangover, hoping the assignment was done but the foreign desk wanted one final story. Cameras had filmed the casket, there were news leads about the transport of his body, plans for the funeral.

The debate back in Australia over the death penalty and treatment of drug traffickers had raged to a level that took me by surprise when I returned. A Sunday afternoon barbecue had been planned at a friend's house and a crowd argued loudly and drunkenly over Van's fate.

One of the women, a friend of years standing, turned to me her eyes fiery, accusing me of being on the side of those fighting to save him, of encouraging the mournful protests in Australia with my reporting.

'What if it was my son who'd ended up taking the drugs he sold back here,' she said. 'How would you feel then?'

I made excuses to leave, feeling like I'd been slapped in the face.

A few days later I was driving on the Western Freeway in Brisbane, a couple of hundred metres from the Moggill Road exit.

It was 11.59 am and I turned on the radio for the midday ABC news.

The first report was from outside the Melbourne church where Van Nguyen's funeral had just taken place. The familiar strains of 'Ave Maria' came through the car speakers – thousands of mourners had sung the song – the same words sung in Van Nguyen's last moments.

I started to cry, the stress of the previous weeks flooding out of me, so much so I had to pull over on the side of the freeway as cars and trucks raced by.

I'd barrelled through my early career, not thinking for a moment of the impact any of the work I was doing was having on me. This was the first time where I'd felt my emotions were out of control. I didn't know about secondary trauma or the result of ongoing exposure.

I didn't know what was ahead.

## CHAPTER 13

# Winging It

THERE ARE SIGNIFICANT moments in life that you only really appreciate long after they have passed. Maybe it was a job rejection that felt brutal in its finality but instead opened doors to a more thrilling career path. Or a passionate, all-consuming romance that faltered, devastatingly, but allowed you to better appreciate the relationships that followed.

And then there are moments that are so magnificent you understand in an instant that they need to be treasured because the universe is offering you something truly inspiring.

It was 2006 and I was in a post-marriage meltdown. I was thirty-seven years old and becoming an expert at procrastination and indecision. I worried that being divorced at that age would rule out meeting someone again in time to have a baby. If I was honest with myself I didn't really feel the urge to have a baby but I worried about that realisation too. Would I feel that way in ten years when it would be too late? Should I simply throw myself into work? Should I try to buy a home by myself? Should I take up Latin dancing and French lessons? No to the Latin but yes to the French. I didn't have the financial confidence at that time to buy property solo and the baby question sat on the shelf. Friends took me aside and said they'd help if I wanted to try to become a parent by myself but that didn't appeal.

I leapt into a relationship which was good, then bad, then not. Nick had charmed me after a black-tie event but what started as a thrilling and rare one-night stand, which made me feel desired again, limped into an on-again, off-again affair that involved another woman who was married and all the complications of an entirely inadvisable and ultimately doomed relationship.

My sister Wendy suggested he'd come along in the 'Nick' of time to help ease the pain of a separation that wasn't my choice. But it was soon time I moved on.

I felt like I was going through a second broken heart and was bouncing from one self-help book or course to another searching for a quick fix. My diary was filled with cringeworthy pep talks to myself. 'Happiness is a learned, practised skill. Be upbeat, a positive lifeforce.'

What nonsense. Not that there was anything wrong with the sentiment or the pursuit of it, but staying positive was not something I'd ever needed to coach myself into. But here I was –

struggling and hoping antidepressants would kick in and let me see through the fog of sadness.

I can't recall who came up with the holiday plan but my friend Leigh Sales and I decided a week in China might be the answer. And if not the answer, at least it would be a distraction.

Leigh had returned from the US bureau to take up a job as the ABC's national security correspondent in Sydney. While we'd started our postings in DC on the same day, she'd stayed on for an extra nine months.

She'd been taking Italian lessons while we'd been in America and when her posting was up she headed to Rome with her husband, Phil, to spend two months indulging in pizza and gelato and hopefully becoming more fluent.

It was while she was there that I started falling into those dark places. It had been three months since Sid and I had separated.

I'd muddled through, sustained by big work assignments. But by the time Leigh was in Italy I was on a downhill slope. She called from a freezing payphone on the cobblestones of Piazza Navona and listened to me sob until the phone beeped in her ear telling her the calling card she'd bought at a newsstand nearby had run out.

Some days I would put on my imaginary Wonder Woman cape and vow never to fall to such depths of despair again. But months after Leigh and Phil had returned to Australia I was still swinging on an erratic emotional pendulum.

China sounded like a good idea, even though heading overseas again so soon, even just for a week, wasn't on Leigh's 'must-do' list. But she was a loyal friend and her level of concern about my despondency outweighed any uneasiness over the fact she was still paying off her last trip.

Neither of us had been to China before but our friend John Taylor was the ABC's correspondent in Beijing and he and his wife, Donna, were adamant that all we needed to do was get the visa and get on the plane, they'd look after the rest.

The tourist visa, even for two Western journalists, was approved quickly. The health form required us to confirm we weren't afflicted with 'psychosis' or 'snivel'. I joked to Leigh I wasn't confident on either by that point in the year but ticked 'no'.

I'd arranged to fly to Sydney to meet up with Leigh for the flight to Beijing rather than travel separately. They warned us in Brisbane that there might be fog delays in Sydney but I'd factored in hours of spare time.

Leigh and I had bonded in Brisbane years earlier when we'd both arrived excessively early for a large group dinner with workmates at a Chinese restaurant. We knew who each other was to say hello but not much more than that. When I'd walked in and seen just one woman sitting at the long table, her fingers tapping out a piano piece on the cream-coloured vinyl tablecloth I smiled.

We confessed to each other that, try as we might, we could never be late to anything, our fathers' dedication to punctuality had been ingrained in both of us. Leigh's dad, Dale, was in the army and military time was the only time for the Sales house. I'd grown up with Dad rattling the car keys at least ten minutes before any departure with warnings that flat tyres and heavy traffic were just some of the unforeseen traps ahead.

But as my plane looped around Sydney, out to Botany Bay and then west towards the Blue Mountains, I realised even several hours of cushioning wasn't going to help this time.

The flight touched down in Sydney as Leigh was being told to switch off phones on her Beijing-bound plane. She had time for one quick text – they weren't holding the flight and she was leaving without me.

It felt like such a blow. I was booked on a flight the next day but I was so short of emotional strength that I was convinced everything was jinxed. I lay back on the bed in the airport hotel room in Sydney that night, after eating something lukewarm and unappealing from room service, and felt overwhelmed with sadness.

While I was in Sydney feeling sorry for myself Leigh was in Beijing meeting friends of John and Donna's. They called their friend Gustav the Swedish prince, but he was actually a count. The regal title made him slightly mysterious to the other expats who lived in the compound in Beijing with our friends.

Gustav and his wife, Marianne, told Leigh that we simply must, must, visit the Great Wall of China, but we had to do it their way.

By the time I arrived twenty-four hours later, feeling cranky that I'd lost a day of what already felt like a short holiday, the plans were in place. Leigh and I would hire a driver to pick us up from our friends' home and take us to The Commune, which, despite its name conjuring up images of a communist retreat, was actually a high-end luxury resort. Its architecture had won awards just a few years earlier at the Venice Biennale and it was being touted as one of the new architectural wonders of China. Inside its gated grounds was a private path to the Great Wall of China.

But rather than spending hundreds of dollars on a room, we would simply make a reservation for lunch in its five-star restaurant. Becoming a hotel guest, even just for a few hours for lunch, would give us the access we needed. And the shared secret among expats was that this was not just any part of the wall, but what was referred to as the 'wild wall'.

Most tourists ended up at the concreted rebuilt sections of the wall. Visiting China's famous architectural feat had become a feat of endurance as they fought their way through the crowd. Noisy buses blowing out dirty exhaust would disgorge visitors from early in the morning. An hour later they'd clamber back on, laden with gaudy souvenirs that would end up gathering dust back home or would be gifted to a young relative who wouldn't question the trinket's authenticity.

The wild wall, we were told, was untouched, and mostly out of reach for time-constrained tourists. This adventure of ours was going to be an all-day affair and Gustav the Swedish count had promised it was worth the effort.

We would make our lunch booking for 1 pm but deliberately arrive far too early. We'd then suggest to hotel staff that we'd take a look at the wall while we waited for our table.

We made the lunch booking for later that week and, on the day, our driver arrived as planned outside our friends' apartment. He had no English and we had no Mandarin but he'd been given a rough outline of the scheme and we joined the traffic jam getting out of Beijing.

Every now and then he'd turn and speak, gesticulating with rapid hand movements while keeping his knees attached to the wheel. We assumed he knew where we were going. We certainly didn't.

An hour later we hurtled past the tourist buses at Badaling, a drop-off place for the regular Great Wall visitors, and twenty minutes later slowed down in front of a private gate guarded by armed security officers. There was nothing to indicate what was beyond it.

Our driver turned to us and shrugged his shoulders, his face questioning if this was our destination. We shrugged back.

Whatever he said to the guards encouraged them to open the gate and we entered a vast expanse of summer greenery, driving past secluded villas built in earthy colours, poking out from behind pockets of trees.

He deposited us at the hotel reception and these two Aussie tourists, dressed in shorts and covered in sunscreen, walked into an almost-empty lobby.

A lone staff member peered at us from the front desk.

'We have a reservation for lunch,' we told her.

She glanced at her watch with a look that told us we were far too early for the reservation.

'But before lunch we'd like to climb the wall,' Leigh added, her voice echoing off the cool tiles on the floor.

In broken English, the woman responded with words that crushed us.

'Oh we are very busy today and the wall is not open.'

Our mouths dropped open and we turned our heads slowly to remind ourselves the lobby was completely empty.

'Not open? The wall's not open?' we asked, bewildered. Our carefully constructed ploy was already starting to fall apart.

'But we want to climb the wall,' Leigh added firmly.

'Which wall?' the receptionist asked, delivering the words in English slowly.

'Um, the Great one?' we tentatively suggested, wondering if we'd missed something.

There was a small sign of acknowledgement on her face.

'Go straight and security will tell you.'

We were so relieved we almost skipped out of there, but as we wandered outside and looked for signs or the promised security officers, we found neither. We strolled along a track that wouldn't have been out of place on a hike through the bush in Australia. There was no sign of any wall, let alone a Great one, and we wondered if our excitement had been misplaced.

We finally spotted a small weathered wooden sign stuck into the ground. It was about ten centimetres tall with faded painted letters. 'To Great Wall', it read with an arrow. We followed the grassy path for another twenty minutes, veering up a steep climb past scattered rocks. We wondered out loud if we were already on the wild wall. Was the wild wall so overgrown that we were walking along the broken remains of it and didn't know?

And then as the trail curved, the bushes opened up and we lifted ourselves into a vista that took our breath away. For as far as we could see, the Great Wall of China stretched out in front of us, up and over mountains and beyond. And for the next hour it was ours.

We scrambled up ramparts, the steps forcing us onto our hands and knees. We posed for photos in the rectangular openings at the top of watch towers, laughing as we mimicked the hotel receptionist asking us – 'Which wall?'

'What if we'd said to her, "Um, the not-so-great-wall? The one built in 1956?".'

Our giggles could be heard by no one. We were entirely alone.

In some places the wall was in such disrepair, with trees growing up through the crumbling rocks, we'd have to leap down into the long grass and find a way to climb back up onto it.

Ants stung our legs and we'd been warned about virus-carrying mosquitoes but nothing could take away our exhilaration. Each turn and bend in the wall opened up another sweeping view.

We walked until we reached a fence and, far beyond it, we saw the tiny dots of human tourists who were crowding into the restored and concreted part of the monument. If only they knew what was on the other side. If only they could see what we'd seen.

We reluctantly turned back. A little while later we spotted two women drinking champagne on one of the peaks, the only other people we encountered. They were hotel guests who were celebrating a wedding anniversary although the mother and daughter acknowledged with a grimace that the husband in question was indeed absent because he'd refused to climb that high. Nothing more could surprise us that day so we took a photo for them and kept walking.

When we reached the spot where we'd first glimpsed the wall, when we'd wondered if we were even on the right track, we hesitated. Stepping off the bricks would signal the end of this adventure and neither of us felt able to do it.

'We may never, ever have an experience like this again,' we said with a tinge of sadness.

On our return we were ushered into the almost-empty restaurant as if we'd been simply strolling around the grounds for the past two hours. We took a stab at the menu and ended up with tasteless chicken gristle but washed it down with a glass of wine each. The lunch had been a means to an end and we weren't bothered.

We felt we'd been granted a remarkable wish, something so rare and magnificent, so uplifting, we glowed with pleasure.

For years after, if either of us felt our spirits sagging, we would remind each other of the awesomeness of that day and the tantalising prospect that another magical moment could be just around the curve of an overgrown path.

# CHAPTER 14

# Catastrophic Loss

IN 2009 I turned forty and limped into the party I'd planned. It wasn't how I'd envisaged starting a new decade but I'd torn a calf muscle playing tennis and instead of stilettos I was wearing flat sandals and reminding myself I'd planned the celebration to mark a turning point in my life. I was divorced, had moved on from the relationship with Nick, was loving my beachside life in Sydney's Bronte and was finally feeling content. Or I thought I was.

But I wasn't entirely ready to settle down so I threw my hat in the ring for the Washington posting again, this time as bureau chief.

When I learned I'd be heading back, I started looking forward to the familiarity of life in the US, even though I'd be going alone.

But it felt like I had a chance at a 'redo'. I was soon reminded of the unpredictability of the job.

Barack Obama had been president for five months and the consequences of the September 11 attacks were still the recurring theme for Americans. Arguments continued over when and how, or even if, they could reduce the number of US military personnel in the Middle East. And the hunt for the mastermind of the attacks, Osama bin Laden, went on.

But all of that had to wait because, just days before I arrived, there was breaking news out of Los Angeles – Michael Jackson had died.

The child star who grew up to be known as the King of Pop had been in rehearsals for a comeback tour in a bid to erase his staggering debts. Child sex abuse allegations had dogged him since 1993 although he'd been acquitted at the end of a chaotic trial in 2005. He still had a massive fan base, though, and the death of one of the most famous people on the planet led the ABC news.

While he died at his LA mansion, fans began gathering at the Neverland Ranch, the home he'd named after the island in *Peter Pan*. It was where he'd built a hobby zoo and a private amusement park although he'd spent less and less time there after it became the focus of police investigations.

As the hours ticked down to my departure, the story was developing rapidly. There were questions about the fifty-year-old's death and a date set for a star-studded memorial service in LA.

While I sat at Sydney airport waiting for my flight, my phone vibrated with a message from my foreign editor, the last one I'd receive before taking off for Washington.

'Don't go on to DC. Go directly to Neverland.'

This direction to land in LA, then hire a car and drive three hours to a ranch, inspired by a children's book, set the tone for my next six years in the US. A period where reality and fiction were sometimes hard to separate.

During my first posting I had often been surprised at the cultural alienness of being in the US. Like most Australians, I grew up on a diet of *Sesame Street* and thought I knew the US. But the minute I was forced to the right side of the sidewalk I was aware of the small differences that could rattle and unsettle.

It could happen in the grocery store where coriander was cilantro, chickpeas were garbanzo beans and ironing spray was starch. Or in the bureau where the American office manager insisted on issuing cheques when the rest of the world had adopted electronic banking, and where the idea that you'd boil water in an electric jug for your tea rather than in the microwave was a foreign concept.

Even something you'd expect to be familiar, like an airport, could be unexpectedly confusing. On an early assignment during my first posting, I was in Oklahoma with camera operator Dan Sweetapple, who'd recently arrived from Canberra.

We'd been covering the anniversary of the Oklahoma bombing. American Timothy McVeigh had been executed for his role in carrying out the deadly attack which partially destroyed a federal building and killed 168 people, including children who'd been at a daycare centre on the second floor.

We'd pitched a few stories to make the trip worthwhile, including a piece on cock fighting, which was then still legal in Oklahoma. We also drove to a massive ammunition factory where the US military was building bombs in anticipation of war in Iraq. The Australian military had signed a contract to buy some of the weapons and we were the first international TV crew allowed to film inside. We were provided protective clothing and plastic glasses which made us look like mad scientists. Inside, we felt like we'd stepped back in time as we watched factory workers hand-paint yellow lines around the nose of a 500-pound bomb on a conveyor belt.

We'd signed contracts promising we wouldn't reveal the extent of work going on beneath the grass-covered mounds that hid the huge factory. The US officials also gave us letters to pass on to airport staff in case they found traces of explosive material during security checks on our luggage or clothes. We were hoping that would be enough to get us through, given this was the year after the terrorist attacks of September 11 and many people were still anxious about flying.

When we arrived at the airport later, the airline was offering a curbside check-in and we couldn't believe our luck. After a week on the road, lugging gear around was starting to wear on us. Our bags plus tripods, lenses, tapes and batteries would average around a hundred kilos.

What a breeze it was as I dropped off Dan and the equipment for the check-in and circled back to return the rental car. If only all airports were like this, I thought.

By the time I walked up, they were attaching the tags to the bags and putting them on a trolley. We gave them a cheery Australian thank you and I promised to buy Dan a beer.

We were twenty metres inside the airport doors when we heard one of the men shouting in anger, 'Yo, we'll be sure to get your bags to DC. Oh yeah, for sure. We'll get them to DC.'

Dan and I paused and looked at each other.

'Oh my God. Were we supposed to tip them?' I asked as the realisation dawned.

We felt like amateurs. Of course no American airport was going to offer a curbside service without a cost. Nothing was ever free in this land of the free.

By then we were halfway across the concourse to security and people were starting to stare. 'Do I go back?' I asked Dan. 'And how much do I give them?'

I couldn't take the risk we'd arrive in Washington without the gear so I darted back across the concourse full of apologies in my strongest Australian accent, hoping twenty dollars was going to ensure the bags didn't end up in Kansas instead.

We had to laugh.

\* \* \*

Working with the ABC crews has been a highlight. Despite moving around so much I never felt disconnected from the friends I'd made over the years. I treasured knowing that the two young camera operators, John Bean and Ben Curry, who'd been my Canberra flatmates fifteen years earlier were still only a phone call away. We often reflected on how that car accident and night in hospital emergency had been the foundation of our strong bond.

Shortly after I started my second US posting in 2009, John and his wife, Pip Courtney, who now hosts *Landline*, were planning a trip. We were short-staffed in the bureau so John and I worked out a cheap option for the ABC. He could have his holiday with Pip, then stay with me in my apartment off 14th Street in Logan Circle and backfill as the Washington camera operator for a month.

It was a magical time for us, two old friends who hadn't worked together since 1996. We covered the world's leaders gathering at the United Nations General Assembly and giggled as we filmed a press conference with our mutual crush, Hugh Jackman.

We were flatmates again. And I was reminded how kind and funny John was. My large seventh-floor apartment looked out across the street onto a Whole Foods supermarket. Each afternoon on a weekend a homeless man would start playing his battered saxophone. But he only had two notes and with those he made an awful droning noise.

When I'd first moved in I thought it was great that the character of the neighbourhood hadn't been totally erased and I'd throw a few bucks into his hat. By the time John arrived a few months later for his stint in the bureau I was stomping around the apartment complaining about not being able to sleep because of the saxophonist. I'd shut all the windows and turn on the air-conditioning to block it out.

John's response was to walk across the street and sit with the musician, listening to his story of a life that had unravelled, and offering the kind of empathy that made me want to be a better person.

John also loved watching the sun set across the Washington monuments from my rooftop. I'd find him there on warm evenings when I returned from work and often after being sent a text, 'On roof, bring more beers.'

When he left Washington to head home to Australia he placed a magnet on my fridge that said, 'Good friends are like stars. You don't always see them but you know they're always there.'

I would never see John again.

The noise of the phone beside my bed woke me in August 2011. It was Stephanie Kennedy – the same Canberra reporter who'd taken me under her wing a decade and a half earlier and had become a close friend. It was after 9 pm in Sydney and, in her role as network editor planning the next day's news coverage, she'd been given devastating news. She'd taken a deep breath and immediately dialled my number.

The ABC helicopter, with veteran reporter Paul Lockyer, pilot Gary Ticehurst and our friend John onboard, had crashed in a remote area near Lake Eyre several hours earlier.

'Lisa, there are no survivors. We've lost John.'

The crisp white summer sheet suddenly felt heavy on my chest, the sound of the air-conditioning roared louder and I remember the whine of a police siren outside.

She said she'd call back but she had to go. The story was about to go online and she wanted me to know before I saw it anywhere else.

John. Gone.

It was almost impossible to comprehend on the other side of the world.

The weight of sadness descended on staff throughout the ABC. All three men had also been admired by many throughout Australia.

His widow, Pip, was overwhelmed with well-wishers. In federal and state parliaments, politicians paused to pay tribute. There was a collective feeling of loss.

I will be forever grateful for the ABC's response. Managing director Mark Scott and news director Kate Torney didn't hesitate in booking me on a flight back to Brisbane and I was with Pip in the home she and John had shared within days.

Speaking at his memorial was hard but I owed it to him. A psychologist, engaged by the ABC, rang to ask if she could help me prepare. Thousands of people would be there. She suggested holding something small and sharp in my hand and to clench my fist if I felt overcome. I gripped a small pink plastic toy dolphin so hard during that speech it left indents in my palms.

A few days later I was back on a plane to Washington, DC, feeling wrung out. I'd been given a chance to grieve with friends, albeit briefly, but I had to get back to work.

Goodbyes were always hard. This one was even tougher but I knew what the expectations were when I'd signed up to go back overseas so I boxed up my sadness and concentrated on what was coming next in Washington.

\* \* \*

In 2012 the wonderful Dan Sweetapple and I were working together again, musing on our first experiences of travel in the US while we wandered around Reagan Airport.

Ronald Reagan Washington National Airport was the kind of airport you wished you could always fly through. It was just a couple of kilometres across the DC border into Virginia and less than a twenty-dollar cab fare from the ABC office downtown. Even if you had half-a-dozen cases to check – which we often did – you'd still only need forty-five minutes to check in, line up for security and head to the gate. Prices for flying out of Reagan were higher due to the privilege of having that quick escape from town. We'd become so casual about flying, and did it so often, that on occasion we'd turn up at Reagan Airport only to discover our producer had in fact taken the cheaper option of booking us on a flight departing from an airport another forty-five minutes west.

On this occasion, it was a mild Friday morning for a December day and the skies were clear. We weren't flying though, instead we were reporting on airline business after a busy Thanksgiving period.

Fridays were always a more relaxed day in the bureau. And on this Friday Australia would be waking up to a glorious summer weekend, kids would be starting Christmas holidays and there was less demand for stories or live crosses.

It was close to midday when our producer Janet Silver called with the first reports out of a small town in Connecticut. There'd been a shooting at a school.

It said something about America that those words alone weren't enough to have us scurrying back to the office. We'd covered so many shootings that it needed to start hitting double figures for us to travel to the crime scene and not simply cover the story from our studio in DC.

We wrapped up our filming at the airport and told her to keep us posted. Another phone call twenty minutes later confirmed this was far worse than anything we'd covered before.

The town was Sandy Hook. A young man had calmly walked in to a school that morning, took aim at frightened little children and shot them dead.

We wouldn't know until late that night that twenty children in grade one and six teachers, as well as the shooter's own mother, had been killed in what was one of the worst shooting massacres America had seen at that point.

We hailed a cab and I dropped Dan back at the office to grab the gear we'd need. His wife, Kathleen, had delivered a suitcase of clothes to the bureau. I lived alone and had to tackle that chore myself. It never took long. It would be below zero in Connecticut so I packed tights, thermal gloves, scarves and a packet of instant single-use hand warmers that would activate when the plastic pack was opened.

Just a few hours after we'd scrambled to the bureau from Reagan Airport we were back there checking into Delta flight 5920 to LaGuardia Airport in New York. Arriving at LaGuardia was still going to leave us an hour's drive south of Sandy Hook but it was as close as we could get that night. And we knew it was going to be a long night.

It was pitch dark and had been snowing when we hit the first police roadblocks a kilometre out of town. We got past them but abandoned the car when it was clear we could get no further. Dense woods surrounded the town and the footpath was already covered in snow. We packed the camera equipment onto a trolley and headed on foot towards the lights of the satellite TV trucks that were already operating.

The Sydney office had been calling us to get set up for live crosses. It was now midday on Saturday in Australia and they wanted reports from their team on the ground immediately. We set up outside the fire station for the first live crosses. It was now eleven hours since the shooting but families were still inside waiting for news about their children.

Later that night we packed up and dragged our gear a kilometre to a nearby sports field where the police chief was holding a press conference. It was well after midnight and Dan and I had both been awake for eighteen hours but we weren't alone with our sleep deprivation. We saw other Australian camera crews, our commercial colleagues who were based in Los Angeles. Our normal welcomes and back slapping were replaced by sombre nods of the head. By 2 am we were preparing for live crosses into the main 7 pm TV bulletins back home.

We wouldn't find out the horrific details until much later. Adam Lanza had killed his mother at their home and then taken her high velocity rifle to the school he'd attended as a child. He shot his way through the glass panel next to the front doors. They were locked every day at 9.30 am as per school security rules but the locks were no barrier to him. He was dressed in black and roamed the hallways as terrified children and teachers hid in cupboards and under desks.

We would not know until years later that he spent less than five minutes inside the school and fired 156 shots before killing himself as the first police arrived on the scene.

Tiny little bodies left bleeding on schoolroom floors.

That night, without those details, I talked into the camera about what we had witnessed: the speechless horror on the faces of the town's residents, the families hugging each other tight. I talked so much in that cold night that the steam from my mouth created a foggy screen between me and the red light on the camera.

An image forced its way into my mind – two of my young nieces, then four and seven and back home safe in Brisbane, lying on a school floor, legs and arms spread out, bullet holes in their bodies.

'I need to stop,' I said to Dan, blinking away tears.

There was a predictable pattern to the horror of these assignments. You spent the first twenty-four hours reporting the details while trying to block out the horror, knowing there was a job to do. Then the reality would sink in and it was harder to push it aside. Memorials of flowers and teddy bears started growing and little notes written in a child's hand were left for others to read. Candles flickered through the night in the windows of households that wouldn't sleep again in peace. Dan was a father and I could feel the weight of the emotion within him.

The local affiliates of the big US networks were the first to arrive on the scene for stories like these and they were quickly followed by CNN and cable TV personalities.

A large sign welcomed visitors to Sandy Hook. It was round with carved-out edges, supported by two metre high white posts on either side. There was gold lettering over the green paint. It was a pretty little town and if you'd come across it in Australia it could easily have boasted of being a Tidy Towns winner.

But the welcome never lasted long when people were facing tragedy. The smaller the town, the harder it was to deal with the presence of strangers roaming the street with cameras and microphones. The same residents were approached once, then twice, then angrily told the next unsuspecting journalist to 'fuck off'. We were doing our job but at that moment we even started to hate ourselves.

On the third day Barack Obama spoke and his voice broke as he read the names of each of the victims. It was enough to break the hardest of hearts.

The bitterly cold weather and long days that ended after 3 am finally took their toll and I started losing my voice. On the fourth day the international editor in Sydney decided to pull me out and send me back to Washington. Our other crew stayed on but the story had already shifted back to the capital where an angry debate raged about gun control.

Two months later I was back at Sandy Hook waiting in a hotel room for a phone call I thought would never come. The ABC's *Foreign Correspondent* program had asked if I could get one of the grieving parents on camera. It was a big ask. The American networks had managed exclusives with one or two families but no foreign broadcaster had had any luck. The support groups that wrapped their arms around the Sandy Hook community were naturally protective when it came to the media.

I had covered a gun safety rally on the National Mall and saw a group of Sandy Hook supporters walking with their banner held high. I walked beside them and chatted till we reached the Capitol and they agreed to put me in contact with someone they thought might talk.

When the phone call finally came I was lost for words. What do you say to a mother who had to bury a son and explain to his twin sister why she survived and her brother did not.

Veronique Pozner was a remarkable woman who wanted a global audience to hear her pleas to get AR-15 semi-automatics off the streets of America. She told us if we came to Connecticut she'd consider speaking to us. She'd wait for our call once we checked into the hotel.

But our first day passed with our calls unanswered. She hadn't told me where she was staying and no one else knew where she was. As the next day passed with no contact, producer Greg Wilesmith, camera operator Rob Hill and I came to the sinking realisation she'd changed her mind.

And then the handset beside my bed at the Hampton Inn rang and Veronique said she was ready to talk. Her house was a few blocks from the school. It was modest in size and we dragged the heavy cases of lights and equipment up the stairs.

Small talk before an interview is often hard. You don't want to end up taking away the spontaneity of what might come out once the cameras are rolling so you try to avoid the subject you're there to discuss. But Veronique's son, Noah, had been shot to death by a mentally deranged teenager. We weren't going to be chatting about her garden or paintings.

Rob sat us down in two chairs, almost within touching distance, and Veronique fondled photographs of a sweet cherub, smiling back at his mum.

Noah had been shot eleven times and his death had given her strength she hadn't felt before – a mum against the National Rifle Association. 'They're weapons of mass carnage designed for the battlefield not society,' she told me.

The gun debate raged during my time in the US and each mass shooting was met with a new round of horror. But America's love affair with guns never diminished.

Years later, when I'd moved to the UK to become the ABC's Europe bureau chief, I watched from afar the outpouring of grief again after a man walked into a nightclub in Orlando, Florida, and shot dead forty-nine people. It was midway through a US presidential election year that would ultimately see Donald Trump win the White House. The shooting sparked another round of soul-searching over gun control and the ABC's DC bureau needed back-up.

I flew into Washington to file stories from the studio while the ABC teams of journalists and camera operators worked around the clock in Florida. I'd been there barely a day when the request came in from the Sydney producers – could I find Veronique and see if she'd talk to me again.

It was three and a half years since she'd lost her son and she had long left Sandy Hook and disconnected her numbers. I'd sent her occasional emails over that time, hoping she was doing okay, but never expected replies.

What I didn't know was that she and her ex-husband had been hounded and tormented by conspiracists who spread repugnant theories that Noah had not actually died and the family were frauds. They were the only Jewish family to lose a child that day and that only fuelled the madness of the falsehoods. They had even faced death threats. Others claimed that the US government had engaged actors to create a fake massacre to ban semi-automatics.

I had been at Sandy Hook in those days after the shooting and had seen the small village plunged into inconceivable grief but entering that online rabbit hole of conspiracy theories made me realise how people could be convinced otherwise. The websites managed to make some of the ludicrous 'evidence' they presented appear plausible and I was less shocked that people fell for it.

Noah's father, Lenny Pozner, had been spending his days taking down hoaxers online, forcing the removal of their rantings and successfully taking them to court. When I tracked both Lenny and Veronique down they agreed to speak to me again, despite the traumatic memories that another mass shooting sparked.

I always worried about the impact of interviewing someone so burdened by trauma – that I was taking too much of their privacy, their strength, their ability to lock away the sadness.

Camera operator Dan Sweetapple who'd been with me on that first awful night in Sandy Hook and the days after had been flown in from Australia to help with the coverage. He'd become a great friend over the years and it was a comforting coincidence that we were together again when we revisited the story.

After interviewing Noah's parents, we flew to Connecticut and found his gravestone in a cemetery so tiny that we drove past the tree-covered entrance before turning back along the single-lane road.

A scarf lay on the ground. Veronique had told me she'd left it there for Noah.

I'd always thought my job as a journalist was to be an observer, respecting the barrier that stopped us touching, intruding, entering or becoming the story. But I bent down and picked up the scarf and tucked it under a rock on the headstone.

Dan sat in the car and took a deep breath, thinking of his two beautiful, boisterous children back in Australia. As he started the rental car my phone pinged. It was my sister in Brisbane sending a video of my niece Eva at an ice-skating competition, her young face beaming out at me from the screen.

It was a strange existence to float between the grief of others and our own completely separate lives. I was reminded of one of the most powerful lines written in the aftermath of the Sandy Hook massacre. Journalist Gregory Korte revealed the weight we all felt reporting on the tragedy.

'How do you write an obituary for a five-year-old?' he wrote. 'And then how do you write nineteen more?'

With the family in 1970. After fourteen years, I was a bit of a
novelty for my siblings, David (*left*), Wendy and Robert.

On the tractor with Dad in 1971. Three
years later he entered parliament and
our simple life in Kilkivan changed.

Getting IEC ready for flight was a family affair. Trudi and
I pushing her out of the hangar on our Kilkivan airstrip,
with the door open to let the hot air escape, 1973.

Grandma was a fearless adventurer
whose postcards would arrive in
Kilkivan from around the world.

With my playmate and baby sister, Trudi.
Our beloved grandma showered us with attention.

Dad flew less after entering politics and
IEC was sold when I was ten.

With my friend Robynne Bishop, ready to escort junior
debutantes along the red carpet in Kilkivan.

Our family left Kilkivan in 1979 but we
always had a fondness for the town
and its residents.

At the 1982 opening of the Don Pancho resort in
Bargara in Dad's electorate. The name made it feel
exotic. So did the umbrellas in our drinks.

With Dad in his Parliament House office in
late 1986. On this trip I had the inspiring
encounter with journalist Richard Carleton.

The night before I almost killed my mother and sister in a car accident. A happy graduation in August 1989 followed by an awful day.

It was all big hair and big belts during our uni years and my flatmate Carolyn Olarenshaw and I followed the call.

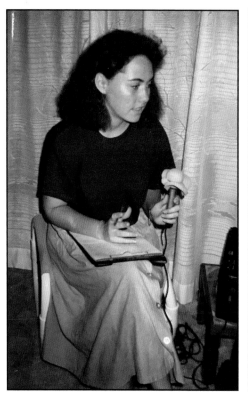

It was only a university radio assignment, but I had a real microphone in my hand and I felt like I was on my way.

My first journalism job and first business card. It was so exciting until I realised they'd spelt my name wrong.

With ABC elections analyst Antony Green, broadcasting from the Queensland tally room for the 1998 state election. I was happy to be on the ground again after struggling badly with my fear of flying during the campaign.

My Canberra flatmates Ben Curry (*at top*) and John Bean. We were bereft when John died in a helicopter crash in 2011.

With Leigh Sales onboard QF11 to LA on 1 December 2001, to begin our postings in the ABC's Washington bureau.

(*Above left*) A fresh-faced correspondent outside the White House. The posting was dominated by the fallout from the September 11 attacks.

(*Above*) My first of two visits to Guantanamo Bay, twelve years apart. This was in 2002, just a few weeks after Australian David Hicks was detained.

(*Left*) Covering the 2004 Democratic convention with John Shovelan in Boston, where Senator John Kerry got the nod as presidential candidate.

My brothers and sisters with Mum and Dad in Brisbane. They'd always find a way to have me at the table.

Finding just the right number of pillows to mimic a soundproof voiceover booth in New York in 2003 during the UN debate on Iraq.

Filing my voiceover using a lip microphone from the van in Bali after the October 2005 terrorist attacks.

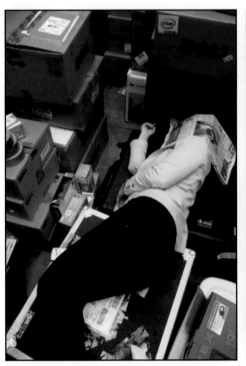

Covering then PM Kevin Rudd at the Pittsburgh G20 meeting, 2009. It was 5am in the US when we'd cross live into the 7pm news bulletins back home.

Trying to bottle the trepidation as I enter the water for my first attempt at a triathlon in 2010 in Washington DC.

The indefatigable Dan Sweetapple lugging the camera, trying to catch the top of a parade in Virginia in 2009 so I could do a piece-to-camera.

Grabbing space at the 2012 London Olympics to file and sleep. With Mary Gearin, Andrew George (*at back*) and Phil Williams.

We were part of the huge media pack watching police detonate explosives and hunt down terrorists in Paris in 2015.

Wearing the black jacket in Paris that offended a Twitter follower in 2015. The subsequent media storm took me by surprise.

Producer Emily Smith and camera operators Cameron Bauer (*left*) and Ale Pavone counting cases off the train after the 2015 Paris attacks.

The earthquake in central Italy in 2016 left 300 people dead. It was confronting watching the fruitless search for bodies in Amatrice.

From left: Robert, me, Wendy, Dad, Mum, David and Trudi getting Dad back into the air for his 85th birthday. I'd come back briefly from the US to join them.

(*Middle*) My final live cross from London with Michael Rowland after nine years abroad and one of the toughest. I knew Mum was likely to die within hours.

(*Below left*) The dress code was black tie but there was nothing glamorous about covering the BAFTAs in 2016 with producer Emily Bryan.

(*Below*) The moment I was captured calling out to Prince Harry the day before his 2018 wedding. 'How do you feel, Harry?' I shouted.

## CHAPTER 15

# Full Throttle

THAT SECOND POSTING in Washington proved to be as challenging as I'd expected but it also allowed me to revisit the stories that had left an impact on me. I returned to Guantanamo Bay in 2014, where some of the same prisoners I'd watched being brought off the planes in 2002, wearing orange jumpsuits and shackled to each other, were still waiting for their trials. I reconnected with a widow of one of the victims of September 11 and saw the pride she took in her children who'd been just toddlers when their dad died in one of the towers.

And it was during that second stint in Washington that I also unexpectedly learned how empowering it could be to overcome a fear.

It's why you would have found me one February morning cursing my long black puffer jacket for barely keeping out the cold and regretting throwing on my running shoes and not my winter boots.

I'd been walking around the intersection of 14th and Q streets in Washington, DC, for five minutes, straining into the gloomy light looking for a rental car. It didn't help that it was a deep blue Mini that wasn't going to stand out in the dark.

The booking said it was called Bertie, which was meant to make the whole experience of car sharing fun, but it wasn't as if I was going to start calling out its name.

Hiring cars by the hour had taken off in Washington, a city where street parking was limited and owning a car was more of a burden than an escape hatch. You'd circle the block three times waiting for someone to pull out of a parking spot and then neatly reverse in, only to discover the sign that warned the next day was 'trash collection' and you'd have to move it by 4 am anyway.

The system of booking short lease cars and unlocking them with the swipe of a card across a reader on the windscreen worked well, until the car you'd booked wasn't there.

Given it wasn't even 6 am I'd assumed someone had taken the car out overnight and slept in, which is what I was wishing I'd done. I was due to meet Lloyd Henry, an African American athlete who'd been tasked with turning me into a triathlete. Lloyd had been coaching triathletes for years and had specialised in long-distance ironman feats that are beyond the capability of the majority of us. They're the races that last for an entire day and end with competitors limping home or being taken away in ambulances.

I was meeting him as part of an experiment I'd agreed to and I was nervous. It had begun when an American friend of mine, Jeff, a marathon runner who'd completed more than one hundred races and then wrote a book about them, took a job at a sports magazine. Jeff had been having a drink with his colleagues one Friday happy hour, arguing over whether you could take a regular relatively healthy person and train them to become a triathlete.

'No way, they could maybe do one of the legs but not all three,' one of them said.

'Too much to master,' said another as he went to the bar to order another round of beers.

'That so?' challenged someone else as he threw dollar bills on the table and got ready to leave.

'Well, I think it can be done,' my friend Jeff, ever the optimist, chimed in, 'but, gee, it's a big call.'

And so The Great Triathlon Makeover of 2010 was born.

They decided to publicly document each step of the experiment in the magazine and, if it ended in failure, then at least half of the happy-hour drinkers would claim victory.

It would be a cross between *My Fair Lady* and *Rocky*. All they needed was an Eliza Doolittle who was happy to improve her muscles instead of her elocution. In exquisite timing I rang Jeff the day after his happy-hour drinks to bemoan my lethargy. My forty-first birthday was approaching and I needed a reboot.

This was the second time I'd lived in Washington, DC, working for the ABC, and I'd quickly fallen into unhealthy habits. I couldn't avoid the late nights in the office. The deadline for the midday news in Australia was late in the evening in Washington, DC. But I could avoid the large wine and bags of potato chips that I scoffed when I got home. I just didn't want to.

I'd never thought of training for a triathlon. I didn't even know what was involved but as Jeff explained what they had planned, and the coaching support they'd offer, it all seemed to crystallise.

'Yes! Let's do it!' I said in a burst of enthusiasm that would be tested and retested over the following six months.

They'd found me a road bike, a wetsuit and triathlete gear and a new pair of runners. And here I was, on what was supposed to be the first day of training, and I'd lost the car.

I made a cursory call to the automated number for the car sharing company to cancel the booking so I wouldn't be charged a penalty. There were no taxis prowling the streets at that hour so I started thinking of how I'd explain to Lloyd that I'd failed at the first hurdle.

But the car sharing company's GPS tracking pointed me three blocks north. The car was on the same downtown street as me but past the homeless shelter that just a few years later would be converted into trendy loft apartments surrounded by restaurants with names like Le Diplomate and El Centro. It was so trendy that reservations were outdated and instead you'd loiter outside hoping for an opening so you could pay an eye-watering twenty-five US dollars for a cocktail.

Locals in my neighbourhood, Logan Circle, were resigned to the inevitable gentrification that was creeping across the city, block by block, like a slow-moving afternoon shadow.

On my first posting to Washington, DC, in the aftermath of the September 11 terrorist attacks, the ABC's office manager, an anxiety-ridden American, had insisted I not walk home from work in the evenings and instead catch a cab. I thought it was an overreaction until my then husband Sid was mugged one night after meeting a friend for a beer and lost his keys and wallet.

But we loved the energy and vibe of the hood, like the sounds of two women shouting greetings across the street at each other in voices so melodic they could easily have slipped into song.

'Yo, gurrlfriend,' came the first lyrics.

'Yo, gurrlfriend. You ain't showed your face at Joes so long I'm a wondering where you been.'

'You better BE there.'

'YOU better be there.'

The sing-song call and response pinged back and forth with neither of them thinking of stepping off the footpath to shorten the distance between them.

I'd walk to work along these vibrant city streets, every part of me tingling with the promise of a new day, with the smell of fresh cut grass and spring leaves and the cacophony of voices and music and honking cars and shouts for someone to 'Pick up after your dog, Ma'am,' in that American tone, a mix of politeness with a dash of intimidation.

A young African American sat on the curb and called out as I walked by. 'Yo, Mama,' he said, his voice gentle yet confident.

I spun around, pulled from my internal revelry and tilted my head in his direction.

'You look black from the back,' he said with a smile and a nod of his head.

I laughed and kept walking, conscious I'd fallen into the languidly hypnotic hip swing of the young African American women of the neighbourhood.

We loved the divey jazz club at the end of our street, HR-57, named after the US House of Representatives Act that designated jazz a 'national treasure'.

A single entry wooden door led you through to the fluorescent-lit bar where you paid ten dollars for the music and got a plastic plate piled with refried beans, rice and brisket.

Local amateurs would sit sipping beers at small round bare wooden tables whose surfaces had the permanent stickiness of nights long gone. A nod of the head from the soloist and they'd step up and join in performances that seemed to have no clear start or finish but just enough of a pause for the few dozen people in the crowd to clap before they kept playing.

Occasionally you'd find yourself in the presence of genius, like the night legendary trumpeter Wynton Marsalis sauntered onto the slightly elevated stage, unannounced, and with a puff of his cheeks lifted his instrument to his lips and blasted us into musical ecstasy.

But the rents became too high for the club and it moved closer to Capitol Hill where the audience were young interns and stiff, suited congressional workers whose regard for the music depended on how many shot glasses sat empty on the table in front of them.

The fried chicken takeout places in our neighbourhood with their simple menus of crispy wings, catfish, collard greens and cornbread started disappearing, too.

The homeless stayed, though, through each reincarnation of the neighbourhood. The numbers of people on the streets skyrocketed during the years I spent in Washington. The mentally ill, the down and out, the ones who'd had the American dream escape their reach and others who never had a shot at it.

It was one of the ironies of this great city that the homeless would gather in largest numbers near the grounds of the White House at Lafayette Park. They'd sleep there on benches, huddled and hiding under donated blankets or sleeping bags, rising when food trucks would come to offer them steaming cups of coffee and bowls of rice and meat.

It was such a stark reminder of the haves and have-nots, just a couple of hundred metres from the president's home at 1600 Pennsylvania Avenue that I sat down with a couple of them once and asked why they didn't want to get out of the cold and stay in a shelter, where there were plenty of empty beds.

'No way,' one of them exclaimed, his eyebrows disappearing into his shaggy matted hair as he processed the question. 'Spend a night in one of those places? Huh, them's crazy people in those places.' And with that he pulled the blanket over his head and shut out the world.

Washington would always challenge me, professionally and personally.

\* \* \*

I'm not sure what I was thinking as I drove to that first training morning but I'd probably lulled myself into believing it was all very doable. Lloyd had decided we would start small – a triathlon in Washington, DC, in a few months' time.

I was meeting Lloyd in south-west Washington at a 25-metre pool that was split into half-a-dozen lanes and looked like it needed a renovation. There weren't a lot of public pools in Washington. The District of Columbia was never flush with cash and swimming pools were not high on the list for public funding among the predominantly black population.

'Show me what you've got,' Lloyd said as I tossed off my winter jacket and beanie and stripped down to my swimmers.

The pool was heated and I slipped into the water, the strength of the warmed chlorine stinging the inside of my nose as I breathed in. I thrashed my way down the pool and back completely out of breath as I popped my head up, removed my goggles and looked up at Lloyd hopefully.

'We can work with that,' he said.

The truth was he went away and wrote in his coaching notes that 'swimming is Lisa's biggest weakness'.

Thirty years after having my head dunked underwater by an enthusiastic swimming teacher at Gympie I was facing that confronting realisation again – that despite loving being in the water, of wearing my Queensland upbringing like a badge, of wanting to run hard at waves and dive beneath the white crests into the unknown, of jumping straight into the deep end of any pool anywhere in the world and knowing that no matter how far I sank I would rise again, I could not swim. Not properly at least.

Lloyd did his best to change that with a lesson each week and two other training sessions. He didn't say much about himself and I hesitated to pry. For Lloyd, this was business. He had an experiment to undertake.

He tossed me a kickboard and we started at the very beginning, but this time there was a gentleness that had been missing in all the other teachers who'd attempted to teach me to swim.

My heart would often race, not so much from the intensity of the exercise but more from the memories that were triggered as I made my way slowly from one end of the pool to the other. Memories of a childhood in Kilkivan where swimming pools were so rare that we treated them with awe and dipped our toes into the water as if it had magical powers. Memories of turning up to a new school in Gympie and discovering my lack of swimming skills was just one more thing that set me apart from my classmates.

Perhaps Lloyd's kindness came from the fact he could see it was tears, not pool water, that had filled my goggles and made me stop halfway down the lane.

I'd accepted the triathlon challenge because I'd pledged on my return to Washington, as a divorcee this time, to say 'yes' more often than not.

'Yes' could lead to regrets. 'Yes' could make you wonder if your head was screwed on right.

But 'no' took you nowhere. 'No' was the end of the story.

The idea of the triathlon alarmed me but I told myself it was just in my mind. I'd overcome my fear of flying and I could overcome this fear too.

Imagine how it would feel to complete it.

I'd thought my fear of flying was immutable but I'd beaten it. So I approached the triathlon in the same way.

My pre-work training sessions with Lloyd became easier as summer approached. Now the sun warmed my legs as I unlocked my bike for the weekly rides with him.

Learning to adjust to clip-in pedals for the first time was another challenge. By clicking the cleats on the bottom of your cycling shoes into the specially designed pedals you could lock your feet in place and maximise your power when you rode. To someone like me who'd never used them before it meant extended moments of panic on the road.

The professional bike riders made it look so easy. It was not.

I'd lock my shoes into the pedals and approach city intersections with trepidation, praying traffic lights wouldn't change to red and force me to dismount. That involved twisting your heel outward and releasing the cleat and then making sure you leaned the bike to the same side you'd just freed up. Countless times I'd release the cleat for my left leg and then lean the bike to the right, where my leg was still locked in. I just could not get my brain to understand – left leg released, lean to left.

Each week I'd have new weeping wounds from where I'd crashed down onto the bitumen. The scars started mounting.

I loved Sundays. That was when a long winding stretch of smooth bitumen inside Rock Creek National Park was closed to traffic and I could ride for thirty kilometres without stopping. And when I did have to come to an eventual stop, it was never rushed and I could recite my mantra several times before following through – left foot release, lean to left.

Lloyd was training a group of us and we'd meet regularly for swimming, running or riding and sometimes a combination of all three to get us used to the physical sensation of transitioning from one movement to another. I had no idea how easily legs could turn to jelly after you'd ridden a bike for forty minutes and then had to start running.

Training for the run was the one thing I felt comfortable doing. I'd completed a half marathon in Sydney the previous year and had kept up my running. I was very slow, but I didn't care. I enjoyed the easiness of an exercise that involved nothing more than sliding on shoes and opening the door, and there was something soothing about the same slow rhythm of heel hitting footpath.

Over the years I'd realised it was better if I had a goal, a reason for running, so I would sign up for races and stay motivated on my slow plods around the neighbourhood.

We'd been a family of 'fun run' entrants. Despite Mum's intense shyness, she loved the idea of being outdoors so much that she would sign us all up for charity runs. There was never any suggestion we'd actually *run* these fun runs. Trudi and I were still young, not even teenagers, and Mum wasn't a runner.

'Just as long as we don't finish behind the ambulance,' Mum would tell us as she encouraged us to keep walking. We'd be a hundred metres or so in front of the rescue squad, which was always the last across the line.

It became a lovely family tradition. On Mother's Days and International Women's Days my sisters and I – and later the next generation of nieces – would join Mum to complete five- or eight-kilometre charity walks. We'd chat along the way and enjoy each other's company. Sometimes I'd break into a run and circle back to find them. Our times and results were never important but we loved the camaraderie and race T-shirts that we proudly wore until they started showing holes under the arms.

Later, when I started doing long runs by myself in foreign countries, I was a little more serious. I still wanted to beat the race sweepers – the officials who would tell those lagging at the end that the road was about to reopen and the race was over. But I also wanted to try to beat my previous times.

There was one particular run in Washington that was so popular it was sold out every year and they began holding a lottery to choose the fifteen thousand people who'd take part.

The Cherry Blossom ten-mile run was held every spring in conjunction with the flowering of the thousands of trees that Japan had gifted to the city at the beginning of the last century. There was also a cultural festival that attracted 1.5 million tourists to see the trees.

The race wound its way through Washington's streets, starting on the National Mall, taking you past the Lincoln Memorial and around the Tidal Basin where the cherry blossoms would be in peak bloom. The fragile buds of the cherry blossoms worked to their own timetable, though. If there'd been a cold snap or early warmth you could find yourself running through streets with bare trees. Forecasting peak bloom was almost impossible more than ten days in advance and the dates for the race were set in place a year earlier.

I was lucky enough to gain a spot in the lottery three times. The last time I ran, it was the end of my second posting in Washington and, after six years, I was leaving the city and country I'd called home. I knew it would be my final race.

It was a cold day, cold enough that I was still wearing a beanie and gloves as I approached the final stretch after an hour of running. A gentle breeze started gathering strength from behind the pack of runners, rippling the water on the Tidal Basin where Thomas Jefferson's statue stood watch, and shaking out the wrinkles of the red, white and blue of the American flags that lined the Mall. And then suddenly it became a gust that shook the trees and whipped up dust and leaves on the ground and then showered us all in a sea of delicate pink and white petals.

It was a magical sight. People laughed and smiled and nodded at each other knowingly. It was as if Mother Nature was willing us to power on, to cross the finish line, even if our legs said otherwise.

I whipped my phone out of the pack around my waist and videoed the last moments of the petals floating around my face and sent it to Mum in Brisbane.

'Look how beautiful this is, Mum,' I said on the video, my nose red from the cold but my eyes shining bright. 'We never got this in Gympie!'

That last race was my slowest. But those numbers don't hint at the minutes I spent admiring the beauty of that shower of petals or the faint lilac perfume that drifted onto my clothes, or the smile that stayed on my face for the remainder of the day.

It reminded me of a line from a Henry Longfellow poem, 'Came the spring with all its splendour, all its birds and all its blossoms.'

All my training with Lloyd was coming to a head and the first day of summer arrived, signalling race day for my first triathlon. It was called a 'sprint', which I regarded from the outset as highly optimistic.

It began with an 800-metre swim, followed by a 20-kilometre ride and then a 6.7-kilometre run, finishing on an avenue heading downhill from the Capitol building.

We'd start the race near the Lincoln Memorial entering into the Potomac River. Temporary floating platforms had been placed at right angles to the riverbank so hundreds of people could enter the water simultaneously. The bike leg would follow a track out of town along the Rock Creek Parkway where I'd been training. I knew all I needed to do after that was put one leg in front of the other to finish the run.

But there were other elements to a triathlon that could make or break your success, including the transitions between each leg. There were techniques to getting out of a wetsuit and into your cycling gear, pulling on your shoes while starting to walk your bike out of the secure area and then at the end of that leg, getting out of those clip-ons and into your running shoes while attempting to constantly keep moving. My goal as an amateur was to try to get those transition times to around three minutes.

Lloyd recommended we take advantage of the pre-race swim the day before, to lessen the shock of the cold and muddy river water during the intensity of the actual race.

My friends Kim and Perry had come to offer moral support and sat in the sun with the newspapers spread out on a picnic blanket, sipping coffees, while they waited for me to come out of the water. The photo they took as I walked back up the grass towards them clutching my swim cap and goggles is a portrait of fear and disbelief.

Every step of the training had forced me into foreign territory. Overcoming my fear of flying had given me strength and courage to attempt this triathlon experiment but it didn't mean I was blasé about the challenge ahead.

It was the start of summer and the water was just cold enough to allow the legal use of wetsuits. A few degrees warmer and they wouldn't have been permitted. Lloyd was thrilled because he was counting on the thick black texture of the neoprene to give me more buoyancy. I was relieved because it created another layer of protection between me and the weeds and murkiness of the deep Potomac River.

A final check was done on water quality twenty-four hours before the start. In previous years the level of E.coli had been considered too high and the swim leg was cancelled, turning the race into a duathlon. I would have been devastated if that had happened, given the months of training and tear-filled goggle episodes I'd endured. If I didn't do it now, I doubted I'd ever attempt it again but the water got the officials' tick of approval.

I barely slept the night before, my stomach churning as I ran through all the scenarios. I imagined getting caught up in the 'washing machine' of competitors in the water at the start and falling so far behind the next wave of swimmers would overtake me. And what if I couldn't find my bike in the secure transition area where I'd left it as instructed the night before? God, what if I couldn't get out of my wetsuit? I read and reread the race instructions even though I'd virtually memorised every word.

Lloyd had left nothing to chance; we even practised our pre-race food consumption and examined our personal toilet needs. There were portaloos along the way but also plenty of crowds and you didn't want to be standing there waiting as the entire race pack passed you by.

Race day was beautiful and sunny. I told myself, 'Whatever happens, you've already achieved more than you ever imagined.'

But I was also feeling the pressure. Articles about my progress had been published in the *Competitor* magazine and hundreds of people had been following the blog about Lloyd's attempts to successfully do a 'Triathlon Makeover' of his Eliza Doolittle.

My workmates at the ABC had been incredibly supportive and were going to spread out along the race route to cheer me on. They knew how hard it had been to keep meeting deadlines while trying to train.

Lloyd knew that getting in the river with 1500 other people was going to be the most daunting moment. We'd be starting in waves of several dozen competitors but he suggested I get in and swim to the edge of the pack to avoid getting whacked in the head or swum over and pushed under. A swimmer had drowned in a triathlon in Philadelphia several weeks earlier and people were still talking about it.

My friend Jeff, who'd hooked me into this adventure, had just one thing to offer. 'Smile and pump your arms when you cross the finish line because you're going to want to keep that photo,' he said with a laugh.

The atmosphere was hectic. Americans love to turn any event into an occasion and music was being pumped out of speakers giving the triathlon the vibe of a rock concert, albeit one starting at 6 am.

My pre-race jitters were peaking. I panicked about blowing a tyre on my bike, about having to be taken from the river by the rescuers in kayaks who paddled in little circles along the race route. But it was too late to back out once I was corralled into my wave of 40- to 44-year-old women. The others all seemed incredibly fit and confident.

The carnival atmosphere continued with cheerleaders who held up signs that had things like 'Clap if you've weed in your wetsuit' written on them.

I was feeling completely overwhelmed but reminded myself of my friend Perry's words to me. 'Just keep going forward, Lisa, even if you end up dogpaddling.' Little did he know how helpful that was as the race siren went and I jumped in to discover cold water plus fear had forced the air from my lungs.

'Just keep moving forward,' I told myself.

I was eventually able to relax into a freestyle stroke but, after a few minutes, I glanced to the shoreline as I took a breath and realised I had veered off course and was only adding to the distance I would end up swimming.

The results would later show I was only in the water for twenty-four minutes but it felt like a lifetime. I got out of the wetsuit and transitioned to the bike in under four minutes and finished the ride in under fifty minutes. Another three minutes to transition to the run, undoing the Velcro on my cycling shoes as I pedalled in, and I was on the home stretch.

I could hear friends cheering me on and as the finish line came into sight I smiled so broadly I thought my face would break. I hadn't needed Jeff's advice. It was exhilarating.

The 'sprint' triathlon took me 2:07:54 and I felt thrilled I'd completed it but even while I was still pumped full of endorphins I vowed I would never do another one.

Except.

Except I discovered quickly that while people were impressed I'd actually finished, they often asked if I was now going to do a 'proper triathlon'.

Were they for real? I'd trained for four months, which included learning how to swim, I'd spent more than two hours swimming, riding and running and it wasn't a 'proper' triathlon?

My friend Jeff and coach Lloyd had both hoped I would sign up for an Olympic-distance triathlon. After succeeding with part one of the triathlon makeover they were excited about writing the next chapter. But I'd been firm with them throughout. It was not going to happen. I don't think they realised how close they'd pushed me to the edge. Completing all that training on top of my job as bureau chief in DC in a mid-term election year had been too much at times.

And besides, the distances for an Olympic triathlon were almost double what I'd only just been able to do – a 1.5-kilometre swim, 40 kilometres on the bike and then a 10-kilometre run.

But after a few days thinking it over, I realised that I'd come so far I'd be cursing myself if I stopped now. The next race was two and a half months away and we had a long way to go with my training.

I won't lie. It was a slog through the hot humid months of summer. I'd started dating a Frenchman in DC whose friends were curious about this woman who would only have half a glass of champagne and call an end to the night at 9 pm, just as the Europeans were warming up.

It had been a humid Washington night when I headed to a bar with my girlfriend Sophie to discuss my latest unimpressive blind date. When I'd arrived in DC newly single, I'd been keen to dip a toe into the American dating scene, but despite confidently believing I'd been well prepared by countless episodes of *Sex and the City* and *Seinfeld*, I soon realised I was completely out of my comfort zone.

I hadn't anticipated that someone I met for a Monday date might also be seeing multiple other women on selected days of the week for months before deciding which of us could earn the label 'exclusive'.

Sophie and I mulled over all this as we kept failing to catch the barman's attention. Suddenly, a gap opened in the crowd as a handsome man confidently strode in and took a seat at the bar where cutlery and a drink had been placed just seconds before.

'Excuse me,' I said indignantly. 'We haven't ordered yet.'

He gave me a withering look and asked what we wanted.

'Bubbles,' I replied.

'Harrison,' he called out to the barman in a thick and clearly exasperated French accent.

'Get these women two champagnes and put it on my tab.'

By the end of the night we'd argued over international politics, the role of the media and agreed on the oddities of American dating rituals. He rang the next morning and before I knew it I had a boyfriend. A French one at that. Although he would tell you he wasn't French but rather, Parisian. According to him, if you weren't living in Paris you were camping out.

For a country girl from Australia it was a romance like none other. He had a penchant for scarves and cigarettes. I was showered with gifts and flowers on any given day simply because he felt like it. But there were multiple cultural hurdles and I immediately regretted that my only option of a foreign language in school had been German and even that had only lasted a year.

I'll call him Philippe, because he was and still remains intensely private. He was the kind of person who abhorred social media and liked people to know as little about him as possible.

Unfortunately for our relationship, sometimes that included me. He remained something of an enigma throughout our seven years together.

*  *  *

Race day arrived. The weather couldn't have been more different from my first triathlon day. It poured through the night. Not just gentle showers but lashings of angry rain that kept waking me until the 4 am alarm finally signalled the end of the restless night.

I almost wept at the endurance I would have to muster to get through the race.

Fifteen hundred people had competed in the first triathlon but five thousand people had signed up for this one.

The water was warm enough that the no-wetsuit rule kicked in so I lost my buoyancy booster and my security blanket. The water was dark and swampy when I got in and it was more than forty minutes before I staggered out of the river.

The results showed I spent eight minutes in the transition area, an inordinately long time. I remember the rain coming down and not being able to find my bike among the thousands that were left there for other competitors. I ended up with so much mud under my shoes I couldn't click them into the pedals. I stopped ten minutes into the ride to pick up a branch to try to scrape out the mud but it didn't work. Hundreds of bikes whizzed past me and I had flashbacks to Mum saying 'as long as we're in front of the ambulance'. I got back on and rode the entire forty kilometres with one foot not connected to the bike pedal, the rain pelting into my cycling glasses.

By the time I started the run leg, my friends could see how much trouble I was in and broke triathlon rules to join me on the road, running alongside me, murmuring words of encouragement.

As the finish line came into sight I'd been moving for three hours and thirty-one minutes. I tried to smile for the obligatory photo but this time there was nothing spontaneous about it. I stopped just a few steps after the end, race officials urging me on to clear the finish line. A friend shoved a water bottle into my hands and I couldn't speak, I simply shook my head.

When people asked me why I did it, I told them it was because I'd overcome my fear of flying. That fear had threatened to hold me back from doing things, from taking opportunities, from making the most of life. And while it took me years to manage the crippling effect of that fear, and then even more years to reduce the impact it was having on me physically and mentally, I did it.

I was still fearful when I competed in those two triathlons. The seemingly confident women being corralled in my starting area probably were as well.

Very few people live without fear.

I feared I would drown, or I would crash off the bike, or I wouldn't finish after months of training and that I'd let everyone down.

Every new challenge throws up new fears. I may develop another fear later in life. But understanding that you have to be proactive – you have to work at overcoming your fear – means I know what I will do if that day comes.

For every paralysing moment of anxiety you can face and move past, another part of your life opens up.

# CHAPTER 16

# Emergency

IN 2015, AFTER six years back in the US, I felt ready for anything, including my third and final posting with the ABC, to head up the Europe bureau, based in London. But I wasn't really prepared. At least not mentally.

I'd planned to take three months' long service leave after finishing in DC before starting in London. Dad was turning ninety and I wanted to be home for his birthday. I also wanted to take Mum on a holiday. She was eighty-five and needed a break from living with and caring for Dad at home. He'd been showing signs of dementia for several years but he was adamant he didn't need extra care. Nevertheless, the situation had become increasingly stressful for Mum.

How to properly care for Mum and Dad had been an ongoing conversation for my siblings and me for a decade. We'd often end up going around in circles because Dad didn't believe he needed a higher level of care, and Mum, who was five years younger, was reluctant to talk about the future.

Mum and I had taken a train trip through Canada a few years earlier and loved it – even though the staff went on strike and then a cargo train crash closed the track and we had to get on buses halfway through. We'd passed the time playing Scrabble on my iPad. Mum had never used a smartphone or tablet before so the idea of using her finger to tap the screen to drag letters into place was a novelty.

Not long after she returned to Brisbane from that holiday she'd bought her own iPad and was teaching herself to send photos and videos of new blooms on her plants. She was becoming adept at sending emails and was now playing online Scrabble with me overseas. The international time zones meant we'd only have one turn each on any given day so games could last for weeks.

Mum was in it to win but there was a limit to what she considered 'acceptable' language. One game was almost abandoned when I played the word 'clitoris'. It was worth twenty-eight points but there was radio silence from Australia for several days.

I rang my older sister, Wendy, who laughed when I confessed our prudish mum might have blushed at seeing that word sitting there each day on the online Scrabble board.

'Oh indeed, she's already been on the phone to me about it!'

While she was quick to adapt to new technology so late in life, Mum didn't adapt to Skype. Even in her eighties, she couldn't shake her crippling shyness. She didn't want to look at herself on screen while she was talking.

Her understanding of how the photos and emails and podcasts all made their way onto her screen was also a bit of a mystery. Each of my siblings would receive a call occasionally to tackle an IT-related conundrum.

Her proudest moment, though, was when she called me to tell me she'd persevered with a particular problem and fixed it herself. She'd been sitting on her chair in the corner of the lounge room, positioned to catch the morning sun but be out of sight of any passing neighbours, when she heard a man's voice emanating from the iPad. Nothing she seemed to do would switch him off so she told me she'd pulled the plug out of the wall in frustration. Of course, with the battery fully charged, that had no impact and the voice continued speaking to her.

Finally she proudly said she hit the eleven button.

'The eleven button?' I asked, clueless as to what she was talking about.

It dawned on me she was talking about the 'pause' button and we both laughed out loud. Mum had a terrific ability to see the funny side in moments like that and I don't think I've laughed so hard as when I laughed with Mum.

We mulled over what trip the two of us would take between my Washington and London postings. We finally settled on another rail journey, this time across Australia from Sydney to Perth onboard the *Indian Pacific*.

By the time June rolled around and I was getting ready to leave America, the family was facing tough decisions. Dad was going downhill quickly. It was hard not to notice his decline on my trips home from the United States.

One morning, on a visit home, I woke early to see Dad in his dressing-gown on the dewy front lawn.

'He's forgotten he doesn't get the paper delivered anymore,' I thought to myself as I went out to remind him.

But as I touched his elbow, he looked at me with confusion and said he was trying to find the chemist. I raised it with my siblings and later with Mum who nodded when I told her, as if none of it surprised her.

Dad woke me once at 3 am, frantic I was going to miss my plane back to America. I wasn't leaving until much later that day and was cross he'd robbed me of a precious few hours of sleep before a restless 24-hour flight.

I regretted the angry words said in frustration as Dad wandered late at night around the three-bedroom duplex he and Mum shared in a retirement village, sleepless and confused. It was devastating for a man who prided himself on his command of the English language to now not be able to rely on his own mind.

He was unstable on his feet as well but would leave his walker well out of reach, often in another room altogether. We all had our share of picking Dad up off the floor where he'd fallen. He'd insist, with a hint of irritation, 'I didn't fall, something tripped me up.'

In the end it was a physical injury that forced us to move Dad into a higher care facility, separating him from Mum after almost seventy years of marriage. He'd broken his hip this time and there'd been discussion with the doctor as to whether he would emerge from hospital at all.

By the time Mum and I were due to leave Brisbane for our train trip Dad was mentally alert enough to insist we go, despite his deteriorating health. We all encouraged him to believe he was going into temporary care after he left hospital and if his condition improved he'd be back home. But none of us believed that.

The first night on the train wasn't particularly restful, bumping along, up and over the Blue Mountains, but I was surprised that Mum found it so hard to get comfortable.

I loved sitting in our cabin watching the dawn light reveal the colours of Australia speeding by. The desert landscape felt so foreign and yet so familiar after six years away. I soaked it all in, knowing that I'd soon be on the other side of the world again.

Mum didn't know, but Trudi, my younger sister who lived in Brisbane, was going to surprise her as the train pulled into Perth. It was the first break Trudi had had without her husband and three daughters since becoming a mum and she was waiting at our carriage as we stepped off. The happy selfies of the three of us on the platform offer just a hint of discomfort in Mum's face.

We'd booked a week of travelling in Western Australia, including a few nights in Broome, where I hadn't been for twenty-five years, not since I was a young reporter sent to camp out in the Kimberley Ranges as part of an Aboriginal Reconciliation Council trip to increase our understanding of Indigenous cultures.

On that first night in Perth, though, it was clear there was something wrong with Mum. She hadn't wanted to join us for dinner and the next morning she admitted she'd had days of chest pains but hadn't said anything in case it put a 'dampener on our time together'.

We called Wendy, whose knowledge as a nurse was still called upon by the family despite her not working in the field for more than thirty years.

It was a Sunday and the best option was to take Mum directly to the emergency department of a public hospital. We thought it was overkill but decided it was better to be cautious. Trudi went in with Mum while I made myself comfortable on a cushioned chair in the near-empty waiting room.

Suddenly the doors flung open.

'Lisa? Is there a Lisa here?' the nurse called out.

'Your mother's heart has stopped,' she relayed as I rushed into the emergency room and saw doctors wielding electric paddles trying to jolt Mum back from the brink.

I could barely take it all in. We'd been on the train just yesterday and yet here was Mum's body on the bed, bright hospital lights focused on the doctors who firmly counted out loud the number of shocks they were administering, nurses rushing, Trudi nodding at me acknowledging that what I was seeing was real.

'I think I'm going to faint,' I remember saying before a nurse slid a chair under me.

They revived Mum but the next two weeks were filled with difficult conversations with doctors, made all the more challenging by the fact we were a long way from home.

Mum was very sick. She'd been suffering from pneumonia during the train trip which is why she'd been so uncomfortable. By the time we took her to hospital the fluid in her lungs had put so much pressure on her heart, it stopped.

She needed a pacemaker but the doctors couldn't guarantee she'd live through the operation.

Meanwhile, back in Brisbane, Robert, David and Wendy were moving Dad into a high-care nursing home, his mental capacity diminished further by the long hospital stay for his broken hip and the heavy medication for the pain. They decided not to tell him about Mum's precarious grip on life, but they didn't know how long they could keep it from him.

'If Mum is going to die in Perth I think we need to get Dad there, to let him see her,' Wendy suggested on one of the hourly phone calls as we deliberated how to navigate a wheelchair-bound ninety-year-old across the country.

Trudi and I were traumatised by the weeks of being on edge, of arriving at the hospital and unexpectedly finding an empty bed and discovering Mum had been moved to another ward; of not knowing if we were making the right decisions.

Mum had the operation and survived. But her health was forever weakened and by the time we got her back to the east coast weeks later she was admitted to hospital for further treatment.

And that was when I was due to leave for my new job in London. I could have said to the ABC I couldn't do it. Or I needed more time. It's odd now to say that I didn't even contemplate that.

From the time the five of us were old enough to understand the message, Dad hammered home the importance of having a work ethic that could never be questioned. If I took a day off, because I was unwell or had simply accumulated hours of overtime, Dad would be alarmed. You could never work hard enough as far as he was concerned. Borrowing money was bad. Spending what you didn't earn was bad. If he saw someone else pop up on TV in my place he'd be alarmed.

'They'll be taking your job, lassie,' he'd warn. And despite my assurances that my job was safe the tiniest niggles of doubt would begin.

Even as Mum recovered from a life-threatening illness, and each day that I shared with Dad was one step closer to his final one, they both insisted I should leave.

# CHAPTER 17

# Controlled Airspace

WHEN YOU FLY into Heathrow there's a moment when you hear the engines switch into descent mode and you catch a glimpse through the clouds of England's coastline and a patchwork of farms in various shades of green.

The slate-coloured Thames, winding its way through the city, appears like a narrow vein from up high. But when you draw closer, it's a powerful artery rising and falling as much as six metres on the tide, like a quietly breathing, living thing.

Those glimpses of London are what so many young Australians see as they embark on their first adventures abroad.

I'd first flown into London as a 23-year-old in 1992 when my boyfriend and I set off on a Contiki trip. For the uninitiated,

Contiki offers a lightning fast, swashbuckling bus tour through Europe of which you'll remember little, courtesy of the speed at which you whizz through centuries-old cities and the intensity of the hangovers.

That holiday appeared jinxed from the moment we boarded our flight. My boyfriend was travelling on a standby ticket because his brother worked for the airline. It wasn't until thirty minutes after departing Singapore when I walked through the plane to try to find him that I realised he'd been bumped from the flight and I was on my way to London alone, without traveller's cheques or a way of contacting him. The young guy next to me said his parents were picking him up and they'd drop me at a hotel.

It took my boyfriend three days to get a seat on another flight and while the holiday lasted another three weeks the relationship was over not long after we got back to Australia. It turned out those few days by myself in London were my happiest of the trip.

Twenty-three years later I was making that same trek from Brisbane to London by myself, only this time for three years, not three weeks, replacing Phil Williams as bureau chief.

Phil and I had first worked together in Canberra in 1994 at Parliament House. He had gone on to become one of the ABC's most experienced foreign correspondents and had remained a great friend and mentor. Luckily for me he was still in England when I faced my first big challenge as bureau chief six weeks after taking on the job.

It was Friday, 13 November 2015. I'd suggested to Philippe, who'd moved to London with me, that we meet at an Italian restaurant near our home. It was down a cobblestone street near Tower Bridge, which was lined with old shipping warehouses. They'd been converted into apartments over the past few decades but a lot of their original brickwork and signs were kept and they still carried the names of the commodities they once stored – Vanilla Court, Wheat Wharf, Cinnamon Wharf and Spice Quays, which was where we were living together at the time.

We soon discovered we weren't the only ones who loved the historic enclave. It was a popular pick for film directors who'd block off the street to use it as their ye olde England backdrop. We'd only find out when we'd read the official letter stuck to our lift warning us we'd be locked in for the day if we didn't leave before a certain time. Australian journalists trying to get to work near Westminster weren't part of the casting call.

This night, though, the street was empty and the night was cool and quiet. It was after 8.30 pm by the time I ordered a veal scallopini at the restaurant and took a sip from an extra-large glass of chianti.

It had been a big day. An Italian camera operator, Ale, had begun working for us and it had been his first day on the road. We'd spent the day out of London filming a story about solar panels floating on a water reservoir and it had been long and exhausting.

I didn't have to work again until Sunday and my boyfriend and I were planning what parts of our new city we could explore. He went outside for a cigarette, one of the very French habits he couldn't shake.

I could see him on the other side of the window and gave a little wave. He was on the phone, probably to friends back in America, and it reminded me to check mine. I could see the brightness of the screen when I pulled it out of the handbag at my feet. There were half-a-dozen missed calls from the office, a voice message and one text from our senior producer Emily Smith.

'Call me.'

Her voice was steady but I'd known her for several years and had already discovered her calm tone was often a complete contradiction to how she was actually feeling. The bigger the breaking story, the lower and slower her voice would become. It was as if she was offering a subliminal message: 'Do not panic. I'm staying completely sane in this shitstorm.'

On this night, she relayed what she knew. There'd been a shooting in Paris. They were reporting ten people dead but likely to be more.

'We've got to get there,' she said as I waved frantically at Philippe to come back inside.

I headed home while he changed our order to takeaway and I called Emily back. We tried to book a Eurostar but we wouldn't make it to Kings Cross station in time. Europe was an hour ahead and the last flights for the day had already left Heathrow.

It was becoming clear a massive attack had been unleashed by terrorists who'd shot and killed diners in restaurants and detonated suicide vests across the city. Their *pièce de résistance* was the coordinated massacre of concert-goers at the Bataclan club while a band was playing live on stage. That's where the remaining terrorists were, holed up inside, as our team in London tried to fight the rising panic of not being able to get there.

A decision was made. Phil, Ale and I would drive to Dover on the English coastline. We'd catch the car ferry and then drive on to Paris. We estimated the whole journey would take close to nine hours but if we all met up at the bureau then hit the road as soon as we'd packed the camera gear we'd make it to Paris in time for the all-important 7 pm Australian news bulletins. The rest of the team would get a flight out in the morning but the French were threatening to shut the borders in the face of this horrifying assault on their country.

Phil had been on holidays in London after leaving the bureau and had kept his car, a tiny four-seater. I squished into the back, surrounded by cases of equipment, scrolling through reports and streaming live news channels. Ale joked that it was becoming the longest first day on the job that anyone had ever had. We were always good at finding the black humour when faced with confronting events. We needed to, to stay sane.

An hour and a half later we pulled in to the border crossing at Dover. The French border crossing was on the English side of the channel, a diplomatic agreement that worked well for both sides despite the oddity of crossing into French territory when you were still on English soil.

That night, the French officials were on edge, treating every approaching car as if it were a potential threat. They had only heard the same information as us, that the hostage situation at the Bataclan was still unfolding and any number of terrorists could be involved.

It was 1.30 am when Phil wound down his window and handed over his passport. He turned to me in the back seat and asked for mine.

The gut-wrenching realisation was immediate.

I didn't have it.

I'd switched my handbag for a backpack at the office before we'd left and that's where my passport was. I'd spent so many years in the US leaping onto planes when stories broke around the nation but we were usually only crossing state borders, not international ones.

Phil liked to think he could speak French. It had been a running joke among his friends as he talked of one day owning a home in the countryside in Europe. But none of his French was working on the border officers as he tried to convince them to let me through with a UK National Insurance card and a Washington, DC, driver's licence. It was never going to work at the best of times, let alone when the biggest terrorist attack ever seen in Europe was still unfolding.

'Lisa,' he said and then paused. I knew what was coming.

They had to keep going. There was not a second to lose. We could already see the ferry and it was into its last moments of boarding.

I grabbed my suitcase and looked at my watch. It was close to 2 am and I was stranded in a dark port in Dover, unsure how I was going to make the 125 kilometres back to London.

But I wasn't going anywhere in a hurry. The French guards took me into a small office and shut the door. I'd tried to cross the border without a passport and that night everyone was a suspect.

I felt sick to my core. I was the new Europe bureau chief who had failed so miserably I hadn't even taken a passport on my first big assignment. I rang the London bureau and could barely say the words. 'Phil and Ale are on their way but I think I'm currently in custody.'

There was nothing they could do. They were too busy organising the coverage, trying to track down Australians who might have been caught up in the chaos and feeding Phil and Ale information about the best route into Paris as roadblocks were going up across the city.

The French officers returned after an hour with a document two pages long. They spoke no English and I spoke no French but they pointed at me to sign it. I prayed I hadn't just agreed to never step foot in France again.

They pointed me to the port exit and I found a number for a minicab stuck to a cork board near the road. I knew it wasn't the safest option – minicabs weren't as strictly regulated as black cabs and there had been recent reports of violent assaults by drivers – but at that point it felt like the only option.

The driver wanted 300 pounds in cash up front and drove me to an automatic teller machine near the port. It was dark and the numbers on the buttons had worn away after years of use. I wondered how many people had stood here in this exact spot, coming off the ferry from France and using this ATM for their first transaction in England.

*PIN number declined.*

I tried again. I had bank accounts in the US and Australia still and a dozen different numbers swirled in my head. I only had one card with me though, my new British bankcard.

*PIN number declined.*

I was sure I'd put in the right number. I'd only just set up the account. But had I put in the wrong number or just hit the wrong digits? My fingers shook as I made the third and final attempt.

Four, seven, eight, two.

The machine started clicking away and twenty-pound notes shuffled out into a neat pile. I grabbed them and handed them to the driver. It was now close to 3 am and I'd been awake almost twenty-four hours. I needed to sleep because I didn't know when I'd next get the chance but I also didn't want to end up dead in a ditch on the side of the road so I propped myself up and watched the back of the driver's head till we pulled into the ABC's bureau at Millbank, a block from Westminster.

Our producer Emily Smith was in the camera room trying to pull together another camera kit. Our senior camera operator Cameron Bauer was in Berlin with the media team following Australian prime minister Malcolm Turnbull. They were on their way to Turkey for the G20 leaders' meetings and Cameron and his friends in the Australian media pack had already downed more than a few whiskeys in the opulent bar of the luxurious Hotel Adlon Kempinski. Catch-ups on the road were rare and checking into a five-star hotel was even rarer and generally only happened when you were trailing a travelling prime minister.

I could hear Cameron on speakerphone trying to sober up and explain to Emily what tripod, batteries and chargers needed to be packed and where to find them in the crew room.

Emily got the rest of us on a 7 am British Airways flight. We had an hour before we needed to leave the office for the drive to

Heathrow and I felt like I'd done nothing but drive all night and produce nothing.

I lay down on the couch in the office for thirty minutes and closed my eyes but it was pointless – the New Zealand TV crew who shared space in our bureau came barrelling in close to 5 am shouting instructions and throwing bubble-wrapped gear into cases with a thump in a bid to catch the same flight.

Meanwhile Phil and Ale, who hadn't clocked off yet from his first day at work at the ABC, were on the ferry chugging towards France. The news producers in Sydney had planned a complex 7 pm bulletin for each of the states and we desperately needed Phil at the live spot to front it.

The live spots were where broadcast agencies like AP and Reuters would set up tents and cameras at the site of any breaking news story then take fifteen- or thirty-minute bookings from clients like us, connecting their cameras to ABC Australia. Channel 7's correspondent had been on holidays in Paris and was already reporting live from there.

It would look bad to have a well-staffed London bureau and not one person on air from the site of the attack. I was blaming myself. We'd been delayed by at least ten minutes by French officials over my passport before Phil had offloaded my bag and left me at Dover border control.

We touched down on a British Airways flight into Charles de Gaulle airport and our phones pinged with a delayed text message from the international desk that the ferry had disembarked passengers at a different port, not Calais, which meant Phil and Ale had even further to drive.

There was just two minutes until every 7 pm ABC TV news bulletin in Australia was going to switch to the live camera on the street outside the Bataclan and Phil was not in front of it.

Zahed Cachalia from the foreign desk in Sydney was on the phone to Emily as we sat on the tarmac waiting to taxi in.

'How fast can you get there?' he asked with a sigh, trying to work on back-up plans as they waited for Phil and Ale to appear at the AP live position.

And then there was a shout of relief I could hear through the phone at Emily's ear. 'He's in sight, we can see him, he's running into shot.'

Phil scurried into position in front of one of the fifty cameras that were now in front of the building where almost a hundred people had been killed less than ten hours earlier.

He patted down his hair and nodded to a woman he presumed was a producer standing there with the camera crew as the ABC news theme started playing into his earpiece. It was only later that he discovered the woman was in fact an eyewitness who had been contacted by Sydney producers and told to meet Phil there so he could interview her live on air.

When we all regrouped in Paris, Ale said that despite them having broken the speed limit the entire way from Dunkirk and arriving in Paris with ten minutes to spare, Phil had insisted on circling the area to find a convenient spot for his car and then neatly negotiated a reverse park. After the stress of the trip, Ale would have jumped the wheels up onto the curb at that point and risked the car being towed as a security threat.

I caught up with Phil later that day and poured out to him that I felt I'd let the team down over the passport incident and jeopardised my reputation. I doubted I could come back from the embarrassment of being a new bureau chief who couldn't even get to the biggest breaking story on the planet.

Phil assured me that by the time we were done covering the massacre no one would remember. And he was right. It was never mentioned after that day and I only began telling the story much later to younger journalists and students so they would realise we all screw up. Mistakes get made. It's how you deal with them that's important. And they don't have to be career ending.

The ABC team spent almost two weeks in Paris, working shifts, taking turns for sleep breaks. There was barely an hour over that period when we weren't on air or writing thousands of words for our digital news page about the attacks. Each day brought new details.

Three groups of men had carried out the coordinated string of attacks that lasted over a four-hour period. It started with three suicide bombers detonating their explosives outside the football stadium in an area north of Paris called Saint-Denis.

Diners at restaurants in popular downtown areas were shot and killed by another group of terrorists who then escaped in cars.

Around 1500 people were inside the Bataclan listening to an American band, Eagles of Death Metal, when three men with assault weapons shouted 'Allahu Akbar!' and opened fire on the crowd.

It was a chaotic scene with some of the crowd able to escape while others hid inside as the shooters stalked them, picking them off one by one with their powerful weapons. At least one attacker was killed but the others took hostages and the scene played out until police stormed the building just before 1 am.

Seven attackers were dead but police knew there must have been a wider network behind an attack of this scale. The French president declared a state of emergency as the country's biggest manhunt began.

The terrorists killed 130 people, including ninety at the Bataclan theatre. Even though the death toll of this massacre had surpassed anything I'd covered, there was a pattern to covering a story like this.

We needed to find out if any Australians were among the injured and try to speak to them or their families about their experience. We provided hourly updates on the hunt for the killers and sent reporter Barbara Miller to Brussels where it appeared the terrorist cell had germinated. And we filmed for hours at the makeshift memorials where mountains of flowers and notes were being left in tribute.

Fear swept across the continent as people realised that young men who'd left to fight in Syria were returning, radicalised and ready to launch war on their own homeland.

Our breakfast programs in Australia were on air from 11 pm in Paris. We would tag-team our shifts and the night crew walked back to the Place de Republique from our hotel, past the bullet holes in the restaurant windows. Inside, glasses of wine were knocked over, meals sat untouched on tables and sawdust had been scattered on the floor to soak up the blood. Hundreds of small candles and wilting flowers made an arc around the front doors.

Sad messages of love for Paris were left in chalk on the ground and a crowd would stand there in silence, crying, holding each other. It was hard not to absorb a little of that grief each time we passed. My boyfriend, whose childhood had been spent just blocks away, was back in our London apartment by himself struggling to comprehend what had happened in his beloved city.

Despite the depth of solidarity felt across Paris, French thieves didn't let the moment pass. Our colleagues warned us to lock our handbags and camera kit around our ankles as we concentrated on our live crosses.

Even though dozens of TV marquees had sprung up and the live-shot position was crowded with international crews, there was no safety in numbers but rather a more appealing target. Expensive equipment was whisked away while we told our audiences about a city in trauma.

The silence was broken as each new hour began at those live-shot positions. It was the lead story everywhere around the world so, as the seconds ticked down to the top of the clock, the camera lights went on and you could hear the rabble of dozens of journalists speaking in multiple languages to their news presenters back home.

Emily was worried we were easy targets. There were terrorists still at large and she couldn't shake the dread that someone could open fire into the line of journalists at the exact moment they went to air and our murders would be broadcast live around the world.

It was exhausting to be constantly on high alert. At one point a teenager rushed up behind Phil as he walked towards us and yelled 'Allahu Akbar'. The kid was harmless but he got the reaction he was looking for.

There were plenty of false alarms, but it didn't make them any less frightening. One night we came back to the hotel, lugging our camera gear through the narrow doors, when dozens of screaming people started running down the street.

The hotel workers pulled down the metal shutters that protected shopfronts in Paris and told us to take shelter. Some of our ABC crew were still outside in the square and, while we worried for them, we hoped they were also filming the scene. We couldn't convince the hotel staff to let us back out. If something was happening we needed to be there.

Harmless firecrackers had sparked the panic that night among the crowd of mourners at Place de Republique. When they heard what sounded like gunshots their instinct had been to run. And others joined the stampede.

Emily was glad she'd decided against booking us into the huge chain hotels the American broadcasters like CNN had chosen. That network alone had more than seventy staff in Paris at that stage and, as the threat level continued to rise and Western media were told to be extra vigilant, we thought they were sitting ducks. We were grateful for the sense of safety at our small hotel. The only other guests were a BBC radio team.

Each day we searched for people prepared to tell their own stories, whether they'd lived through the attack or knew others who'd witnessed it. Phil waited outside the hospital to speak to a man who'd been visiting his friend who'd been admitted. They'd both been inside the Bataclan. He said he'd looked into the gunman's eyes and had seen 'pure evil'.

The crew met briefly early each morning in the lobby, away from the front windows, to discuss our plans for the next twenty-four hours of coverage. Some of us walked in after filming through the night while others would be getting ready to head out to produce stories for the evening bulletins back home. The days blurred into each other and it seemed like months since I'd been caught at the border without my passport.

I was shocked to see a Twitter follower criticise what I was wearing on air. I'd packed extremely lightly that Friday night when we'd heard the initial reports and was relying on a black jacket with different scarves to get me through the assignment.

The viewer, Stephen, tweeted: 'don't you think when time permits a visit to "David Jones" for a few more clothes might be a priority?'

I understood the point he was trying to make, despite the fact that there was no David Jones in fashionable Paris, but I couldn't help myself and responded with a 'huh?'.

He tweeted back: 'the same jacket ... report after report ... I'm sure you follow'.

I was astounded and responded to the tweet – 'Funnily enough I didn't have time to shop. Mental note to self – pack better when covering breaking news tragedies.'

It went viral. The support from colleagues was immediate. Channel 7's Hugh Whitfeld tweeted that he'd been wearing the same jacket since the night of the attack and no one had criticised him. And Channel 9's Karl Stefanovic who had famously worn the same suit on air for a year on the *Today Show* and discovered no one had noticed, sought me out to say, 'forget about it'. A national newspaper ran a story online headlined 'Lisa Millar's coat from Paris reporting is sending Twitter abuzz'.

Hours later I was getting interview requests from others seeking to confirm the story. I told them we needed to concentrate on what we were there for – 130 dead and a hunt for terrorists.

My jacket was a small thing that attracted more attention than it should have given the gravity of the story we were covering, but it was a reminder of the different standards to which women and men were held.

Clothing was a problem but it wasn't the jacket in the end. None of us had realised how long we'd be away from home and we'd run out of clean underpants. Emily offered to find some while I kept reporting.

'To be clear, Lisa, I'd do this as a friend not a producer,' she said, drawing the line on her work duties.

Time was precious and we needed it to be a lightning-fast shopping expedition, but she rang me with a problem. All she could find was elegant French lingerie, mostly G-strings, all of it sheer and sexy, when all we both really wanted was a pair of good old-fashioned cotton undies.

Here we were, covering a massacre, and becoming increasingly frustrated as we tried to translate French definitions of bikinis and European-size options. We had to laugh.

Emily had better luck buying lunch. Phil had insisted on using his rudimentary French to order sandwiches from a boulangerie for the team but the miscommunication was terrible and it was clear no one was going to get what they'd ordered.

'Please, Phil, just order in English, I'm tired and I just need to eat,' Emily pleaded with him as she took charge.

When she went back the next day, Emily discovered the owner spoke fluent English. He told her one of the Australians had left his notebook behind.

'Oh, the older man who spoke a little French?' Emily suggested.

The owner was emphatic. '*Non!* He spoke no French!'

We would laugh about that story for days at Phil's expense. We needed the tension release. It had been five days since the attack.

That night sometime after 4.30 am my phone rang. It was the Sydney desk alerting us to a raid underway in Saint-Denis, half an hour north of central Paris, close to the stadium where the terrorists had launched their attack. I stumbled out into the corridor in my pyjamas. The tourists had cleared out and more news crews had piled in. Our hotel was now something of a media hostel where social niceties had long been ditched.

Emily was already awake, persistently knocking on Cameron, our camera operator's door. They worked hard and they slept hard but we finally got him and Phil out the door and on their way. It was their turn to chase this breaking news story but within half an hour we realised this was going to need the entire team on site. More than a hundred police and soldiers had tracked down the mastermind of the attacks, Abdelhamid Abaaoud, and had several blocks in Saint-Denis circled.

Emily and I grabbed more gear and ordered an Uber but each time we told the driver where we needed to go they ordered us out of the car. They didn't feel safe. Most of the drivers were Muslim and our reporter Barbara Miller had told us when her driver had stopped for directions in daylight the day before, the policeman had reached for his gun. Eventually we got a driver who accepted the extra cash and dropped us half a kilometre from the scene. That was as close as he was going.

We could see TV cameras set up near a church and beyond them an impenetrable row of military tanks. The scene was chaotic and confused as locals began crowding into the streets, pushing into us as we tried to protect ourselves and our equipment. The predominantly Muslim population had felt targeted since the initial attacks and were angry their suburb was now the focus for authorities.

We found Phil and Cameron near a CNN crew. The big international networks often had their own security teams, or 'back-watchers' as they were called, and it gave us a bit more confidence. We set up for more live crosses, trying to establish if we were in the best spot, hearing sporadic gunfire but feeling like we were too far down the block to get a good look.

Explosions rocketed down the street. All we could report was that the assault was ongoing. Reinforcements arrived as helicopters circled overhead.

It went on like this for hours and eventually Emily and I needed a toilet. A female CNN correspondent told us a shop owner up the road was letting media in for five euros but you had to take your own toilet paper. That wasn't unusual for France.

Police had barricaded the road between us and the toilet and they demanded our ID before waving us through. Emily quietly admitted she'd showed them her hotel room key by mistake instead of her ABC press pass and they hadn't looked twice. This was not making us feel any safer.

Around 8.30 am the police line separating the locals who'd been gathering in large numbers and the media seemed to melt away and the mood changed. Police with battering rams smashed in the doors of the church just metres behind us as they hunted for attackers. We weren't sure anymore where the safe line was. The reality was, there wasn't one.

The police killed Abaaoud and a female accomplice during those morning raids. Another eight suspects were captured.

But no one was relaxing. The November 13 attacks had been multi-pronged and extremely well organised. Experts were convinced multiple terrorist cells were growing in strength across Europe.

Our bosses in Sydney decided to get us out of Paris, staggering our departures so some of us kept reporting while others were en route back to London. A few of us boarded the Eurostar at Gare du Nord after two weeks in France, bought a round of beers and collapsed into our seats.

We had no idea what was coming. It was probably better we didn't.

# CHAPTER 18

# Rapid Descent

FISH IS A dish best ordered in a restaurant. Any attempts I've made to prepare it at home rob it of its flavour and juiciness. The skin never crisps but retains a soggy grey texture that is unappealing on the plate. And I also tend to make a mess.

One of my colleagues in the DC bureau, Michael Vincent, once asked me if I was ever worried about cooking fish when I lived alone and could choke to death on the bones.

'You don't even have a cat,' he added.

I'm not sure what assistance a cat could have offered but I could confidently say the thought of scrambling to remember how to cough out fish bones while the oxygen drained from my body, leaving me slumped over my dining room table, had never, ever, crossed my mind. Once it was there though, it had the effect of creating suspicion about seafood.

But at the end of 2016 I was ready to make some changes and cooking fish at home again was one of them. A little over a year had passed since I'd begun my posting in Europe and the bureau had already covered half-a-dozen terrorist attacks. One of the worst was in Nice in July 2016. An Islamist terrorist drove his nineteen-tonne truck into crowds celebrating Bastille Day and killed more than eighty people, including ten children. Some of them had been lining up for ice-creams along the boulevard while their parents gazed out at the calming Mediterranean waters.

We had a new coordinating producer in 2016, another Emily, who was thankfully just as brilliant as our first Emily, who'd reluctantly given in to the pull of her Australian home and desire to have a more settled life.

I had been having a beer at the pub with my fellow correspondents James Glenday and Steve Cannane. It was one of the first times the three of us had managed to get together. Steve was the newest recruit and it had been so busy we hadn't been able to welcome him properly.

He'd had an interesting career path, hosting Triple J's Hack program as well as *Lateline* and he came with an impressive reputation for no-nonsense investigations, which included a book on Scientology. He also loved cricket and couldn't wait to play in the home of his beloved game.

But he'd arrived into a vortex of news that even he admitted was a steep learning curve as the Brits decided to leave the European

Union in what was quickly nicknamed Brexit. The international ramifications were huge and we'd been working around the clock, including some quick turnarounds to various parts of England and Scotland, to test the mood on the ground.

On that day we felt we could draw a line under the story, for a while at least. Theresa May had become prime minister hours earlier, replacing David Cameron who'd been forced to fall on his sword over his handling of the referendum. The story requests from Sydney had already started dropping off.

It was a warm evening and we stood outside watching the young suits who worked around Westminster down their schooners. The pub was so close to Parliament House it had an old bell inside which would ring if the chambers were being recalled and any wayward politicians were needed for a vote on the floor.

'You've worked in a few bureaus, Millar,' Steve started saying. He paused before adding, 'Does it get busier than this?'

Ha! It sure does I told him as I finished the last mouthful and headed home. The Tube was hot and crowded on that summer's night but when I got off at London Bridge for the ten-minute walk home along the Thames the air had started to cool and picnickers were packing up.

I kicked off my shoes and slumped on the couch with Philippe to watch the late news. The 10 pm BBC news was essential viewing, although I'd flick over to ITV to check if they had anything fresh. The headlines were dominated by the new prime minister.

A young Sydney producer whose name was unfamiliar rang me to say he'd seen reports of a truck crash in Nice on social media and asked if I knew anything. I didn't take a lot of interest. It didn't sound like much and there was no breaking news strap across the bottom of the BBC news. After the Paris attacks we'd had several false alarms from enthusiastic producers back in Australia who didn't want to be the one to have missed something.

But within fifteen minutes it was clear something catastrophic had happened. A large truck was deliberately driven into hundreds of people celebrating Bastille Day along the Nice promenade. Eighty-six people would die and almost 500 would be injured.

I told the foreign desk in Sydney I'd grab a cab and head back into the office with a travel pack just in case. I always had a 'go bag' near the dining room table that included all the European phone and laptop chargers, Euro currency and my passport.

All I needed was to slip the laptop in. Summer made travel a little lighter and as long as I had cool long pants, flat shoes and a few uncrushable tops I was right.

Sydney rang again. James and Steve weren't answering their phones and weren't at home. 'They're just a couple of blocks from the office,' I said, 'I'll get them,' not letting on they were probably now a couple more schooners along than when I left them. But nothing sobers you up like a breaking story and they were both on air by the time I got back to the office.

We ribbed each other about jinxing our one night off with the conversation about busy bureaus and then got down to the challenge ahead – trying to get across the English Channel this late at night.

So many evening attacks were happening in Europe that I had even discussed with our bosses in Australia if we needed to temporarily have someone based outside of the UK to enable us to get to a story quicker. But the cost and logistics of keeping a team semi-permanently on the continent meant the idea went into the too-hard basket.

Emily found a 2 am flight from Stansted Airport, normally our least favourite departure spot because it was ninety minutes north of London, but this time she rushed to book tickets before CNN or the big networks snapped them up. They'd send so many crews on an assignment like this we'd have no chance of getting seats if they'd decided they wanted the same flight.

The flight would land close enough to Nice and we could hire a car and drive the rest of the way, arriving in time for the ABC's primetime evening TV news back home. There wouldn't be any sleep but that wasn't the priority.

James or Steve would come with me and the others would stay in the bureau and keep filing. They were both incredibly capable reporters but I was under instruction from Sydney to make sure that, as bureau chief, I was still part of the first line of coverage on big breaking stories for the first few months.

It was well after midnight when I rang home and told Philippe I was heading off – for how long, who knew?

'Wow, again?' he asked. We'd been together now for six years and while he'd moved from Washington to be with me I'd barely been home since taking on the job.

His response made me baulk. I then made a call I hadn't made in all of my previous years overseas. I rang one of the senior editors in Sydney, someone I considered a friend, and told him, 'I don't think I can go. I reckon I'll bugger up my relationship if I do.' I had always put so much pressure on myself, remembering Dad's emphasis on work ethic, trying to do the right thing, to keep showing up, to not let people down that it seemed unthinkable to pull out of an assignment at that point in the night.

I had a moment of regret but, given my track record of making the ABC the priority over my personal life, I knew something had to change. Both James and Steve headed to Nice and did the bureau proud. But we were only ever as good as the crew we were with and producer Emily Bryan and camera operator Niall Lenihan ensured the coverage was spot on. And, besides, it had only been a few months since camera operator Dave Sciasci and I had been in Brussels covering a terrorist attack there.

The two of us had been sent back to Paris in March to film a story for the ABC's *7.30* program on the spike in police recruitment after the Bataclan attacks a few months earlier. The city was still on edge but we'd had a fun day with the latest batch of enthusiastic young French trainee police officers who wanted to wear the uniform and protect their country.

We'd stayed at one of the same hotels we'd used during the Bataclan attacks in November. Simply turning up at a hotel in a foreign country and seeing a familiar face behind the reception desk made it feel slightly more routine, something we yearned for in our peripatetic lives.

We were eating breakfast downstairs, espressos and croissants, discussing the day of filming ahead of us on the police story, when the London office rang. Something had happened at Brussels airport. They'd seen a tweet from someone saying they'd been sitting in a departure gate when there'd been a shudder. Did anyone know what was going on? they'd asked.

It could be nothing but by this stage we were on such high alert that we started moving. By the time we were in our rooms packing bags, confirmation came through – there'd been a bombing.

We had too much equipment to take it all. We'd been preparing for a long-form current affairs story with extra cameras and lights. You had to move quickly on a breaking story and we didn't need all the bells and whistles. We left half of it in one room and checked out of the other, telling the hotel we'd be back in a few days and to keep it all safe.

We hailed a cab and headed to Gare du Nord, the main train station in Paris. The London office was booking the tickets while Dave and I were scanning news sites and social media, looking for any details. We pulled up in front of the station but there was bad news. The line to Belgium had been closed. France was shutting its borders.

Our driver didn't speak a lot of English but he could tell things weren't going well. I tapped him on the shoulder and said 'Brussels?'

'BRUSSELS?' he asked with alarm.

It was a five-hour drive but there was no other way to get there. Brussels airport had come under attack and so had its metro system. Planes and trains were grounded.

He wanted cash and reckoned it would be at least 600 euros if he left the meter running. We negotiated him down, but not by much. He was happy as he navigated us out of Paris with the wheel between his knees.

We were getting plenty of details while we drove and I was on the phone doing live crosses into our 24-hour news network and radio stations back home, telling them about the police roadblocks we were encountering and the reports coming through from eyewitnesses.

Dave was filtering information he was finding online and taking requests from program producers back home as well as starting work on a filing plan with the international desk. There were so many outlets on radio, TV and online now at the ABC that locking in filing plans and schedules was the key to a successful assignment.

Despite the lost hours, when the taxi dropped us at the military cordon that now circled Brussels airport we found only a couple of other TV crews. The international crews that would normally rush to a story like this were stymied because this time the airport was the scene of the attack and they couldn't get in. Others were coming from France as we'd done but we were a step ahead of them.

Passengers had been kept on planes on the tarmac for hours after the two explosions, while others had been taken to a nearby sports centre. Airline blankets were protecting them from the chill of the March air as much as the shock of what they'd been through.

We interviewed some of them as they left for hotels and then we headed into the city centre where another bomb had been detonated at a metro station. We spent the following nights doing live crosses from Place de la Bourse where flowers and candles and chalk messages of grief and solidarity had been left. There were warnings that the large crowds there were an easy target for terrorists but our biggest concerns were drunk Belgians who lurched into our shots and hassled us.

We were using LiveU for our crosses, small portable packs that enabled us to reliably go live without paying huge dollars to agencies like Associated Press. But we'd often set up next to the big agencies' marquees and the bigger networks for protection. We had to weigh up being in the middle of the crowd and conveying the atmosphere with the safety that being on the perimeter brought. And we needed to be able to make a quick exit if things went wrong. It was one of the key lessons from the hostile environment courses the ABC made us do before postings – don't go into a situation if you don't know how to get out.

Back-up had arrived from our London bureau and, five days later, Dave and I were out of there, heading back to Paris to collect the equipment we'd left at the hotel. The *7.30* producer who'd initially sent us to Paris asked if we could finish filming the original story on police recruits but we were shattered after working around the clock and being surrounded by a country in national mourning. We told her it would have to wait.

Thirty-two people were killed and hundreds more were injured in Brussels. The terrorists who claimed responsibility were connected to the Paris attacks in November the previous year and Europe remained a tinderbox of tension.

Every month of 2016 seemed to bring news of another attack, sometimes an unsuccessful knifing, or an attack in a train carriage, or a priest dead after having his throat slit. We barely had time to take a breath. Islamist terrorism – terrorist cells founded within the hatred of Islamic State and lone wolves whose plans were even harder for authorities to infiltrate – was succeeding in creating an atmosphere of fear.

Each time the news would break we'd make the calculation whether it was a big enough story to dispatch a crew. Death toll, location, possibility of Australians involved, method of attack all played in the decision.

\* \* \*

A month after the Nice attack I was woken at 4 am by our international editor, Michael Carey. There'd been an earthquake in central Italy and they were debating whether to send us.

Philippe got up and made me coffee, turning on the television and calling out the latest reports as I threw things into a bag.

'There's only twelve dead,' he sniffed, getting used to the brutal way we'd make decisions on which jobs to fly into and which to cover from the London bureau. I rang him from Heathrow two hours later to tell him I was heading to Italy.

The quake had struck a town called Amatrice, a name I failed to pronounce well enough for my Italian colleagues in Australia for the four days I spent on the ground there. It was 170 kilometres north-east of Rome and rental cars were in short supply.

I was working with Geoffrey Lye, a camera operator who'd been flown in from Australia to try to lessen the load on the London crew in what was becoming a relentless news year.

When we lugged our half-a-dozen protective cases filled with camera gear to the rental spot and saw our assigned car, we didn't know whether to laugh or cry. It was a Fiat with two doors and barely any space. We had to make a decision – did we risk losing another hour in the rental car queue in a European summer to try to switch it or did we just squeeze in? We squeezed.

It turned out to be a brilliant decision because, while other TV networks in big four-wheel drives were stopped at military roadblocks closer to the quake zone, we zipped by with a quick beep of the horn and a wave.

Many of the roads had been damaged in the quake, though, and secondary shocks were still being felt. Everything was shut down, including hotels, and the closest place our producers were able to book us into was an hour's drive away.

Our producer Emily Bryan in London would ring them each day to beg them to make a meal for us and we'd return after midnight to find a ham salad in the hotel's empty kitchen waiting for us. We wondered if it would be simpler to sleep in the car. It could have been safer as well. One night at the hotel I slept through a particularly strong aftershock that rattled the wardrobe and had other guests racing outside in their pyjamas.

On the fourth day we found ourselves confined to one particular square of Amatrice. Hundreds of people were still missing and Italian rescue crews were searching for survivors in the crumpled buildings around us. They had blocked off the small road leading in. There were so many military vehicles and ambulances that even our small car couldn't fit through and extract us from the cordoned-off area.

There were regular aftershocks and while the tallest building in town was only a few storeys high, the effect of the tremors would send pieces of debris raining down.

I rang Mark Colvin, the renowned former foreign correspondent and presenter of *pm*, to tell him I was struggling to collect any 'news' for my cross to him later that day because I was going to be stuck for hours in one place.

I was exhausted and covered in the dust of the town's devastation. I couldn't remember when I'd showered last because when I had the choice between sleep and a shower in our brief respites at the hotel, sleep would win. I was relying on dry shampoo and baby wipes from the Red Cross to make myself presentable for TV. Geoffrey the camera operator had gone off on foot to try to find us food and water from one of the volunteer tents that had been set up.

At that point I was lucky enough to call Mark Colvin a friend, and it helped to have his calming voice on the other end of the phone when I explained my dilemma. His support meant so much to all of us in the field.

'What's around you?' he asked.

I told him I'd just been watching one search for several hours now. They were looking for an elderly woman. Bulldozers were lifting massive slabs of concrete to try to locate the bedroom where she would have been sleeping at the time of the quake. Every time they thought they'd found something a whistle would blow, the bulldozers would stop in their tracks and everyone would fall silent as crews carefully picked their way in on foot.

It was a process being repeated across this historic village in the mountains. Hundreds of people were missing. If a body was found they'd hold up a white sheet to protect the extraction from view.

I had been sitting watching the meticulous operation for hours, feeling frustrated that I couldn't get to the press conferences or where I thought the 'news' was happening.

Earthquakes robbed the colour from a village. Rugs and religious icons and colourful curtains from thousands of homes had disappeared under the cloud of fine soot that had settled on them.

After one whistle the elderly woman's family, who had been standing like sentinels, were called in and I stretched to see what they'd found. A worker carefully placed a beautifully crafted wooden jewellery box in the hands of a granddaughter. She opened it and pulled out a necklace and sobbed. I cried with them. Ten minutes later a Red Cross volunteer gingerly placed a framed picture and documents in her hands.

Two dozen people – media, locals, rescuers on a break – stood watching her pain and grief in absolute silence. There was not a sound until the bulldozers started up again to dig deeper but we knew what they were now looking for: a body, not a survivor.

Since I'd met him, Mark had given me so many lessons in journalism and he reminded me of one of the basics that day.

Just tell the audience what you're seeing.

And what I saw was harrowing.

Five days later, on the plane back to London, I could still feel the dust on my clothes and in my hair. I was sitting two rows from the back and, oddly, the large passenger plane had no compartments separating us from business class. I could see all the way to the cockpit door and a revelation popped into my mind.

I'd left London thinking a dozen people had died in the earthquake but in the end the death toll was around three hundred. More people had died in the earthquake than were on the plane with me. I dropped my head and tears escaped.

I've never been ashamed of crying. I was always the crier of the family and could easily melt at magical moments as well as difficult ones. For me, tears could relieve a stressful moment, like taking a deep breath.

But these days my tears were more often in despair at the trauma I was witnessing, at the depth of the sadness that had swallowed up families who, without a moment's notice, had grief crash into their lives.

I knew I was absorbing that grief simply by being a bystander but, if I ever doubted myself, Mark Colvin would tell me tears were also a sign of understanding and he encouraged me to not shy away from showing empathy in my reporting.

When I walked in the door to our home on the Thames it was quiet. My partner had decided to go back to America for a few weeks, tired of being in London when I was rarely there.

I dropped my bag on the floor, had a shower and then poured a gin. I silently thanked my English friend Claire who'd told me to measure a decent G and T by reciting 'one elephant, two elephants, three elephants' as the gin gurgled out of the bottle. It hadn't even been a year since I'd arrived in London and already the posting was becoming incredibly challenging, both professionally and personally.

Christmas in Europe was a beautiful season of festivities but I wanted to get home for a few weeks to see Mum and Dad. I promised the team I'd be on call over New Year's Eve if they could get through December.

Dad was in the high-care nursing home and I was only able to speak to him when one of my brothers or sisters was with him and we could organise a call.

We'd bought him a mobile phone with large numbers on it, especially created for the elderly, but that was mostly beyond him now. It wouldn't go back onto the charger properly or he'd forget to hang up. Sometimes he'd work out how to use it and I'd end up having a teary conversation with him in the middle of the night because he'd been unaware of the time difference.

I'd created a picture book for him. The cover was all of us standing in front of a small charter plane that we'd organised for a joy flight for his eighty-fifth birthday.

Inside were pictures of our Piper Cherokee from the farm, India Echo Charlie, and grandchildren and great-grandchildren. The photos were meant to prompt the memories in his increasingly demented mind. But that felt ambitious. Simply getting him to drink water and avoid dehydration was an effort now.

My calls with Mum also alarmed me. She sounded depressed and was struggling with both her and Dad's inevitable decline. She was determined to try to keep her licence so she could drive the eight minutes to Dad's nursing home most days.

My sister Wendy's partner, Tom, was also very unwell. And my younger sister, Trudi, seemed to be lacking her usual chirpiness on the phone with me.

I needed to get home.

Once there, I realised I wasn't much help in lifting my family's spirits. I had upsetting phone calls with Philippe, who was still back in America, about the future of our relationship. I'd sit in Mum's car with the windows up in the dark garage so she wouldn't worry about my tears.

One sleepless night I wrote an email to Trudi, who was just a few suburbs away.

*Sis, I'm sorry I'm snappy but I don't think I'm doing so great. I'm going to ring the ABC counsellor tomorrow to schedule a session. I'm irritable, and quick to cry, can't sleep and I have a deep, deep sense of foreboding – all the signs that things aren't right mentally. I woke up after dreaming of watching bodies being pulled from the earthquake, one body after another, just bodies. Love, me*

After years of covering trauma, I knew what the signs were. I'd been involved in the peer support program at the ABC for ten years and I'd urged people to make use of the ABC counsellors. I was also a director on the board of the Dart Centre for Journalism and Trauma and was always encouraging others to recognise the impact the job might have on us. I was relieved in a way that I recognised it in myself.

Each time I'd get on the plane to fly back overseas I'd wonder if it would be the last time I'd see my parents. The knots in my stomach would often last halfway to Dubai no matter how many distractions I tried to find onboard or how many drinks I had.

Dad was ninety-one and Mum was eighty-six. I struggled with why I couldn't accept that death was the natural end to life, that we'd been so lucky to have them as long as we had. I wondered if not having my own children, my own nuclear family, increased that impending sense of loss.

While I was in Australia there'd been yet another terrorist attack, this time on Berlin's Christmas outdoor market. A 24-year-old failed Tunisian asylum seeker hijacked a truck and drove it into a crowd of people, killing eleven. James covered this.

If the team in London hadn't been shattered and exhausted before I'd left for Australia, they were now.

By the time I got back to London the bureau was pretty much done with 2016 and, as I'd promised, they all took time off and I was on call.

And that's when I decided to try to start cooking fish at home again.

It was New Year's Eve and authorities were concerned there might be another attack somewhere in Europe despite the heavy security that was now commonplace.

I was happy enough to stay home but I was on call for any emergencies. I opened a bottle of champagne, put aside my suspicion of home-cooked fish and successfully ate and drank without choking before heading to bed at 10 pm.

The mobile phone beside my bed woke me a minute before 2 am.

It was 1 January 2017. The bureau producer Emily Bryan told me there'd been a shooting at a nightclub in Istanbul. Dozens were dead and the Sydney desk wanted me and camera operator Niall Lenihan on the first flight out.

'When the fuck did Turkey end up in our patch?' I asked her, slightly irritated that I'd spent the day worrying about an attack in France or Germany but was going to be sent off to a country that was normally covered by the Middle East bureau.

We always joked that for people who specialised in communications we were not very good at it. It turned out the Middle East team had taken leave but the message hadn't come through to us.

I'd been to Turkey on my honeymoon when Sid and I had traipsed around the country on public buses, sipping tea and buying carpets. But that had been twenty years earlier.

Did we need journalist visas to get in; could we get a carnet (a complex set of forms to avoid duty tax taking camera equipment in and out of countries and the bane of our lives) completed before the flight; was there a fixer (a freelance producer who was always a local and could set up interviews and translate) to work with us; could we even get a flight?

The last question was answered quickly enough because the flight had already been booked and it departed Heathrow in exactly four hours.

I've never been a huge fan of New Year's Eve. There's always so much pressure to have a wonderful time when the actual 'party' part of the night doesn't even begin until long after I want to be in bed. I've ended up stuck sitting on a couch talking to someone who was a stranger just a few hours earlier and who I'm hoping will stay a stranger and disappear just as quickly once the new year kicks in.

The only New Year's Eve when I regretted midnight passing was in 1997 when a group of friends and I fled Canberra and rented a house at Peregian Beach on Queensland's Sunshine Coast. We ventured down to the sand to build bonfires and someone had a guitar and we sang and danced and drank cheap wine. We could see faint fireworks further down the coast but there was just us on our patch of sand and it was perfect.

Getting a taxi on New Year's Eve anywhere in the world would always make me question my life choices. Did I really need to have come to this party? Did I really need to drink? Why, why am I now stuck here at this house in some suburb I never wanted to visit waiting for a cab that's never going to turn up?

But then there was London on New Year's Eve. I grabbed a suitcase, throwing in my warmest jacket, and started walking. Happy drunks slurred 'Happy New Year' at me while I kept scanning for the light of a vacant black cab.

Niall had made it to the office before me but he was not in good shape. He was twenty years younger than me and had been partying with a crew of Aussie media. Their phones had started ringing with the same message as mine. Get to Istanbul. The trouble for Niall, though, was that he'd already ended his night, curled up and asleep. But he was a long way from his home or the office.

Despite being in fierce competition with each other, he and the other crews were all good friends and they poured him into a cab. I found him in the camera room trying to sober up enough to pack cases of equipment.

'Happy New Year,' I said, drolly.

We made the 6 am flight and we spread out on seats for a couple of hours, our sleep occasionally interrupted by a beer fart or burp from another passenger. The smell inside the cabin was toxic by the time we touched down but at least we'd made it. We bought visas at the airport, got our gear through customs despite the lack of language, and met up with our fixer, Mahmood, at the hotel. With the time difference it was 3 pm when we got there and I knew we only had an hour of daylight left to get the lay of the land.

We spent two days reporting from outside the nightclub, crossing live into bulletins throughout the day and evening. Reporting from a scene like that had changed so much since I started as a foreign correspondent fifteen years earlier. At least the ABC had streamlined the communication process so you were talking to only a handful of people back in Sydney but you'd have to have the filing plan clear in your head. There would be at least two or three thirty-second radio news stories to voice and then send back to Sydney for the early morning bulletins, perhaps a live cross with the *AM* presenter which you would fit around a live TV cross for *News Breakfast*. Depending on which country and time zone you were working in you'd have to isolate which hours could be set aside to collect new information, including talking to witnesses. There was a piece-to-camera to film, sometimes two, depending on what was required.

There were occasions on big, developing stories where you'd be setting up for a live cross to Australia and producers in Sydney would be feeding you information in your earpiece that you would then repeat back live on air. They had access to agency wires and were sometimes further ahead of the information than you were if you'd been trying to follow different leads and angles.

The situation in Istanbul was tense but nothing we hadn't seen before. This one happened at an exclusive nightclub called Reina on the banks of the Bosphorus when hundreds of people had been celebrating New Year's Eve. A gunman had taken a taxi to the trendy suburb, pulled out a gun and shot dead the police officer outside before killing another thirty-eight people and then fleeing. When Niall and I met up with our fixer about twelve hours later, dozens of heavily armed police were milling around outside. They'd covered the broken windows and the bloody scenes inside with blue tarps. It struck me as odd that the street was so empty apart from the police and the media. Many of the victims had been foreigners and we confirmed pretty quickly none were Australian.

Niall had already covered half-a-dozen terrorist attacks for the ABC and it was one of the first questions we always asked – are there any Australians among the dead? If the answer was yes, the pressure on us would be even more intense.

You got a feel for how the hours would progress. Competing for space with the vast media pack that flocked to tragedies like these could be frustrating but it was also reassuring to have them close by. But when the American and European networks switched off their lights and packed up their cameras it could feel pretty lonely.

Due to the time difference, Asian and Australian crews would be left behind after midnight waiting for our next live cross, sitting on camera cases, trying to ignore the ache that comes when the temperatures drop to minus 10 degrees.

We were the last to wrap up on our final night. We'd let the fixer go hours earlier to save money when two police officers came over to speak to us. We couldn't understand what they wanted.

'Australia,' I said, hoping a smile would get us through the encounter. But instead of a nod of approval they were clearly agitated with hands on their guns.

I opened the cover of my passport to show them and with a swift movement they took it and disappeared into the dark. I looked at Niall with alarm. We were on an empty street in a foreign country that had an aggressive approach to the media and I'd just failed at the one thing we were always told to do – hang on to your passport.

I tried to ring the fixer to help with some on-the-spot translations but he didn't answer. It could all be harmless but we were exhausted and cold and our brains had stopped functioning properly hours earlier. We debated heading back to the hotel to get help when the police re-emerged from the dark, handed back the passport and disappeared again.

'Let's get out of here,' I said, both of us glad we were booked on a flight first thing in the morning.

When we arrived at Istanbul airport there was no sign of the customs officials who had to confirm the equipment we'd brought into the country was the same we were taking out. I pushed the trolley to the end of the departure hall and looped around to start again. Niall wanted to know what I was doing.

'Getting my steps up,' I told him, waving my fitness watch in his direction. I often felt the need to find the normal in abnormal situations. I thought of the Channel 9 camera operator I'd seen at breakfast at the hotel. He'd ignored the plates of Turkish delight on offer at the buffet and was opening a jar of Vegemite he'd brought with him. He said he needed reminders of home on stories like this.

The journey back to London was eleven hours door to door despite Istanbul being only a three-hour flight away. There was no rush. My partner was seeing family in Paris.

I opened the door to the apartment and sniffed the air. In my rush to get to Istanbul days earlier, I'd left the heater on and the fish scraps from my New Year's Eve dinner were still in the sink.

I walked into the bedroom to dump my bag and laughed. For some reason, I'd made my bed at 2 am four days earlier. Maybe it was the need to feel like there was still routine in my life.

I found the note I'd written to myself the evening before I'd left, when I'd been sipping champagne and contemplating the year ahead.

'Get my life back,' it said.

I hadn't even made it through the first few days of the new year.

I was clueless about what was ahead. Or that 2017 would be a year that would test me like no other.

## CHAPTER 19

# Crosswinds

THE RHYTHM OF the overseas bureaus was always set by the clock in Australia. In the US, the mornings tended to be your own. Australia was going to bed and the last program of the day, *Lateline* when it was still on air, was broadcast around 6.30 am, give or take an hour or two depending on the time of year. It was rare they'd want you out of bed for a live cross. But as Australia woke up our day got busier the later it got and it wasn't unusual to still be in the office after 9 pm if big stories were breaking.

In London you were on duty from the minute you woke up. Australia had been awake and the foreign desk would be waiting for a respectable time to call if it wasn't urgent. If it was urgent then no one worried about sleep anyway.

I only missed one early morning call from the foreign desk and it was the day David Bowie died. I'd dislodged my phone from the charger near my bed and it had slowly drained of juice through the night. By the time I heard the home phone ringing in the lounge room it was too late to get on air and they'd located one of the other reporters.

The London bureau could have frantic mornings of filing for the *pm* program on radio, the 7 pm news, the international news TV program *The World* and at least a handful of radio news voicers for the ABC's evening bulletins.

Then, for a few hours before Australia started waking again, looking for material for *AM*, the *News Breakfast* TV program and online digital copy, there'd be a few hours of peace. Sometimes we'd duck down to the pub for three Ps – a pie, peas and a pint. But that didn't happen often.

There were around ten of us working in the London bureau, including Anne who sold ABC programs to other countries, but on any given day there might only be a few of us in the office.

On 22 March 2017 we were all on deck and we'd remarked how unusual it was. We wrapped up a chat about our coverage plans for the French election campaign and bureau manager Simon May, a terrific Englishman in his late thirties with a great sense of humour, said he was off to the dentist. We didn't know if he was joking given the loose arrangement many Brits seemed to have with dental hygiene.

He looked out the window and saw dozens of people running away from the Houses of Parliament, shouting at each other. He could hear the word 'bomb'.

We hesitated for a moment. This was something we'd discussed in our security plans. We were so close to Westminster that if something happened we needed to know if it was safer for us to stay in the building or try to escape down the fire exit if terrorists stormed the building.

But now it was actually happening.

We had no idea what was happening but at least some of us had to get out with camera gear to film it – and quickly.

Exactly a year earlier Dave and I had covered the Brussels airport and metro attacks and Emily had dealt with the logistics of trying to get news crews in to back us up after we'd driven five hours there in a taxi. This time we simply ran downstairs. But not before I quickly applied makeup with shaking hands.

We called out to people running past, Dave carrying the camera and running alongside me. 'What's happened?' I asked them. 'What did you see?'

A knife, a man, a car, a car bomb, two men. Everyone gave different answers. It was chaotic. Information gathered in the aftermath of an attack by shocked eyewitnesses can often be wrong and you needed to be careful how you used it.

I started filming a piece-to-camera with the scene behind me but the police shouted instructions to move back, further away from Westminster Bridge. Dave kept rolling and I kept talking to the camera as the police pushed us along.

The crime scene tape went up and a cordon was established. Our office and the rest of the team were on one side. Dave and I were on the other.

Thankfully Dave and I had grabbed enough battery power and the LiveU equipment to enable us to go live to Australia for the hours ahead that we'd be on the street.

The cordon was in place for thirty-six hours but once they were sure the initial threat had passed, much later that day, they allowed us back into our building through the back entrance staffed by security officers.

Khalid Masood had driven his car across Westminster Bridge, ramming pedestrians, injuring at least fifty of them before crashing into the gates of Parliament House, leaping from the car and stabbing an unarmed police officer, PC Keith Palmer. Four people were killed. There was no car bomb but Masood's actions shook the city to its core.

It was one thing to be covering terrorist attacks in foreign countries but this was an attack on our home.

Simon hesitated to bring his young children back into the city. Anne, another Brit, said she felt anxious on the Tube, eyeing every backpack as a possible bomb. It took exactly three minutes to leave the train deep underground at Westminster Station and follow the crowds up the long series of escalators to street level. Anne said it had become the most stressful three minutes of her day.

Every day since I'd started working at the London bureau unarmed police officers had stood outside Parliament House, patiently posing for photos with tourists. I had watched them smile, give directions and answer questions about tours. I'd been thinking about doing a story on them because I was constantly amazed at how cheerful they remained despite the extra duties that came with the shift.

Forty-five minutes before Keith Palmer was killed, a tourist from Florida walked up to him and asked if he'd mind if she took his photo.

'No problem,' he told her.

'He was really nice,' she told reporters later that day.

It was the last photo of him.

Two weeks later bombs went off in the metro in St Petersburg, killing fifteen. We covered it from the bureau. Getting into Russia at short notice was impossible because of the visa restrictions. But a few days later, when a truck was driven into crowds in Sweden, we sent a team from the office. Five people died.

We didn't need the official terror alert system to be raised to its highest level for us all to feel the magnitude of what was happening.

Niall and I covered Emmanuel Macron's election night victory outside the Louvre in Paris but it was an anxious night. Thousands of people were packed into the area but just hours earlier, when we'd been setting up equipment, a bomb scare had seen the area evacuated. Packs of armed military roamed Paris while their tanks lined the streets.

It had only been a few weeks since I'd been pulled from a meal with American friends at a Chinese restaurant in London by a phone call telling me there'd been an attack on the Champs-Élysées. We caught the next Eurostar and arrived in Paris before they'd even washed the last of the blood away. An Islamic extremist had tried to shoot tourists before killing a policeman. The extremist was shot dead before he could escape. The beautiful boulevard now held vigil for another victim.

There seemed to be no end to the grim news and some of it was becoming personal. On 9 May 2017, a day after returning from covering Macron's victory, I was in a cab with a freelance camera operator heading to Trafalgar Square when my phone rang. It was Mark Colvin.

'Is this a convenient time?' he inquired in a voice that was made for radio.

Mark was a mentor, a wise owl and a friend. And he was dying. I'd been told to expect this phone call. He wanted to say goodbye. When he asked if the time of his phone call was convenient the only answer was yes.

In typical Mark style we talked about Macron and the assignment I'd just completed. He always knew more about any subject than I could possibly hope to know. He spoke a little of the pain he'd been in, now dulled by heavy drugs. And after six minutes he said, 'Oh well, we'll talk again.'

We never did. He died two days later. His loss was felt across the ABC and I still felt sad and flat when, a matter of weeks later, the phone rang again late one evening.

The terrorist attacks and late breaking news had become so regular I'd started answering the phone with two words. 'What's happened?'

This time there was uncertainty. There'd been a concert in Manchester. An American singer, Ariana Grande, had performed to an excitable fan base – mostly young girls, teenagers, their mums and older siblings. It was 11 pm and there were reports that a speaker had exploded and caused panic. No one was quite sure. The details were slow to come out.

Emily and I headed into the office just in case. By now I was keeping my go-to bag with extra clothes in the bureau rather than my house because we were having to react so quickly so often to breaking news stories it didn't seem worth taking it home.

At midnight Emily, Niall and I were in a taxi trying to locate a rental car in a London suburb. It was going to take us five hours to drive to Manchester but we'd get there by morning and in time for the evening news bulletins in Australia.

We spent the first hour checking news alerts, streaming the BBC and Sky TV on our phones and planning what we'd do. A suicide bomber had detonated a shrapnel-laden homemade bomb as the concert was finishing. We knew more than a dozen were dead but our experience had taught us that number would climb.

It was the first suicide bombing in the UK since the attacks on buses and the Tube in 2005.

There was heavy traffic despite it nearing 2 am but suddenly it started slowing. There'd been a car accident and the police told us it should be cleared within the hour. It wasn't going to derail our timing but it wasn't good.

We rang Sydney to warn them and the bosses suggested at least we could get some sleep. I wondered what kind of reporter could snooze while trying to get to a story to cover the deaths of dozens. It wasn't me.

And this attack was different. Ariana Grande was a huge star and parents and her teenage fan base had travelled into Manchester from far afield for the concert. I'd never heard of her before that night and struggled to remember how her name was pronounced in the days that followed. But those eyewitnesses wouldn't be hanging around in Manchester. They'd be leaving as soon as they could and every moment was valuable.

Our car was boxed in by semi-trailers on either side and a large concrete median strip. We couldn't go back the way we'd come. And we couldn't slip along an outside lane to find an exit off the highway and an alternate route. We were going nowhere.

Niall went for a cigarette and came back with bad news. The police had told him we could be there for at least three hours. It was a serious crash and they couldn't clear even one lane to get us moving.

My phone was ringing constantly with producers from radio programs wanting me to go live from the scene and I told them I was nowhere near it. I thought of all the hours I'd spent in cars trying to get to terrorist attacks. To the Bataclan, to Brussels in a taxi and now to Manchester. The panic of the heart-racing rush to get to a story followed by the frustration and helplessness.

We investigated trying to book a driver from somewhere nearby to pick me up on the other side of the road and I'd climb over the concrete median strip.

At least if I got to Manchester I could connect with the agencies like AP and EBU, the European Broadcasting Union, and be able to cross live into the Australian night-time bulletins. But we knew it was a pretty weak Plan B.

Finally the traffic started slowly inching forward after 4 am and by the time we made it to the Manchester city limits Niall steered the car up onto a footpath and started dragging equipment out of the boot. I couldn't tell viewers I was at the Manchester arena where the attack had taken place but at least I could faithfully report 'from Manchester'. Just.

As I'd suspected, many of the eyewitnesses had already left the city and others weren't hanging around to talk to the media.

Twenty-two people died that night, many of them children, and hundreds more were injured. It was the worst kind of terrorist attack – a young lone wolf with help from his brother. There was no grand terrorist network that could be successfully busted open, reassuring Britons that they were safe.

Instead, Prime Minister Theresa May ordered nearly a thousand troops onto the streets of the UK. And Britons, who prided themselves on the fact they were guarded by bobbies with batons, felt like they were at war.

The presence of troops was a constant reminder the threat level had been raised from severe to critical. That meant another attack was imminent. We braced ourselves.

Amid all this, Britons were going to another election campaign. The Brexit vote of 2016 had sparked even more furious debate and Theresa May was looking for a mandate to push on with her plans. We needed to file stories, not just focusing on terror but on what the Brexit decision had meant a year on in places far out of London.

I wanted to revisit Derek Mead, a multimillionaire seventy-something dairy farmer in Somerset, who'd been frank and entertaining for a *Foreign Correspondent* story I'd filed the previous year before the Brexit vote. I wondered how he was feeling twelve months later when there seemed no clear path to leaving the European Union.

Derek was a tweed-coat-wearing character who ran a huge adventure park with farm animals and water slides and miniature trains. He was entertaining and, as predicted, as blunt on camera as he was off it about Brexit. We filmed an interview before he insisted on buying us lunch, promising to take us to one of his posh members' clubs in Pall Mall next time.

It was a long day of filming but I knew I wasn't on call the next day for the first time in months. The day off couldn't have come soon enough. We were all exhausted but the string of attacks and Mark's death had knocked me for six.

I was seeing less of my French boyfriend, who was restless living in London, and while I knew he loved me, he didn't love the life we had.

The following evening I arrived at a friend's fiftieth birthday party swinging a bottle of champagne and laughing at the surprise on their faces that I had actually turned up. I'd been missing in action for most of 2017.

Sometime after 10 pm, and well after I'd finished most of the champagne, my friend's brother-in-law came up to the deck and asked whose handbag was ringing.

It was mine.

An attack had taken place on London Bridge. We were so close we could see the flashing blue lights in the distance, but we'd been oblivious to the terror that had taken place.

I grabbed my bag, called an Uber and ran out the door.

I made it to within a block of the attack scene and watched as people were walking out, their clothes splattered with blood. Young girls cried and a man, wrapped in a silver emergency blanket, told me he'd hidden in the back of a restaurant as the attackers went on a stabbing spree through Borough Market.

Niall the camera operator was desperately trying to get through roadblocks to meet me but for a couple of hours all I had was my phone. I would take a photo of each person who agreed to speak, send that and their name and correct spelling to the Sydney producers and then put the person on the phone telling them they would be live on air to Australian television.

The photo would be used as a graphic as their voice could be heard relaying the terrifying story. During big events like that everyone is on their phones and the mobile networks are so jammed that getting a video feed up would have been impossible. This was the next best thing.

I would leave them standing there with my phone attached to their ear while I searched for other people to interview.

Many restaurants and cafes had kept people inside, fearing further attacks. It meant for hours after there was a steady stream of people coming out past the police cordon.

A woman riding a bike rushed up to the taped-off area and begged to be taken through, telling the officer her friend had been on the bridge. She broke down and he wrapped his arms around her.

I took endless photos of what I was witnessing and tweeted them, knowing the ABC producers would be trawling my feed for pictures they would then publish on the ABC website.

Around 3 am my phone battery was running flat. I'd met up with Niall and we decided to go back to my flat, less than a kilometre away, so I could get warmer clothes and recharge my phone.

Eight innocent people were killed that night, including two young Australian women. The three terrorists had used a van to run down dozens of people on London Bridge before stabbing dozens more with thirty-centimetre ceramic kitchen knives.

It was only a handful of days until the election and, while we covered the terrorist attack, we also needed to give attention to the debate that had sparked the election in the first place. But would it seem odd to run the story I'd filmed in Somerset with Derek Mead as planned the day before the election? The decision was made to not let it go to waste and I was relieved when it finally aired.

Donna, one of our other long-time producers, rang Derek to let him know where he could find the piece online and tell him Niall and I were keen for our date at his club.

'Oh, I'm so sorry, we're thinking of you,' I heard her say.

She put the phone down and paused before telling me, 'He's dead.'

Derek Mead had been killed in a farm accident two days after we'd filmed with him. His dog had knocked a lever in the tractor cabin and the machinery had squashed Derek against a fence.

He wasn't a close friend. I barely knew him really. But I was speechless. He'd been dead before we'd even put the story to air.

Everything I touched seemed connected to death. The grim foreboding I'd felt at the start of the year had grown and I felt a heavy weight descending.

I walked downstairs, through the heavy doors of our Westminster office building and heard the screeching of brakes. A motorcyclist was hit by a car and careered into a tree in front of me. Others ran to his aid. I couldn't move. Something very bad was happening to the world and I couldn't process what I was seeing.

My internal threat level was constantly elevated. The tactic by terrorists to drive trucks or cars into crowds made me stand back from street corners. I'd watch a bus turning a corner and be convinced it was coming for me. Backpacks were bombs, cars were weapons, and no one could be trusted.

The election a day later gave no clarity to politics in the UK. In fact the result was so close it was unclear when it would be called. I felt like I was reporting in a fog of exhaustion and emotion.

My friend and former bureau chief Phil Williams had come back to London as the ABC's chief foreign correspondent to help with the coverage and I'd offered him a spare bed at my place. Some days at least one of us never made it home, snatching a few hours' sleep in the office instead after filing late into the night.

And when we thought we could bear witness to no more trauma, we were wrong. Just days later Phil came out of the spare bedroom at 4 am and saw the flicker of the television screen. 'What's happened,' he asked.

'Just watch,' I told him. I had no words to explain what I was seeing.

A 24-storey building was ablaze. There were people on the top floors, silhouetted by light and flames. Steve Cannane and James Glenday and our camera teams were already at the scene reporting live as the desperate rescue attempts took place. It was a horrifying sight that left us feeling utterly helpless.

Seventy-two people would die in the Grenfell Tower and we would be reporting on the atrocity of the failures that led to that fire for months to come.

The weight within became that much heavier.

In another attempt to pretend I could construct moments of routine in my life, I went to the dentist. She didn't know what I did for a living and as she reclined the chair, she asked me how I was.

I told her I was good. All good.

Any problems with the teeth, she asked.

Nope. Everything is good.

'Have you been flossing?'

I hadn't.

I didn't like to floss. I never had.

And her question seemed loaded with judgement.

A tear dripped onto the inside of the large plastic safety glasses I was wearing, then another. I wiped them away as her back was turned, arranging equipment on the bench.

But her simple question had triggered something deep within me; it was one more demand on me when I had nothing left to give. I began to sob and I couldn't stop. I was sobbing for every victim's mother I'd met that year, for Mark Colvin, for Derek Mead, for the residents trapped on Grenfell's twenty-fourth floor.

I was sobbing with physical and mental exhaustion.

And then I started to laugh. The dentist spun around in alarm and I tried to reassure her I was okay.

Well, I wasn't okay. But at least I understood why I wasn't okay and that the tears were okay.

I had spent a decade trying to help colleagues see the signs of traumatic stress, to understand that it could be an unexpected moment that sent you over the edge and here I was, living through one of those moments.

The dentist downed her tools and sat beside me. We talked about Grenfell and how she could still smell the smoke up to ten kilometres away and how she dwelt on the fate of the victims who never made it out. We talked about how depressed so many people were. And then she checked my teeth and didn't mention flossing again.

As soon as I left I rang my friend Cait McMahon back in Australia. A renowned psychologist in her field, she was also managing director of the Dart Centre for Journalism and Trauma and I couldn't wait to tell her I'd experienced something she'd been warning me about for years. All of the trauma training had left its mark on me and I was confident I was going to be okay.

Just five days later, though, our ABC team would be tested again. There'd been an attack at a mosque in a north London suburb. A van had been driven into the crowds as they left late-night prayers.

I'd been fast asleep when the phone rang and as I stumbled out of the bedroom I heard the key in the door. Phil was just returning home from the office. It was close to midnight. I changed out of my pyjamas and we left to find a cab.

We'd previously discussed how many dead was enough dead to warrant us covering stories or getting on planes and travelling to the scene. It was a brutal conversation but one our bureau had to have as one attack after another occurred.

This one was in Finsbury Park, north of the city centre, but we debated how many of the bureau should go to the scene – adding to safety concerns if the situation was hostile – and who should stay back and file from the office.

We were discussing it again when the black cab in front of us clipped a cyclist and sent him crashing off the road. He'd braked suddenly and so did our taxi.

'Keep going,' I told our driver firmly and looked over at Phil. 'We could be going to forty dead, Phil, we don't have time for this.'

It was a moment that later shook me. That I had reached a point of such intense exposure to violence that I had calculated so quickly and with so little empathy that a possibly seriously injured cyclist didn't warrant my attention.

We were all burning out.

Niall was the first to call it quits. The young Aussie camera operator who'd joined us as a freelancer during the Paris attacks and then became a dedicated part of the team asked to see me in the camera room. It wasn't a large area and it was filled with equipment for every occasion, including bulletproof vests and helmets we'd all been fitted with when we took the posting.

He handed me a piece of paper on which he'd written a long note explaining his decision. It could be summed up in one sentence though. 'I can't go to bed at night wondering when the call will come, what horror I will have to film next.'

I was gutted. Finding good camera operators was hard and I'd tried to look after the team. I slid down the wall and he sat beside me as I begged him to change his mind, offering him several weeks off to recharge. But his decision was made.

Our coordinating producer Emily Bryan, who'd been my rock, had also decided she wanted to go home to Tasmania to restart her life, get married, have babies.

The ABC paid staff well in the bureaus but there was no amount of money that could help people deal with 2017.

Niall's and Emily's decisions came as a body blow to me and my tears flowed at their joint farewell. What the team didn't know was that my relationship with Philippe had ended a few days earlier.

I went home to Australia for a couple of weeks and then extended it on the encouragement of my bosses. They asked if I was 'done' and needed to come home permanently.

Every day I'd sit with Dad in Brisbane's warm winter sun just outside his room at the aged care home. Some days we'd talk about flying and our little Piper Cherokee. Other days he would nod off asleep. Mum and I would play Scrabble on our iPads together before we crept out, making sure to put the alarm back on to alert the nurses if Dad tried to get out of bed and start wandering.

The flight back to London was tough. I left Dad for what I suspected would be the last time and I knew there'd be no one to welcome me back in London. The apartment would be empty.

The news came in November when I was on assignment in Dublin. Dad's breathing had been slowing during the day, his organs gradually shutting down. He'd been surrounded by love and music and Millar family chatter. Trudi was the last to leave and she rang me from his room. We talked and cried while he still slept in the chair nearby and then she hung up and reluctantly went home.

I was filming a piece-to-camera with a wonderful camera operator called Tim Stevens, a gentle soul with incredible talent behind the lens. I needed to get the story finished and asked Tim to film as much as we could before the next call came. I stumbled over the first take of the piece-to-camera but dug my nails into my palm to transfer the pain in my heart to my skin and signed off, 'Lisa Millar, ABC News, Dublin.'

We were in the taxi and had just pulled up at the hotel when my older sister, Wendy, rang. Dad had passed away a few hours after Trudi had left him. The family had always teased me that Dad was the leader of the Lisa Millar Cheer Squad. And now he was gone. Tim packed my suitcase for me and checked us out of the hotel.

I didn't go back to Australia for Dad's cremation. He'd always made it clear he didn't expect me to.

At 8.30 am Mum and my brothers and sisters and their wives and husbands gathered under a rotunda at the cemetery and I joined them by video from Vienna. They toasted Dad with sparkling wine and I opened a bottle of wine from room service. We told loving stories of his ninety-two years.

'We had some good times on the farm,' Wendy said.

'Which day was that?' my brother David quipped. It *had* been hard work for my older siblings. Trudi and I knew we'd got off lightly with the chores.

We'd been told Dad's body would be cremated at 9.05 am and we fell silent for a moment. I could hear Mum's sharp intake of breath. And then, as if on cue, the faint sound of a passenger plane high above this group of mourners made them look up.

'Bye Dad,' they chuckled as I smiled from afar.

We said a prayer and I told them I'd be home for Dad's memorial in six weeks' time. I disconnected the video and went to bed on the other side of the world.

I had started the year writing a note of encouragement to myself to 'get my life back' but instead I'd witnessed so many others lose their lives, in inhumane and murderous ways.

The year 2017 was one of the most challenging I faced. By the time my posting ended the following year I had covered eight terrorist attacks in Europe, two of them frighteningly close to the bureau and my home. I reported on others from the bureau while my colleagues – my friends – headed into the devastation.

My family back home in Queensland did the best they could to lift me up – surprise care packages in the mail, video calls over dinner, endless games of online Scrabble with Mum and the smiling, laughing sun-kissed faces of the newest Millars, little ones I'd soon get a chance to know and love.

Mum encouraged my sister Wendy to fly to London to help me pack up my life. Mum secretly hoped it would also be a holiday that would finally let Wendy breathe again after losing her own partner just months after Dad died.

We dangled the temptation of her finally using her schoolgirl French in Paris, a city she'd only dreamed of visiting. But, in what would be wretchedly sad timing, Wendy arrived in London as Mum entered her last days of life. She'd become critically ill and when the days became hours we waited for the phone call from Brisbane.

I had one last job to do, a final commitment as foreign correspondent.

The ABC *News Breakfast* program had asked for one last live cross, a goodbye to viewers after almost a decade overseas. None of them knew we were about to lose Mum. They didn't have to know.

The most recent addition to the London bureau, a wonderfully skilled producer called Roscoe who'd just arrived from the US bureau, asked them to avoid personal questions for fear I'd fall apart.

I chatted and laughed with host Michael Rowland on air, boxing up the grief I felt so I could get the job done.

In Brisbane, just hours later, Mum died, with Trudi holding her with the strength of all of us.

I felt cheated – after all this time, after so many years overseas, when my ticket home was in my hands, I wasn't going to have even one final tantalising hour with Mum. I knew it came with the territory of taking an overseas posting but it didn't make it any easier. There was a long list of reporters, camera crews and producers who'd lost those closest to them when they couldn't be further away. All you could do was try to support each other.

You were nothing in those bureaus without the team around you. In particular, the camera operators who stood by my side over the years were often great company as well as terrific professionals and I leaned on their friendship. We spent hours together huddled in cars, waiting outside buildings in blizzards for a bureaucrat in a foreign land to open a door, editing stories perched on beds in cheap hotel rooms into the early hours and sharing more lukewarm room service food than I wanted to recall.

We all knew it was a privilege to be posted overseas for the ABC but there was also a price to pay.

\* \* \* \*

Thankfully there were moments of joy in those difficult years otherwise we all may have been tempted to pack our bags and head home early. I would pinch myself sometimes. I felt so far removed from that little girl in Kilkivan, with her tape recorder and earnest questions for the family, and I wished I'd been able to tell her that dreams could come true.

Grandma was born in England and while I wouldn't have described her as fanatical about the royal family, she was certainly fond of them.

What would she have made of my prime position outside the chapel at Windsor Castle waiting for the newly betrothed Harry and Meghan to walk past the magnificent mass of blooms that had been plucked for the occasion?

Britons had been through so much, with the terror attacks and Brexit heartache, that they were ready to party, whether they were royalists or not and the royal wedding in May 2018 was a ready-made celebration.

We'd been reporting from Windsor for several days. Roads were barricaded, security was high, and thousands of people were thronging into the area. We got word that Harry and his older brother, William, would stroll down the street from the castle on the eve of the wedding and greet fans.

One of my classmates from journalism lectures at Queensland University had risen through the ranks to become an assistant private secretary to the Queen but even that connection wasn't going to help us with the problem we faced that afternoon. We needed to work out which side of the road the two princes would walk down so we could get into position before police locked off the road. We took a punt and stayed closest to the castle, settling in to wait for an hour as the crowd grew. The two young royals finally walked out through the castle walls and straight over to the opposite side of the street with their backs to us, disappearing into a sea of outstretched hands.

We were going to miss the shot we wanted – the royals walking behind me as I did a piece-to-camera from the scene.

When they turned to come back up the street I leaned as far as I could over the metal barricades, pointed the microphone and shouted out as loudly as I could – 'Harry, Harry – how do you feel?'

He turned his head in my direction and raised his right hand and tapped his heart. I immediately started delivering my lines and it was perfect television for us. I hadn't seen the dozens of photographers perched high on ladders across the street who captured the moment. It ended up on a gossip and entertainment blog called 'Celebitchy' with the caption, 'Look at this lady, she is my spirit animal.'

The photo quickly went viral and it proved too much for the anti-monarchists back home in Australia who bombarded me with criticism for appearing to be too joyful covering an event they considered irrelevant to most Australians.

But I made no apologies. I was only doing my job. And, besides, they hadn't been through what we'd been through for the past two years. It felt good to be covering a happy news story for a change.

## CHAPTER 20

# Inflate Lifejackets

I NEVER EXPECTED trauma and fear would be the dominant themes of my working life. The trauma was something I experienced second-hand, as a witness to the aftermath of school shootings, earthquakes and suicide bombings. The fear was very much a personal battle that lasted a little over a decade. But both are intrinsically linked.

When I returned from Singapore in December 2005 and struggled with the two weeks I'd spent waiting outside Changi Prison for Van Nguyen to be hanged, the ABC was just beginning to investigate a new way of helping staff.

I was flown down to Sydney to be a guinea pig in a focus group early in the new year. The ABC had been watching what the BBC was doing in this field and wanted to play us a training DVD and discuss where our organisation could take it. Inside the airless room at the ABC's headquarters in Ultimo were some of the ABC's greatest journalists, all former foreign correspondents – Peter Cave, Mark Colvin and Philip Williams.

A psychologist stood at the front, gauging whether this exercise was going to be a lost cause with the hardened men in the room that day who'd spent years in the field. Her name was Cait McMahon and she ran the Asia–Pacific branch of an international organisation called the Dart Centre for Journalism and Trauma, a group none of us had heard of.

When Cait began talking about the impact long-term trauma could have, one seasoned war reporter who'd spent the previous few years in and out of Iraq and Afghanistan, sat with folded arms and an expression on his face that read 'what would you fucking know?'. But by the time we left that session we'd 'drunk the Kool-Aid', as one of our colleagues put it, and became great supporters of Dart.

Since then, Dart and the concept of trauma-educated reporting has become part of the language in the media.

In the days after the Paris attacks in 2015 at the Bataclan and other venues, Mark Colvin wrote an email to Mark Scott, the then managing director of the ABC, in support of the work that Dart had done with the organisation.

*'Dart training has made a lot of journalists better at their jobs – more sympathetic as interviewers, more capable of drawing people's stories out without ugly intrusiveness or damaging the dignity of victims.*

*'That's why I mention the Paris bombings: both Phil Williams and Lisa Millar have had a long association with Dart, and it really shows. Their reporting and interviewing from the atrocities sites has made me proud to be part of the ABC.'*

Cait was convinced trauma was misunderstood by media organisations. The statistics were clear about the damage that could be done. Substance abuse and broken relationships were more common among people in the media than they should be.

She saw it as a problem that could impact on the freedom of the press. 'Trauma silences people. It silences societies, individuals, communities. When you're traumatised, physiologically you can't speak often,' Cait said. 'If a journalist is so traumatised and so burned out by what they've been exposed to professionally and can no longer work, or chooses not to work because they'd just have to go and do flower shows because there's been too much of the dose of trauma, they are silenced as much as someone like Peter Greste who was physically silenced when he was jailed in Egypt.

'It's really important to help journalists remain articulate, to remain resilient enough and robust enough to keep telling those stories.'

The way to do that involved training organisations to look after their people, teaching trauma awareness and self-care strategies to ensure that the accumulative effect of exposure was something journalists could manage rather than something that derailed their career.

This concept was considered vital among first responders like ambulance and police officers and yet, despite reporters and photographers often being the next to arrive on site at a big story, it had not played much of a role in conversations at media organisations.

It reminded me of my time at *The Sun* in Brisbane in the early 1990s, a job I had for eighteen months. After that I'd worked at WIN TV for a year before I got the ABC job in North Queensland.

The job at *The Sun* was memorable for two things. The stand-out moment came on 10 December 1991. I'd been working the early shift starting at 4 am until around midday when I'd leave the office. I would ring the taxi company late each afternoon to confirm my booking for the next early morning start. It was often the same friendly voice on the switchboard and we would exchange pleasantries before she locked in the time and driver.

When I rang this time, she was surprised I was going to work.

'You going in, love?' she queried.

'Um, yes, why not?' I replied.

'The place has shut down, love. They've booked our cabs to drop off all your redundancy cheques.'

Between midday when I'd left the office in Fortitude Valley and late afternoon when I phoned the cab company, security guards had moved in, staff had been kicked out (and had headed immediately across the road to the pub) and we were all jobless.

Despite the shock, it wasn't all bad. The $2500 payout enabled me to buy a car with air-conditioning, which meant I could extend my job search north of humid Brisbane a little more comfortably and I ended up working for regional television in Townsville.

It remained one of my most unexpected career developments.

My other memory from *The Sun* was the time I spent on police rounds, my last role at the paper. I used to ring police stations around Queensland to see what had happened overnight and then meet up with a photographer at whatever fire, death, murder or kidnap had happened within driving distance to carry out a 'death knock'. It didn't always involve a death but it did involve knocking on a victim's door and speaking to them or the grieving family.

I was twenty-one years old and would be lying to say it wasn't confronting. Perhaps my naivety and tentative approach helped but I became quite successful at encouraging people to talk. Maybe they felt sorry for me. Sometimes they wanted to ensure their loved one was remembered as they wished.

The photographer, Tom, was an old hand at it. In his early forties and with a sensitive heart, he knew when to indulge in black humour to alleviate the stress. It was a technique used by so many in the media to get through tough jobs.

One day we were sent to Ipswich, about forty minutes west of Brisbane.

The paper had been following the case of a missing 22-year-old woman. I'd written a front-page story the day before about the discovery of her broken-down and abandoned car. She'd rung Queensland's roadside assistance company RACQ at 8.30 pm from a public phone box a four-minute walk away. And then disappeared without a trace.

Twenty-seven hours later police had found her, questioned her and sent her home. Police believed she'd been abducted and held captive. My job was to get her story.

Back then the White Pages and the electoral roll were gold when it came to working out where people lived. Everyone had a home phone and the idea of listing it as a private number barely crossed our minds.

We had no idea what this woman had gone through as a captive and, as we drove out on that winter's morning before dawn, we discussed our tactics.

The photographer kindly said he'd be happy to back me up if I told the bosses that we'd knocked and no one responded. They called that a 'grass knock' because no one would hear it. But I knew I couldn't carry off a lie like that and so we sat and waited in the winter fog, cursing that we hadn't brought food as the temperature barely climbed past zero.

Finally, a light went on and someone picked up a newspaper off the lawn. The house was awake.

We walked up the wooden steps of the old Queenslander and only a few seconds after I knocked the door opened. The face that peered out belonged to a young woman. It was bruised and her eyes flickered as she tried to process who these early visitors were.

Blame the cold, hunger or shock but the last thing I remembered was introducing myself to her before I fainted. When I came to, I was inside the house and she was offering me a glass of water. I pleaded with her to give me a few lines for a story, which she did, as long as we didn't take her photo. She told me she'd been taken from her car on the highway and kept in a dark room with a bucket for a toilet.

When we left the photographer spun around and snapped a photo and I could see the dismay in her eyes. The photographer gave me a shrug as if to say, 'I had no choice'.

The commercial TV stations had sent satellite trucks and reporters and they were waiting outside as we rushed off to find a public telephone. I inserted twenty-cent coins into the phone to connect to the paper's copy-takers, who would type my dictated story into the system. By the time we got back to the office, the paper was hitting the streets and my story and the photo was the front-page splash.

When I walked in, one of the senior editors started applauding and others joined in. He handed me a cardboard cut-out of an Oscar that they'd dummied up which read 'For Best Acting, Lisa Millar'.

It struck me that they thought I'd deliberately fainted to get the interview. And they were proud of me.

Years later I was at a barbecue in Brisbane as news filtered through that Princess Diana had been injured in a car crash in Paris. A journalism lecturer, nursing a beer as he stood at the grill, espoused on paparazzi tactics. And then he began to tell a story that he said he told his students about the journalist who faked a faint to get an interview.

I jumped in and told him *I* was that journalist and I *hadn't* faked the faint. Instead, I'd been afraid, cold, hungry and shocked when the kidnapped woman had opened her door – all the things a young reporter couldn't admit.

Years later, when the ABC began training staff to become more trauma literate – in not only the way we looked after ourselves but how we treated those we reported on – I found the whole concept eye opening.

But it also made complete sense and I understood why I'd reacted as I did hearing the strains of 'Ave Maria' at the beginning of the radio news story covering Van Nguyen's funeral in Melbourne. His death, as difficult as it was, wasn't necessarily the worst thing I'd covered. But it came after almost two decades of covering stories of grief and tragedy.

Cait McMahon made me realise that my feelings were all perfectly normal. It would be abnormal not to be affected by the things I'd witnessed in some way. The two of us became friends and continued to talk about trauma for the next fifteen years.

'It can be the one event that bowls people over,' she told me one day as we sat with our coffees at a beach in Melbourne. 'But it tends to be the accumulative effect that you're not aware of, that you might be doing the self-care strategies but there's something that just is corrosive about trauma … we think we're okay but there comes a moment that knocks you off your horse well and truly, or you just slip off the saddle a little and you can't get back up.'

She explained that most military organisations had set tours of duty for a reason but in journalism that doesn't happen. Being told to just get back out there and do it was how we'd progressed through our careers.

She wasn't recommending pulling people from the field but, rather, giving them the tools to look after themselves so they could also better understand the grief of those they were reporting on.

'If you become trauma literate, it also helps you understand the punters you're covering, the mum and dad who just lost their kids in a drowning accident, what they might be going through. It gives you a framework and an understanding. To help yourself but also to do better journalism.'

I found Cait's explanation of fear fascinating. Fear responses start in the brain area called the amygdala. This small part of the brain, in the temporal lobe, detects how much something impacted us, or its emotional salience. The amygdala fires up when we see anger or fear in someone's face. When we experience a threat such as having a gun pointed at us the amygdala becomes activated, which in turn stimulates the release of stress chemicals and readies the sympathetic nervous system for the fight, flight, freeze response. Our heart pumps, pupils dilate, and blood flow increases as our body prepares for our survival action. With the gun pointed at us we need to fight, run or play dead – fight, flight, freeze.

The hippocampus and prefrontal cortex were next to be activated, she explained. These parts of the brain were intricately linked to the amygdala and were involved in higher-level processing. They helped us understand the context of what was happening and whether a perceived threat was real. We might have seen that the gun was a toy and it was our friend pointing it at us. In that moment the information is processed and this part of the brain – the 'thinking' part – lets the amygdala know that it can 'stand down'. Things are okay, so our blood pressure drops, our muscles relax and our system returns to its equilibrium.

An unresolved trauma response happens when the system gets 'jammed' or stuck and it can't return to balance. It could mean we'd see danger and threat when there wasn't any, like the war veteran who'd hear a car backfire but react like it was a bomb exploding. We'd start priming ourselves for threats all around us.

When you started experiencing this kind of trauma, social support was important, especially connecting with people who understood what you were going through. Sometimes it wasn't just those closest to you, like your partner or family, but people going through the same thing, other journalists and camera crews who were best placed to help.

The ABC created a peer support program to encourage those conversations. And there was a long list of techniques to deal with covering traumatic stories including things as simple as walking. 'If we experience trauma and we just sit, it does get locked in our bodies, it does manifest, so we've got to, at a bare minimum, walk it out,' Cait said.

As Cait explained, trauma and fear were interconnected. 'There's a sense of a foreshortened future and it's because we lose our sense of safety, because when we're exposed to trauma it impacts us and we don't feel safe in the world. We start to see threats and we have fears.'

After the series of attacks in Europe, many of them involving cars ramming into pedestrians, I started finding ways to get to work that would avoid major roads. If I had to stand and wait for a walk sign I'd step back against the nearest building, never waiting on the footpath. It became second nature and I confessed one day to SBS reporter Brett Mason that I felt I was overreacting. His face immediately relaxed and he rattled off all the things he did to avoid what he thought were threats to his life. I realised I wasn't alone in my survival techniques.

'It's the fear parts of the brain that are activated when we're exposed to trauma, even if it's not our own trauma,' Cait explained. 'It's very basic and primal and not a personality failure as some seem to think. It's just this thing that happens to animals like a dog that gets attacked that has the same fight, flight, freeze response. There's no shame in it.'

At some point in their career almost all media members would cover at least one story that could be a trigger to induce PTSD, according to research done by American professor of psychology Elana Newman.

It could be the sports journalist who thinks they'd never witness trauma but was there to see the tragic death of cricketer Phillip Hughes after he was hit by a ball. And then there were reporters and camera crews who would have those experiences over and over again.

'The average person would see one of those things and be traumatised and journalists keep going back and back. It's not corrosive for everyone but it can be. There are plenty of people who can function and function well and we need to teach people how to find that resilience,' Cait said.

Camera operator Niall Lenihan was drinking at a London pub watching the Champions League football final when a text made his phone vibrate on 3 June 2017. It was the night of the attack at Borough Market and the producer Emily Bryan told him to get to the office, grab his camera kit and try to find me somewhere amid the chaos.

Niall had already covered half-a-dozen terrorist attacks by then and we'd started the new year together in Istanbul covering the deaths of nearly forty people. The roads were grinding to a halt and Niall waited with a BBC crew for taxis that never came. An Uber driver saw the large camera at his feet and pulled over, winding down the window and asking if he had any more details about the attack. It was the only invitation Niall needed to jump in and promise the driver cash to get him there as quickly as possible.

He saw the familiar flashes of silver as he got closer. They were the space blankets that were thrown around the shoulders of people to keep them warm. He'd first seen them when he'd started out, covering the rescue of a yachtsman in rough seas off Australia. But he'd been seeing them more regularly, outside the Bataclan the night of the Paris attacks and at every event since then. For Niall, the silver blanket became synonymous with tragedy.

Niall met up with me and we spoke to a man wrapped in silver who went into a long story about watching the football. We started to panic – time was racing by and we needed witnesses not dull stories.

But the man wrapped up his sentence by saying, 'and that's when I jumped on my friend to protect him but he'd been stabbed'. And he lifted his blanket to show his friend's blood saturating his shirt.

Niall remembered each moment of that night. The sounds of explosions as bags were being detonated, the riot police constantly moving us on, a young woman sobbing, the chaos, the tension.

Niall was an ambitious young camera operator who thought his first terrorist attack was a lucky break. It was the kind of story that could make your career and he'd moved from Australia to get those gigs. 'But as attacks went on you started to feel not so lucky,' he told me. 'You started to feel as if you were cursed.'

He knew he'd had enough.

He wasn't alone. We all knew we couldn't keep doing this forever.

# CHAPTER 21

# Final Approach

DESPITE THE DIFFERENT paths all of us Millars took over the decades we'd still think of India Echo Charlie and wonder what had happened to her. I hoped she'd found a family who loved her as much as we had.

Dad had a large aerial photo of his homemade airstrip framed above his desk at home and family Christmases would often find us huddled over a phone, searching Google Earth to see if there were any traces of those runways, despite them no longer being in use. We also tried to fix the broken propeller on the tiny plastic model of the plane that had been given to him by the Piper dealer and I'd included photos of IEC in Dad's photo book – friends waving from inside the cabin just before take-off, me as a young child, standing on the wing and hugging the door.

We knew IEC had had a succession of owners and Australia's register of small planes suggested she was still flying somewhere out west towards Longreach.

With Dad gone but the memories of our childhood and his dreams still rich in our minds I started tracing the plane's owners. We'd sold it to a Christian organisation that took their messages of scripture to isolated properties and they sold it to a farmer who later went bankrupt. IEC was part of the fire sale.

It was six months before the next owner, Dave, noticed the imprint of words left behind by a large sticker that had been removed from the door. 'While we were yet sinners Christ died for us,' it said.

When I tracked Dave down he told me he'd been a regular churchgoer so the words stayed with him as the decades passed. Owning IEC was a tremendous joy and selling her was a mistake he came to regret. 'It was easier to land that plane than park a car and you could never overload her,' he said.

He did wonder though if 120 kilograms of mangoes plus four people on a trip in North Queensland might have been pushing it.

It was Dave who almost crashed her when the engine flooded with water, the day before he was due to hand her over to the next owner.

IEC had a new propeller and engine and a new paint job which replaced the original gold and blue. She flew around Australia and spent a decade in a mining town called Paraburdoo in Western Australia.

But then she was back in Queensland and the register told us she was on a property at Tambo. It was fifty years since we'd bought her and I pictured her sitting in a shed, old and worn out, gathering cobwebs.

On a Sunday morning in Melbourne, when the coronavirus forced us all to stay locked inside, I rang the number for a farmhouse thousands of kilometres away. A grazier called Adrian Bucknell told me that IEC was far from gathering dust. She was flying every week. And, more extraordinarily, after flying around Australia for half a century, she was being kept in a hangar on a private strip less than fifty kilometres from the Millar farm at Kilkivan.

We made plans to visit but weeks turned into months and state border closures prevented me heading north. When my sister Wendy and I finally made the road trip to Murgon, Adrian stood waiting for me at the hangar door, pushing back his dusty Akubra and apologising for his grease-covered hands. He must have sensed how important this moment felt.

'Before you get excited, I'm not sure if it's the same plane,' he warned.

But how could it not be? I could see the initials IEC along its rear and while it was now white with black and blue stripes and the seats were green not beige, surely Grandma's initials there towards its tail were confirmation.

He'd noticed differences in the photos I'd sent him. There was an extra hinge on the cowling that covered the engine. The boots over the wheels were missing. He hoped we hadn't come all that way to be disappointed.

Maybe our IEC, which had been bought by Grandma and named after her fifty years earlier, was now scrap metal and another plane flew with her registration.

We circled the plane from tail to nose and back again and I yearned for it to be our plane. It had been three years since Dad had died and two decades since I'd first set off as a foreign correspondent. And it had been even longer since the Millars had left this area and farewelled a simple country life.

I needed this to be IEC to make me feel connected again – connected to my childhood and to a part of Australia that had felt so far away.

Adrian apologised for not taking us for a fly but the plane's hours were up and he needed to get it to a scheduled maintenance appointment up north.

I took a photo of the seven-digit serial number on the rusted metal plate screwed onto its belly and later that night trawled through Dad's logbook and documents, hoping to find the corresponding number.

Then I found it.

There was an obscure aviation enthusiasts' website with pages of small passport-size photos of light aircraft sitting on airstrips around Australia. There was a photo of IEC from 1977 at Maryborough airport. The date corresponded with Dad's logbook. His electorate office had been in Maryborough and he would sometimes fly to work. And there below the photo was the serial number that matched the one I'd seen on the plane in Murgon, our plane.

I shouldn't have doubted it was India Echo Charlie that we'd found in that hangar decades later. She looked a little bit older, a little worn out around the edges, but so was I.

We'd both been flying all our lives but had found our way home.

# CHAPTER 22

# Juliet Oscar Yankee

SOMETIMES WHEN I'M on the phone to a call centre I'll slip into using the aviation alphabet. Juliet Oscar Yankee, I'll tell them, the very act of reciting my middle name bringing me a little joy, a reminder that despite the years, the connection to those childhood memories of repeating the words with Dad, remains strong.

I hadn't expected when I moved back to Australia to find myself so far from family again. I'd taken a job in Melbourne as co-host of the ABC *News Breakfast* program but within six months the borders were closed because of a devastating virus and Queensland may as well have been on the other side of the world.

Melbourne went into lockdown. Michael Rowland and I still turned up every day at 4 am at the ABC studios to prepare for the breakfast program. But as soon as it was done, I returned home, suddenly facing long days of solitude.

I had no choice but to slow down. And I realised how little stillness there'd been in my life.

Before dawn in winter, when there's no hint of the day to come, the water of Port Phillip Bay resembles a large slick of black oil. The orange lights of a gas storage site send reflections that stretch their flickering tentacles out into the darkness. Green and red markers blink on the horizon where a huge cargo ship sits, like a child's drawing that's been carefully cut out with plastic safety scissors and placed delicately on top of the water.

The water stays so still. Closer to dawn the smallest ripples are created by the *Spirit of Tasmania* silently gliding into the pier. Back and forth, back and forth it goes each day between Melbourne and the small state seemingly just out of sight, beyond the cargo ships on the horizon.

A light is turned on in the apartment near mine and I can see the glow it's leaving on my empty balcony. It's the first sign of a day starting, followed by the sounds – a dishwasher being emptied, a whimper of a baby, a TV switching on, an ad for life insurance.

The water remains still, until a kayak slides across the sand and a paddle breaks the surface. I have always wanted to swim in this water but, after a year of living in Victoria, I haven't. I don't know why. It draws me but discourages me.

The dark surface I see at night can hold so many secrets beneath. The cruise ships used to berth at the pier and then wait for hundreds of passengers to get on trams and into taxis and spend days sightseeing. I wondered how much pollution those hotels of the sea were leaving in the water.

The port is only slightly further away with ships coming from across the world. Surely they'd be leaving their mark on the water as well.

What about the fish? Or something else? I've never loved the sensation of swimming among marine life, no matter how colourful they might be. I don't want to accidentally connect with them, to feel the rush of a school of fish passing by, tiny grey fingerlings close to my fingers as my arm rotates for that first stroke through the water.

'What's on the bottom of the bay?' I ask a friend, a regular swimmer, who responds with a quizzical look.

'On the bottom, under the water, is it sand?' I ask again, thinking he hasn't understood.

'Oh, just some broken glass,' he replies, laughing.

He doesn't know that I don't joke about the water.

One year in the middle of winter Philippe and I escaped from Washington, DC, to the Dominican Republic. It had been snowing and there was more cold weather to come. The wet flakes delighted me at the start of the season but a few months in I dreaded them. Salt trucks ploughed the streets and the sun's warmth turned the glistening white mounds into dirty melting ice traps hiding torn rubbish bags slowly losing their contents.

I soon understood why the Americans had a name for the retirees who fled to the south during winter – snowbirds. They'd go for months at a time.

We were going to be snowbirds for just under a week. It was January and my Facebook was filled with photos from Australia: cold beers on hot sand, the blue–green sparkle of the Pacific Ocean reflected in sunglasses smudged with sunscreen. I could almost hear the squeals of joy as colourfully painted summer toes touched water and waves crashed into sunburnt bodies, watched over carefully by rugged young lifesavers.

I longed for that feeling but the travel pages had only endless offerings of all-inclusive deals at huge resorts that promised five stars but delivered three, where poolside banana chairs were claimed by families of ten from Kansas or Oklahoma on trips of a lifetime, who dumped their towels before filling themselves at the breakfast buffet with pancakes and bacon and gallons of maple syrup. They were happy. They were together. But I didn't want to share their holiday.

We found a small hotel instead, outside the secure tourists' compound, further down the beach where a security guard sat on the sand, paid to protect the resort next door. The owners had gone broke during construction and, day by day, small parts of the resort were whisked away by locals. Blue and white tiles disappearing one by one.

The anticipation of a holiday can be so joyful. The swimmers thrown in the suitcase, the buzz of excitement knowing the heavy winter coat won't be touched for a week, the sight of the water as the plane circles lower over the island until it touches down with a thump and the first whiff of warmth enters the cabin as the flight attendant shoves open the heavy door.

But, oh, the misery when expectations fail to deliver. We walked onto the sand and I saw dozens of plastic bags floating on the surface and throwaway coffee cups bobbing on the crest of a wave before being dumped onto the sand for a moment and then swept back out.

The water itself was thick and cloudy with grit. I couldn't see the bottom. A man on a small blue yacht a couple of hundred metres out stood on the rim and used the ocean for his toilet.

I didn't go in. I found space at the resort pool with the other Americans who'd fled winter.

So when I ask my new friend, Will, in Melbourne what's on the bottom of the water in Port Phillip Bay and he says broken glass, I don't laugh.

'It's sand,' he says, with a smile. 'You should go in.'

But still I hesitate. Despite the many lessons in DC with Lloyd Henry and other attempts to learn and enjoy swimming over the years, it still feels like something that just doesn't come naturally to me.

But on a Friday night Zoom call with other friends in the neighbourhood in the middle of the coronavirus pandemic we decide to swim on Sunday at 11 am. There are four of us who promise each other several times we won't back out, despite knowing our courage has been strengthened by several wines while we sit in the comfort of our solitary lounge rooms.

I arrive at the beach early. I always arrive early.

'The news goes to air at 7 pm, not a minute before or a minute past,' I'd say to friends who wondered how long I'd been sitting alone at a restaurant table waiting for tardy companions.

I'd be told to deliver a TV news report from a disaster zone that was no more than two minutes and ten seconds in length, not two minutes thirty.

When your work decisions revolve around a few seconds here and a few seconds there, I was bound to become a loyal servant of time.

At the beach, none of us has a wetsuit and, as we start stripping off layers of clothing on the sand, a man building castles with his daughters, rugged up warmly, waves to us and sings out, 'Good luck.'

The others in my group are Victorians, they're used to cold water, not like me, the only Queenslander. They've done this before. But even they have a moment of doubt.

'Are we really doing this?' they ask, the warmth of the Friday night wine long gone as we watch other swimmers zip up head to toe in thick wetsuits. We debate whether thermal caps should have been worn to conquer the cold, or if a summer rashie makes any difference to your body temperature or just leaves more wet material clinging to you when you emerge.

We've stood on the water's edge for too long. If I don't start moving it will never happen.

The water is clear and, as promised, I can see sand on the bottom and a smattering of smooth stones. It's so still the sun creates small octagonal shapes of light in the water and I feel like I'm disturbing a just-completed jigsaw.

I take a few steps and then start to run, picking up my legs and causing bubbles to form around my feet. I run until the water is at my knees and it starts to drag on me, slowing my speed, every step still kicking up sprays of water into my face.

A two-metre yellow marker stands out of the water, staking out the area for swimmers, a warning to the jet skis and power boats to stay clear.

It's still too shallow but I'm desperate to just dive in and start swinging my arms. It feels like I'm moving through melting ice cubes left out of the freezer for a few minutes too long.

The others are behind me, going slower. I can hear their groans, cursing Friday night promises fuelled by alcohol.

Finally it's deep enough to dive in and I'm under the surface, my lungs squeezing tight, protesting at the piercing cold.

I am numb but happy. There is no elegance about my strokes. I clumsily push my head under and up again, laughing and waving to some friends on the shore who've come down to watch.

It only lasts a matter of minutes. It's too cold to stay in any longer but I still linger on my way out, relishing the endorphins surging through my body.

I can't stop the joyful laugh bubbling out of me, the same sensation I had when I fell over the finish line of that triathlon in Washington, DC. But each time I questioned what I was doing, when the anxiety crept up, I reminded myself that I'd already overcome my most debilitating fear, a fear of flying that had weighed so heavily on my life for so long.

And if I could do that then I could do anything.

When I crossed that finish line I watched other runners fold their bodies in half, collapsing in relief, some frowning at disappointing times, others desperately lunging for water to rehydrate.

All I wanted to do was laugh.

So many times over the years, I called on that sense of endurance and determination. I tested myself and sometimes came up wanting.

I had dreamed of a big life but discovered I could be immobilised by fear.

But I also knew my middle name, Joy, had been a gift that had given me a zest for life. Years later, in that biting bay swim in Victoria, I was pushing the boundaries of my comfort zone again, embracing the chance to try something new.

I'd still been anxious about the water – what was in it, what was on the bottom, what the chill would do to my body left uncovered by neoprene.

Fear was always going to be a constant but I'd discovered while I might not ever eradicate it, I could face it, I could break through.

And by plunging in, I'd been treated to an exhilaration that had become utterly addictive.

# ACKNOWLEDGEMENTS

To say I was a reluctant memoirist is to put it mildly. If it were not for a socially distanced coffee encounter with the tireless Louise Adler in the early days of the pandemic this book may never have come to life. Thank you, Louise, for refusing to be put off by my hesitation to become the story when for the past thirty years I have been more comfortable telling other people's stories.

I am so grateful to Jacquie Brown and Deonie Fiford, who took my offerings and with their expert eyes helped craft them into something worth publishing. I felt protected by the safety net of your editorial care. Emma Rusher and her team from Hachette have worked hard to ensure it had the widest audience possible. Thank you.

I started down this path knowing that my memory may not always serve me well. Photos, emails and notes buried in boxes that haven't been opened for years helped but I'm indebted to my colleagues and friends who have taken endless phone calls from me during the process and I hope they feel I've done justice to their stories. To the people of Kilkivan and Gympie and others who so readily gave me your time and memories and helped spark my own, thank you.

Thank you to Neil McLean and Les Posen for their invaluable insight into the fear of flying and to Neil especially, who created the course that changed my life.

My friends at the Dart Centre for Journalism and Trauma both here in Australia and the US, in particular Cait McMahon, have taught me so much about trauma reporting and helped pick up the pieces and get me back on my feet.

I have been so lucky to work with the most incredible reporting teams both in Australia and overseas. To the camera operators, producers, reporters, editors, makeup artists and office managers, thanks for the laughs, the tears, the beers and the unflagging collegiality. Many of you are more than workmates, you are lifelong friends. It has been a delight to reunite with Michael Rowland on ABC *News Breakfast* after first becoming friends in Canberra in the 1990s and he and his wife, Nicki, were early supporters of my writing efforts, urging me on during Zoom cocktail hours.

I am indebted to Tracy Bowden, Andrea Jonson, Jane Wilson and Christina Lamb for casting an eye over the manuscript and Marian Wilkinson for the kind of friendship that meant she dropped everything to help work on the title.

Huge thanks to Fleur Bitcon who took on the task I set her of being the harshest critic of the manuscript in its final stages. Fleur held my hand on a flight in 1996 when my fear of flying was mounting and I felt the warmth of her hold again as we went through this process.

# ACKNOWLEDGEMENTS

The year 2020 was terrible for so many people and for Melbournians especially who spent so much of it in lockdown as the deadly coronavirus swept the globe. The hours I spent walking with Georgie Tunny, Rob Mills, Deb Beale and Danielle Watts helped me process the conflicting emotions many of us felt and allowed ideas to germinate while we strolled.

My friendship with Robynne Dodds, Carolyn Olarenshaw and Sharon Fewtrell withstood the distances between us, and their support never wavered. I appreciate their openness to having their own stories shared as well.

It is difficult to find the right words to explain how deeply grateful I am that my friendship with Leigh Sales has withstood the test of time. Her humour is matched by her intellect but both are overshadowed by her intense loyalty to her friends.

Finally, to my siblings, who retold their stories and checked and double-checked facts about our family history and read the manuscript many times over. No matter where I have been in the world, I have always felt your love. My brothers Robert and David and sisters Wendy and Trudi insisted I keep pursuing my adventures even when our beloved parents were entering their final years and needed their family around them more than ever. The foundation of our family was fortified by the loving presence of my siblings' partners Dorothea, Dianne, Tom and David and I'm so grateful for the support they have given me. Their children and their children's children put sunshine back in my life when sometimes skies darkened.

This book would not exist without you all.

**hachette**
AUSTRALIA

If you would like to find out more about
Hachette Australia, our authors, upcoming events
and new releases you can visit our website or our
social media channels:

hachette.com.au

HachetteAustralia

HachetteAus